Maucher and Malik on
Management

Maucher | Malik | Farschtschian

Maucher and Malik on Management

Maxims of Corporate Management –
Best of Maucher's Speeches, Essays and Interviews

Translated from German by Myrna Lesniak

Campus Verlag
Frankfurt/New York

The original edition was published in 2012 by Campus Verlag with the title
Maucher und Malik über Management. Maximen unternehmerischen Handelns.
All rights reserved.

ISBN 978-3-593-50025-6

Copyright © 2013 Campus Verlag GmbH, Frankfurt am Main
Cover design: Hißmann, Heilmann, Hamburg
Typesetting: Fotosatz L. Huhn, Linsengericht
Typesetted with the following font: Scala and Scala Sans
Print and binding: Beltz, Bad Langensalza
Printed in Germany

This book is also available as an E-Book.
www.campus.de

Contents

Part 3
Discussion between Helmut Maucher and Fredmund Malik
Thoughts on Management and the Economy

Part 4
Helmut Maucher's Thoughts on the Future and Recommendations
for Improving our Democratic Constitutions

Preface by
Farsam Farschtschian

This book is about one of the greatest success stories in the history of corporate management and about one of the most accomplished business leaders ever.

Dr. Helmut Maucher is one of those very rare top managers who have an exceptional and equal command of three things: acting, reflecting and writing.

The quality of Maucher's entrepreneurial action is apparent in his successful and exemplary management of Nestlé over two decades. Moreover, his reflections on management are highly sophisticated and he applies his considerable intellect to an analysis of his actions. Finally, as the book shows, Helmut Maucher is also a master at expressing his thoughts and actions both orally and in writing. These three dimensions unite to form a harmonious entity.

Based on Dr Helmut Maucher's speeches, publications and interviews the work is a unique testimony to the outstanding entrepreneurial results which can be achieved by good and right management. The contributions for this book were written with a number of aims and contexts in mind, at different points in time from 1988 to 2010 and for a public that included leading international business executives, politicians, employees, students and also grammar school teachers – a cross section of society.

In Maucher's publications a certain number of repetitions with respect to the various topics have been retained in order to lend greater emphasis to the major points he makes. However, because of the change in contexts similar formulations, too, acquire a new meaning and highlight the extensive range of his statements. Only then is it possible to appreciate how comprehensive Maucher's knowledge and practice of management are – through time, space and purpose. Each situation may be entirely different but the message he wishes to impart could not be more to the point.

This book is a first-class work presenting guidelines for new generations of managers. Helmut Maucher's style and methods of management are annotated in a comprehensive introduction by Prof. Dr. Fredmund Malik, who Peter Drucker, the doyen of management, considers to be one of the leading management thinkers in Europe. Malik regards Maucher's life-time achievement in the light of his own system-cybernetic work on good and right management. At the same time he particularly emphasizes those dimensions that are universally valid in Maucher's management performance and that will consequently last well into the future.

The book is complemented and rounded off by both experts exchanging opinions on the core issues of management, business and society in a comprehensive dialogue lasting several hours. Maucher's own aphorisms form the conclusion to this work, which gets to the heart of the most complex topics in a succinct and elegant way that makes them easily comprehensible.

I have held numerous conversations with Maucher and Malik in the course of the last few years and these enabled me to become familiar with the views of both these management masterminds and to follow their development closely. Although their views are expressed and reached in different ways, they arrive at the same or very similar points of view in many key areas. However, in areas where they place emphasis on different aspects, they reach new common solutions. These find brilliant expression in the section containing the extensive dialogue which took place especially for this book.

Where Maucher is too modest to praise himself, it takes Malik with his management expertise to provide the correct context for Maucher's unique management accomplishments. Malik attaches the appropriate importance to the achievements of a person of Helmut Maucher's standing and demonstrates the significance that Maucher's management has for meeting the enormous challenges of the economy and society both today and in the future.

Malik himself predicted the current economic crises and the fact that these were caused substantially by mismanagement. He recognized very early on that the major driving forces behind these crises were the Anglo-Saxon approach of corporate governance and shareholder values. He felt that on account of their short-term orientation these would lead inevitably to one of the greatest misallocations of economic and social resources in history. Showing keen foresight and on the basis of his knowledge, Malik has developed the solutions essential for responding to the current challenges in his holistic management models and his innovative change management tools. It is in this context that Malik shows the immense significance of Maucher's management for current and future generations of business leaders.

This book is one of the most outstanding works on management and portrays the quintessence of unparalleled entrepreneurial success due to right and excellent management. With its unique picture of the lifetime accomplishments of Helmut Maucher, who celebrated his 85th birthday last year, it is for entrepreneurs, managers and politicians and is intended to act as a »lighthouse for sailors in times of storm« by providing reliable navigation for mastering the fundamental worldwide transformation. Moreover, in times when managers and management are greatly misunderstood, this book – using Helmut Maucher's achievements at Nestlé as an example – is intended to provide a wide range of readers with a new understanding of the social importance of large-scale enterprises, right management and socially responsible leadership.

Farsam Farschtschian

Part 1
Introduction by Fredmund Malik

Good Management –
Good Food, Good Life

Global company Nestlé and the name of Helmut Maucher are inextricably linked together. Within only two decades Helmut Maucher, with breath-taking dynamism, made Nestlé into the largest and greatest food company in the world and at the same time into one of the few truly global corporations.

Under Maucher's management Nestlé's sales tripled and in fact it would have risen even more but for negative currency effects. The stock market price, ex dividend, increased more than 15 times compared to when Maucher took over. He developed promising new product lines which proved to be successful, acquired and successfully integrated a total of 250 companies, effected some of the largest acquisitions ever and opened up a great number of new markets all around the globe. Even more significant is the fact that not only was Maucher highly successful in managing this huge expansion but that in doing so – as is generally acknowledged – he did not make any mistakes.

All this was made possible by the exemplary management which Helmut Maucher established at Nestlé. *Good Food, Good Life* is the company's motto and Maucher's *Good Management* made Nestlé what it is today.

Today, management continues to be misunderstood what frequently has dangerous results. For example, it is often primarily seen as a means of becoming rich, famous and powerful. Then there is the misunderstanding that companies are first and foremost machines for maximizing profits. Indeed, companies can always be abused if one is so inclined, but in that case management and the economy cannot be seen as responsible and sustainable.

I regard management in the following way: management is the profession for ensuring proper functioning. So, it is management that enables social organizations to function or fails to do so and therefore, management is one of the key functions of modern society. Managers are the very people who practice management as seen in this way – as a profession at the various levels of the organization.

Consequently, almost entirely everything that is most precious to us as members of modern societies and that makes life in them also worth living – from economic prosperity to a high level of education and from health, science and research, and the strength of innovation and creativity and finally to the quality of life – depends on the competence and quality of management.

Thus management is the social function that enables everything else to function. It is also the function that transforms economic and social resources into results and value for society.

In order to achieve this, management has to be carried out in the right way and it has to be done well. It has to be right and good management. Much of what is termed management up and down the country fails, to a large degree, to meet both these requirements or complies very badly with them. The prevalent understanding of management is a minefield of errors and false doctrines. That was why the crises which threaten our affluence today were able to arise, crises which were and are largely due to wrong and bad management.

Consequently, with Nestlé and Helmut Maucher's unique management performance as examples, this book is intended to show what right and good, and even excellent management is in practice and what this can achieve. It was for that very reason that I recommended that Helmut Maucher should publish his speeches and writings as a collection, should place them in the context of the significant challenges facing us today and in the future, and thus provide present and future generations of managers with a universally valid navigation aid.

The book presents Helmut Maucher's management philosophy and management practice in his original texts, placed, within the framework of this introduction, in the context of my own management theory. It illustrates why Maucher's management is right and why this enabled him in his position as Nestlé's CEO to be so successful for so many years.

Helmut Maucher's management performance, which is exceptional in many respects, is to become apparent to readers far beyond those with only an immediate interest in this subject matter. Moreover, the book is to demonstrate what it was about his person in the many decades of his career right to the highest position in Nestlé that distinguished him from other top managers.

Maucher's approach not only stands for an extraordinary management performance in the past but – which for today is more important – as a template for a new future of socially responsible, right and good management. This is of the utmost importance because the economy and society are in the midst of one of the greatest transformations there has ever been. For some time I have been calling this the »Great Transformation 21«, which means the global change of the 21st century. In a sense it is comparable with the change from an agricultural to an industrial society about 200 years ago but it is much larger and more profound due to its staggering proportions.

It is no exaggeration if this transformation is seen as the transition to a new world parts of which can already be seen quite clearly whereas others are still unknown and where much will be radically new and revolutionary. The current crises can be understood far better, above and beyond mere economy, as the birth pangs of this new world. The »Great Transformation 21« is already confronting the structures of every society, and first and foremost their organizations and their management with enormous challenges.

At this time, over and above revolutionary technologies, right management, as can be seen so clearly in Maucher's success at Nestlé, will be the key to a peaceful, organic and human change. The power of right management today is founded and manifoldly reinforced by innovative change management tools and completely new methods for mastering enormously complex and dynamic challenges.

This book affords a unique insight into the thoughts and work of one of the most successful business leaders ever. It shows how with his management, governance and leadership Maucher transformed Nestlé, which at that time lagged considerably behind its competitors, into the largest and most successful food company in the world within a period of only two decades. Moreover, he also saw to it that the company remained successful and dynamic after he stepped down from office upon reaching retirement age and that it was able to build considerably on his success.

Helmut Maucher became the Delegate (CEO) of the Board of Directors in 1981 when he assumed overall management of Nestlé. This was the first time that a non-Swiss national became head of the largest company in Switzerland; in many respects this was a novelty, the full significance of which can only be assessed by those with a profound knowledge of Switzerland. In 1981, Nestlé generated a turnover of around CHF 28 billion, made a net profit of just under CHF 1 billion and had 146,000 employees. As of 1990, Maucher was both Delegate and Chairman of the Board of Directors until 1997. Peter Brabeck-Lethmate with an excellent team of top managers succeeded him as Delegate in 1997. Helmut Maucher continued in his position as Chairman of the Board of Directors until 2000, when he was succeeded by Rainer E. Gut, a long-standing member and Vice-Chairman of the Nestlé Board. Helmut Maucher has been Honorary Chairman since then.

When Helmut Maucher stepped down from his position of Chairman at the annual general meeting in 2000, turnover for the business year 1999 amounted to almost CHF 75 billion; net profit was almost CHF 5 billion and the company had a good 230,000 employees.

Maucher's successors took over the helm with great vigor and continued the success of the company without any further ado. In the business year 2011, Nestlé generated a turnover of around CHF 84 billion, a net profit of almost CHF 10 billion and had 328,000 employees. The company has around 500 factories in more than 80 countries and with almost 100 international brands is present in almost every country in the world.

We may also ascribe some of this continuing success to Helmut Maucher himself on two counts: firstly, some of the conditions necessary for the lasting business success were created early in the period when he was running the company; in particular these included the strategic expansion of the product portfolio and of the company's presence geographically. Unlike those managers who aim primarily at maximizing the annual results, Maucher possessed the rare courage of rejecting the reporting of short-term results in order to make the company all the stronger in the long term. Maucher's guiding principle for this was notion of the »healthy company«, which goes beyond short-term or even mere financial results.

Secondly he had successors, especially the new CEO, Peter Brabeck-Lethmate, and his former long-standing members of staff and pupils, who, for many years, had been effectively prepared under his direction to succeed him. As a result they even acquired the ability to surpass their predecessor when changed circumstances and opportunities made this necessary. One of the noblest achievements of successful leadership is having pupils who become even better than their master.

Secrets in Helmut Maucher's management

It can be ascertained that there are no secrets in Maucher's management in the strict sense of the word, for he has been open and generous when talking about his views, principles and actions, as is obvious in the speeches and publications contained in this book. However, there are also many issues with which most managers are unfamiliar because they never cropped up in this way in their own education. The main reason is that in conventional business schools since the beginning of the 1990s different and often entirely wrong contents were taught as the ultimate truth, which frequently the exact opposite of Helmut Maucher's management principles.

In this respect we are faced to a large degree with the huge challenge of re-learning and reorientation. Consequently by looking more closely at Maucher's achievements this book provides an invaluable guide and shows a way out of the labyrinth of misapprehensions about right management. I have chosen some of the key aspects of Helmut Maucher's concept of management for what is to follow because I consider these to be particularly crucial to coping with the future.

Amongst other things it is easily recognizable how early – and also impressively – Helmut Maucher's mindset corresponded to what I call integrated cybernetics and systems thinking. It is a holistic way of thinking in terms of multidimensional relationships which goes beyond the individual corporate divisions and their respective specialty and combines them to a functioning whole.

It will become evident that it is quite normal and natural for Maucher to see things in their entirety and in their interaction, in their cross-linking inwardly and outwardly, and thus to recognize their inherent complexity and dynamism. This ability is one of his outstanding strengths, an ability which many top-executives do not possess.

Multiplying top management intelligence

Early in my management research I discovered the meaning of both cybernetic control intelligence in terms of self-regulation and its practical realization through principles which I term *Master Controls*.

The function of these *Master Controls* is comparable to laws of nature such as the genetic code in biology, laws relating to harmony in music, or the principles of bionics. From these, among other things, I derived the controls with the objectives of right management in mind and this resulted in natural laws of functioning, about which I have written frequently so that top management can exploit their power.

Helmut Maucher, like few others, has at his command the consummate skill of using this kind of cybernetic control intelligence. What does that mean?

Maucher is a man of principles and of thinking long-term and on a large scale. Long before the rather vague concept of »sustainability« appeared in reaction to the prevailing short-term orientation, Maucher took the lead with clear, well thought-out principles – which applied both to himself and the entire corporation. Helmut Maucher is one of the few master craftsmen in this respect.

It was for Nestlé that he devised those timeless principles that go far beyond mere long-term orientation which has long ceased to suffice in view of today's complex conditions. Thus he provided the corporation and its employees with orientation and direction which reached right to the very foundations of the organization and enabled them to act independently, according to Maucher's own governance intelligence.

If, for example, companies do not grow sufficiently, even though their markets provide them with ample growth potential, then the reason is usually that the executives have not learned to manage on the basis of precepts, principles and policies with the result that they limit the growth of their companies prematurely and unnecessarily.

Master Controls understood in this way allow the managerial intelligence of those at the highest corporate level to be multiplied by the number of all the executives who apply the Master Controls within the organization. By this method, they spread the intelligence at the top to the outermost boundaries within the scope of the organization and make them effective in their operations. As a precautionary measure the most intelligent *Master Controls* also include rules for deviating from the rules if necessary. For example, for accepting sound compromises; moreover they even include rules for altering rules.

Only such precepts or general rules of this kind permit decentralization to function reliably within a company and thus achieve far-reaching cybernetic self-regulation and self-organization that in turn are indispensible competencies in complex and dynamic conditions.

More than merely long-term

The concept »long-term«, however, is far from sufficient to achieve this enormous effectiveness. It is in this respect that Helmut Maucher has achieved something much more important. He brought the corporate analogue of the Categorical Imperative propounded by Immanuel Kant, the great philosopher of ethics, to bear globally because he assessed his decisions against the key question: *How must I decide at present so that in principle my action may be correct for an unlimited period?* That means in practical terms that a decision remains correct until there are signs of basically changing circumstances which necessitate a rethinking of policies and strategies and under certain circumstances also demand new decisions.

In Kant's version the Imperative states: *Act as if the maxim of your action should – by your will – become a universal law of nature.*

In the context of corporate management that means »the law of the corporation« instead of the »law of nature«. That is precisely the effect of right policies.

30 years before ethics have become a general management fad due, among other things, to the excessive manager bonuses and there are attempts everywhere to artificially superimpose ethics in retrospect, Maucher succeeded in smoothly integrating the right ethics into the activities of the corporation and in blending both of them to form an organically harmonious whole.

Immune to fashions through better governance logic

Thus another of Maucher's »secrets« is uncovered. Due to the fact that he also made use of the powerful impact of such principle, Maucher had a great advantage over other top executives in that he was immune to the ever-changing fads and fashions in management and to the financial temptations from the zeitgeist – which during the economic boom was more of a demon of the times. It was this very Zeitgeist, however, which during his entire regime demanded, in almost every aspect, the opposite of what he in his position as CEO considered right. He defied these temptations, especially with regards to the most crucial issues, with great success, discipline and responsibility, as I will show later.

It is natural for Maucher to think in terms of great future dimensions. For this, however, he rarely uses the word »vision« because he wasn't deceived by the euphoric stock market- born hypes of his time.

His broad view again becomes apparent in his comprehensive understanding of holistic, economic, social and political interdependent contexts – and particularly of the responsibility which a corporation has towards the whole of society. As a result, his corporate policy and strategy decisions are far-reaching because he sees them holistically and consequently he is able to take the total dimensions of a challenge into account.

On the other hand, this was entirely contrary to the neo-liberal doctrine of shareholder value, which occasionally Maucher ironically referred to as share-fetishism. To see corporations primarily as machines for generating profits did not correspond to Maucher's understanding of a functioning company, for he regarded the functioning of a company strictly in terms of the market and the customer.

Thus he was able to keep firmly in view two of the cast-iron benchmarks that enable right corporate governance in the first place. Reasons for these can be found in my books where I dub them the »polar stars« of management navigation. They are the twins »customer value« and »competitiveness«, the only benchmarks in the economy which cannot be manipulated. In contrast, »shareholder value« and »enhancement of value« correspond to the ever-changing »position of the planets« metaphorically speaking. They are subject to the vagaries of the stock market and, to a large extent, to the lack of understanding of management logic in real economic terms. For that reason they are easy to manipulate, as has been proved in the scandals surrounding Enron, WorldCom and many others.

Right management based on the »polar stars« of customer value and competitiveness aims first of all at creating economic performance and only after this has been achieved does it aim at its distribution – which then naturally includes the shareholders. It was precisely because Maucher understood managing in this way that Nestlé generated even larger profits under his regime and created more shareholder value than those CEOs who all too frequently submit obsequiously and immediately to the dictates of shareholder value and its apostles.

On the basis of these precepts, Maucher, as can be seen later, practiced an exemplary and effectively functioning corporate governance, which was far ahead of and superior to the Corporate Governance Codes that were pompously emerging at that time.

Profound expert knowledge of his business

As the last of the »secrets« of Maucher's success I have singled out something which can hardly ever be found in books on management and which – because it is largely not understood – and is therefore frequently mistaken for gut feeling and intuition.

This secret is his exquisite, downright perfect expertise in Nestlé's business. Maucher knew Nestlé inside out. His vast knowledge was almost unparalleled. He had grown up in this business and had been actively involved in organizing many things down to the very last detail. Consequently, he knew everything there was to know about the numerous things that constitute a business – products, markets, consumers, brands, marketing, advertising and packaging; raw materials, quality, prices and manufacturing processes; about trade, suppliers and banks; finance, risks, the stock market and shareholders; the media, local and international politics – and first and foremost he knew about people.

Intimate knowledge of the business is what it takes to make excellent management possible in the first place. However competent executives are, they cannot manage just any company without further ado, as is often assumed – let alone other types of organization. To put it another way: if you want to ride a horse properly, you have to know a lot about horses.

It goes without saying that the most successful executive in the steel industry should not be entrusted with the management of a bank and on the other hand even excellent bank executives are more likely to have difficulty understanding manufacturing companies.

It was the early insight into such facts that enabled me to incorporate precisely those elements of right and good management into my own management theory that are universally essential irrespective of the particular type of organization and also culture. It was then only a natural step to make management into a profession with its own craftsmanship and with its typically universal precepts, tasks and tools: into a profession that can be learned to a greater degree than most people believe nowadays or are able to imagine. After these results had been successfully expressed in easy to learn models for right management, it was possible to develop new forms of advanced management, leadership and governance education, forms that were often revolutionary in their effectiveness.

The better CEOs understand the business, the better they can utilize their management for the benefit of the customer and for competitive advantages. They understand things faster and better than others; they do not require detailed analyses, often grasp connections at a glance where others first need to study long reports, and for that reason are able – as it were shooting from the hip – to take right and good decisions at lightning speed and then act upon them. What laymen often and rashly think of as gut feeling and intuition has its origins more frequently in a thorough knowledge of the business.

If you have no professional management at your command, you quickly reach your limits, especially in complex businesses; and if you have no knowledge of the business, then your management will very quickly come to an end. Both are needed in a flexible balance, capable of changing quickly and unpredictably, according to the circumstances.

His immense expertise combined synergistically with his management professionality was the decisive reasons for Helmut Maucher being such a powerful and in essentials such a brilliant CEO and, what is more, an entrepreneur in the best sense of the word.

Against the mainstream, and therefore more successful

It is crucial to this book that Helmut Maucher achieved his highly unusual business success in a way that is almost diametrically opposed to the concept of management that has prevailed from the early 1990s to the present day. The financial, debt and economic crises are making it more and more evident just how gigantic the misdirections of mainstream management were.

It was half way through Maucher's active service as CEO that a period began with an onslaught of the greatest ever errors and false doctrines in management theory and practice. From about 1992 on, the real economy and the financial economy began to drift apart, imperceptibly at first and then more intensively until they literally became two different worlds.

The indispensable parameters of entrepreneurial navigation were displaced by purely financial parameters based on short-term performance. Decisions were geared more and more towards movements of the stock market and evaluations by financial analysts instead of towards customer value and competitiveness. The opinions expressed by the finance media counted for more than the customers' decision to buy. Shareholder value became more important than technological innovation and real investments. Maximizing the return on equity capital had priority over healthy financing and liquidity reserves. Observing a socially acceptable approach to large reconstruction programs and heeding social responsibility were frequently and arrogantly dismissed as »romantic or crazy leftist ideas«.

Thus began the systematic misallocation of financial and social resources from the real economy to the financial system. Capital leveraged as much as 100-fold flowed into the financial markets, and there was a brain drain from corporations with factories to the Wall Street industries.

Therefore, Helmut Maucher's great success was created with precisely the style of management which was fundamentally contrary to that taught to generations of students at many universities and numerous business schools in particular. It is much of this business administration that is the direct cause of today's financial crisis, the rise in unemployment particularly among young people and increasing social tensions. The booster mechanisms of the respective consulting industries including corporate governance consulting, strategy consultants, executive search and executive compensation and also the accounting firms, have exacerbated these errors a thousand times over and caused them to impact on the economy. So far the question of their responsibility has not even been addressed.

If, on the other hand, Maucher's management expertise had been widely applied, a financial, debt and social crisis like today's could never have arisen. On the contrary, we would have corporations that were healthy to their very core and therefore there would also be a healthy, strong, real economy and a financial economy, too. In this social situation – perhaps the most threatening since the 1920s – with its danger of a deflation that has still not been properly perceived, the example set by Helmut Maucher gives rise to great hope, for it goes beyond excellent management. It is in this dimension that Maucher stands for genuine leadership in the best sense of the word, a leadership which sets an example also for other areas of society.

For that reason, this book also has significance beyond business. It will help to clear up and eliminate many misconceptions about business activity and management which are entertained especially by those at the highest decision-making level in numerous public organizations, in politics and in the general public, too. Excessive bonuses, major bankruptcies, scandals involving banks and the stock markets and all the crises in the financial system would never have arisen if management had been carried out in the right way.

This book is also a convincing illustration that not all the business world corresponds to the many clichés in the media, but that there are companies which function superbly. These include such organizations as Nestlé, who not only know how to be successful in business but also fulfill their social and ecological responsibilities, where they even take the initiative in an exemplary way. Thus the wide divide between business and the people can be bridged and some of the gaps closed.

Encounters

At our very first meeting it struck me that Maucher essentially thought and acted differently to the majority of people and that his principles and guidelines were fundamentally more different than they had been generally represented. You obviously need to know what to look for if you want to see this clearly; if you want to distinguish between right and wrong and between good and bad management.

Helmut Maucher and I have met very rarely and until the idea of this book was conceived we had only met three times. Our first meeting took place in the fall of 1998 when Helmut Maucher and myself had to deliver speeches at an event for invited guests, where one of the topics was shareholder value, a topic which was in vogue and very prevalent at the time. The first edition of my book *Die Richtige Corporate Governance* (The Right Corporate Governance) had appeared in the previous year. There I had stated that the shareholder value approach which originated in the USA was a misconception and was based on misunderstandings of right management and also misunderstandings of the American economy and its merely apparent strengths and successes; these were by no means the result of particularly exemplary management, which had been the general uncritical assumption at the time.

I showed that this approach meant that fundamental mistakes in management were going to be inevitable and, as already mentioned, would result in the huge misallocation both of economic and human resources. I had been addressing this topic in my publications for years and I had given numerous lectures and seminars on the subject and my experiences at the time are outlined in the above-mentioned book.

It was the time when the new-economy boom was heading towards its zenith; when most of the economic world was dancing round the »golden calf of the Internet«; and when the new perverse factor of success was the so-called »money burn rate «. Shareholder value, key financial figures and Anglo-Saxon management generally were considered to be the new truths for corporate management and had been accepted as such almost worldwide except mainly for the segment of family owned businesses in Europe.

In his presentation Helmut Maucher expressed himself among other things in words which were directed at myself »*I agree with you there. At present we are performing a huge balancing act at Nestlé on account of shareholder values. Tomorrow morning I will have to tell the financial world what they would like to hear and in the afternoon I have to see to it that we do the exact opposite in the company without the financial world being aware of the fact.*«

No one had ever expressed this so clearly and unequivocally. At that time, admittedly, few of the guests got the message, for at that point in time the majority of them were so fixated on shareholder value that it was hardly possible for them to think of alternatives. However, Maucher was one of the few CEOs who did not shy away from an argument with the financial world and often informed them in no uncertain terms of his diametrically opposite points of view, as for example when it came to the price of acquisitions, about which he simply knew considerably more than young financial analysts.

Our second meeting took place in 2006, on the occasion of a dinner given by a major Southern German entrepreneur. Maucher and I were sitting opposite each other at the table and we got into conversation about the power of brands as well as brand strategies and marketing. I was surprised to note that Helmut Maucher, the architect of the world's largest food company, had addressed these issues in person and in very great detail during his active service with the company. In most cases CEOs leave such issues to their specialists and relevant agencies but that was not Helmut Maucher's way.

With a mischievous look he told me that his people had wanted to abolish the original corporate logo and replace it with something more up to date. Nestlé's logo is a small bird's nest in which a caring mother bird is feeding her three young. It is derived from the name of the company's founder, Henri Nestle, who came originally from the Swabian area of Southern Germany where Nestle means »little nest«. Maucher energetically vetoed this intention, however, for this logo was a constitutional element in the identity of the corporation. Just because of the design, he was prepared to do without one of the three little birds so that the proportions of the logo would show to better advantage in small font sizes, too. What emerged in the course of this extremely interesting conversation was the considerable attention to detail and great expertise that Nestlé's CEO brought to bear on the key issues in the business, which is, as I have mentioned, one of the characteristics of his way of management.

The idea for this book was conceived at the third meeting when we were invited to dinner by Dr. Farsam Farschtschian, one of my doctoral candidates, to celebrate his PhD. It was I who had proposed the theme of his dissertation and had supervised it in conjunction with a colleague, Prof. Martin Hilb. The central figure of the dissertation is Helmut Maucher because the research project dealt with his impressively successful acquisitions and above all his exceedingly professional handling of the Board of Directors in that connection.

Dynamic and growth with successful acquisitions

The title of Farsam Farschtschian's doctoral thesis was: *The Secret of Successful Acquisitions – Abandoning the Myth of Board Influence* and it is one of the best dissertations I have ever received during my academic career.

It addressed the subject of why Nestlé was so enormously and sustainably successful with its long-standing acquisition strategy, whereas the then Swiss Airline »Swissair« failed so miserably in spite of applying the exact same strategy and finally went under. In particular Dr. Farschtschian considered which role the Board of Directors in each company had played in the events.

My reason for proposing this subject for the dissertation was the particular feature that this was a golden opportunity which made a comparison of the two companies unique because we had almost controlled laboratory conditions such as exist in science and technology. To a large extent both companies operated under the same conditions, were subject to the same legal system, were globally active, were exposed to the same *zeitgeist* and the same trends; their headquarters were in the same country and both of them had Boards which were studded with top-class high-ranking personalities.

The crucial difference was the quality of their management – it was Maucher's professionalism as Nestlé's CEO and his sovereign cooperation and interaction with the Board of Directors that made all the difference. We only need to remember once again that it is right management which gets things functioning.

In effecting acquisitions Maucher set an example by acting according to his strategic principle of »Be first, be daring, be different«. An acquisition is of all strategies the one that fails most frequently and in most cases most dramatically and for that reason experts consider it to be the most difficult of all strategies. However, Helmut Maucher met the challenges presented by acquisition strategy so brilliantly that there was never a single failure.

One of the reasons for this is the fact that Maucher himself not only had a command of acquisition management – something which others can also do if they have plenty of funds or huge credits – but he also had a brilliant command of the management required to integrate new companies into the complex brand and organization structure of Nestlé and above all to combine the corporate cultures, which in the case of most of his acquisitions could scarcely have been more different.

A fast-moving company

Nestlé is in the business of »*fast-moving consumer goods*«. Under Maucher's regime, Nestlé also became a »*fast-moving company*«.

One of the company's key success factors was in fact Maucher's daring acquisition strategy, which he pursued in the period between 1980 and 2000.

All in all, while he was in office, existing businesses were sold for CHF 9 billion and new ones were acquired worth CHF 40 billion – an amazing total of 250 companies, as has been already mentioned. That was about 13 companies a year – a tremendous challenge for Nestlé's management.

These included some of the largest and most spectacular acquisitions of the time whereby, in the light of the standards which prevailed then, gigantic sums of money were involved. In 1985, for example, Nestlé acquired Carnation, an American corporation, for $3 billion – until then one of the largest takeovers ever. Shortly afterwards, in 1988, Rowntree, the English company, was acquired for $4 billion, which was the largest takeover of a UK company by foreigners. In the same year Buitoni, the Italian company and later Perrier, the French company, were added – to mention but a few of the more well-known brands.

Thus Helmut Maucher perceptibly reduced the one-sided dependence on Nescafé and rapidly gained a foothold on the market for the company's new products such as ice cream, chocolate bars, pasta, pet foods and water. Moreover, this strategy was a significant lever for expanding the company's geographical presence in the USA and in the former communist states in the east.

Despite the diversity of the products and the speed of the acquisitions Nestlé never lost its identity. On the contrary, this was steadily strengthened because Maucher was an expert at creating a functional basic logic. He provided Nestlé with rules which hold the company together to its very core – biology calls it the genetic code. In this instance we could call it the *Maucher Code*, one of the most universal and significant Master Controls.

At the dinner given by the newly qualified Doctor of Economic Sciences to celebrate his PhD, Helmut Maucher and I had the opportunity, for the very first time, to discuss in detail – against the background of the dissertation with its very abundant results – his management philosophy and his management methodology, the results of which, in the context of his strategy and his co-operation with the Board, were portrayed so impressively in the research project.

Plans for this book

When, on the spur of the moment, I suggested to Maucher that evening that we undertake the project of writing this book, he declined at first. He said that he had written everything already and that it was only a short time earlier that his *Management-Brevier* had appeared in which he had outlined all the key points once more.

Maucher is decidedly modest in such matters. For example, he had never for one moment thought of aping the trend of writing his biography or having one written for him. This is an admirable exception in a time when many at the age of only 50 think that their biography could be of interest.

I had already benefited from my reading of Maucher's *Management-Brevier* and for that reason it was clear to me that there was still much more for him to say. It was easy for me to recognize this fact, for not only did I have a sharper perception of Maucher's uniqueness on account of my own management theories but also because of my co-operation with many hundreds of top executives for almost 40 years and because of my active engagement as a member and Chairman of Corporate Governance Boards. Last but not least, there was also my management experience in my own organization, which has been a leading pioneer of exemplary management innovations since 1984.

CEO, Board of Directors and right Governance

Helmut Maucher was an uncommonly strong CEO. He placed great emphasis on the freedom and authority vested in him. He was both CEO and Chairman of the Board of Directors for a long time, which is permissible under Swiss corporate law but would not be possible under German law.

Maucher appeared almost uncompromising in the figure he presented as CEO, the strong man at the head of the company, as the only functioning management principle for the top management. Occasionally the effect could appear somewhat dogmatic.

CEO and autocratic rule

This is one of the few topics where our opinions seemed at first to diverge. It is true that I too stand for the principle of a strong CEO and in practical terms this means that the unrestricted decision-making ability of a company and its capacity to act must be ensured unfailingly at all times. However the solution to this is not only to be found in unrestricted autocratic rule by one person, which is often the way it is construed.

The solution of the one-man autocracy reaches its limits, when a CEO who more or less rules alone, for whatever reason, simply proves to be the wrong man for the job.

Starting in the early 1990s it became common practice for executive searchers to introduce lateral hires into companies as CEOs. Due inevitably to frequently limited knowledge of the business and the company, such CEOs can make wrong decisions within a very short time, which can have irreparable consequences for the company.

On the other hand, Maucher and I share the opinion that where the man at the head of the company is in fact strong, reliable and particularly competent, the results can be second to none. Many commercial empires have arisen or could actually only do so because of this constellation.

If we look more closely, it also becomes very apparent that Maucher carried out his exceedingly strong CEO position with much greater sovereignty than complied with prevailing opinion, text books and the image of the CEO created in the media. Above all, in his position of CEO he acted quite differently from many of his contemporaries in the most senior executive positions at that time, contemporaries who frequently yielded to the temptation to give free reign to their own egomania. We have dealt with Maucher's extremely instructive and special methods as CEO in our conversation, which has been included in this book as a transcript.

Maucher used his power which was in principle almost unlimited and his unique position much more wisely and therefore far more effectively than is usual in top-level management. As he was well aware of the fact that power corrupts and that, as is generally known, absolute power corrupts absolutely, he had the greatness to restrict his unlimited power of his own volition.

It is therefore consistent that because he possessed the expert knowledge of Nestlé's business himself, he made most of the decisions by himself without consulting the Board of Directors. However, he brought personalities onto the Board of Directors who had other attributes; who were strong, capable and independent enough to protect him from the dangers of his enormous power should that have proved to be necessary. Thus, he also established, amongst other things, a Board Committee which had the right of veto where more significant investments were to be decided.

Maucher's corporate governance principles went far beyond the governance codes emerging at that time. Maucher's methods were actually in direct contrast to some of their key points and were superior to the recommendations of the customary codes. For example, he decidedly opposed the excessive manager incomes which were becoming customary at that time, especially if these were also associated with or could be linked to cutbacks in the workforce. He pursued a different avenue than is usual when it came to the remuneration of the Board of Directors preferring a set payment instead of variable profit-related bonus payments, which are always fraught with the risk that decisions are made in favor of short-term improvements in earnings in the interest of one's own income.

Maucher did not need to make use of his formal position of power, for he had a considerable natural authority due to his continuing successes with his right management and due to his profound business knowledge. Added to this was the fact that he treated the members of the Board of Directors with high regard. He enjoyed great respect and he was trusted in his position as head of the company and also as a human being.

A leader with a team instead of a team of leaders

One of Maucher's bold principles is *a leader with a team* – and not, as many would prefer to see, *a team of leaders* at the top. This is a universally valid principle for the organization of a top management, for scarcely anything paralyses a company more than the potential indecisiveness of teams, their frequent self-paralysis and mediocrity.

As stated, Maucher rejected many of the foundations of Anglo-Saxon corporate governance which have dominated for years or accepted them solely as a matter of form; he rejected such concepts as shareholder value, a short-term increase in market value and management with purely financial parameters or with quarterly financial statements. He regarded these elements as objectively obstructive to right and good management. This finds beautiful expression in his quotation on shareholder value.

However that is precisely why his Board of Directors functioned so well and why he also had their unrestrained trust, which is depicted impressively by Farsam Farschtschian in his dissertation.

Thus it was that the members of the Board of Directors could rely on Maucher to always keep them informed about everything – openly, unreservedly and accurately, whether it was positive or negative. When large investments were to be considered – such as the acquisitions mentioned above – Maucher provided the Board of Directors, in good time, with a short but comprehensive exposé that he, the CEO, had produced in person. Usually it was not more than ten or twelve pages long and contained all the information that was relevant to any decision that was to be taken at the highest level.

There were no long-winded discussions and no presentations en masse, but crystal clear management information, which was why decisions by Nestlé's Board of Directors could be reached professionally and quickly.

During our talks, Maucher frequently stressed that the Board of Directors knew that he would have resigned if the Board had good grounds for rejecting his requests two or three times. There can scarcely be any higher degree of personal integrity than to link your own fate to management decisions at the highest level.

Especially when co-operating with Nestlé's Board of Directors, Maucher considered truth and openness, as values of corporate culture and unambiguous morals, to be important. He also emphasized to the shareholders the importance of values for right corporate governance and used to tell them: »*I hope we share more value than just share value* ...«

A distinctive feature of Nestlé's corporate governance is also the fact that Maucher had no employment contract. Just imagine the CEO of the world's largest food company working without a contract.... Knowing the elaborate and highly complex contracts which are usually considered to be indispensable in top management, it is hard to believe and we wonder what the point of it was.

Maucher was reappointed every year and therefore it would have been possible to part with him each year without observing any formal requirements and without any difficulty should there have been any grounds for such action. In order to make this possible in practice, too and in case anything unforeseen happened to him, he informed the Board of Directors every year which persons he recommended to be his successor. His great power was also expressed in his dual function of CEO and Chairman of the Board of Directors, positions which he held simultaneously for ten years. As long as it is possible to part from a CEO every year and at the same time to settle the choice of a successor any time, power can lose many of the negative aspects that are feared. But a strong CEO, who knows the company and the business to the very last detail, who has the authority to decide and whom the Board of Directors trusts, has the advantage.

People and corporate culture

Maucher's principles of personnel policy, promoting young and potential managers, management development as well as management education and training are completely different to what most text books want.

Even his own career path was almost the opposite of what is regarded by HR and executive-search experts as obligatory today, for Helmut Maucher worked »only« for Nestlé all his life. As of 1964, he had held different positions in management in Frankfurt until he became General Director of the Nestlé Group in Germany in 1975. As mentioned, he became the Head of Nestlé AG Switzerland on October 1, 1980 and in 1981 he became CEO of the Nestlé Group. From 1990 until 1997 he held both the position of Chairman and CEO. After he stepped down from his post of CEO, he continued as Chairman of the Board until 2000 when he was appointed Honorary Chairman.

According to this principle he filled the key positions in the corporation preferably with people who had a similar career path. He positioned people who had always »only« been with Nestlé to succeed him. Thus it was that when Peter Brabeck-Lethmate was appointed his direct successor, he had more than 30 years experience at Nestlé, where he had begun work as a product specialist. It was precisely for that reason that these executives were consistently and exceedingly successful. After 30 years with Nestlé, tried and tested by ever increasing and challenging tasks, the man knows the company and the company knows the man. When Maucher handed over leadership to Peter Brabeck-Lethmate, he left the headquarters in Vevey and returned to Frankfurt. Maucher said his successor had to be able to go his own way.

Selecting the right executives

In other matters pertaining to staff policy, Maucher had basically different principles to conventional HR practice and theory. Maucher said a guideline for his staff selection was: »*Look more in the eyes than in the files* ...« which is only one of the many very apt formulations for which he is well-known.

He placed particular emphasis on the education of executives. This found expression among other things in his personal involvement in Rive Reine, Nestlé's own international training and education center, with its pioneering and innovative training programs in management development. It was also evident in his efforts to ensure a leading position for the International Institute for Management Development (IMD) in Lausanne.

However, it was to the *selection* of the right people that Maucher attached most importance. Moreover, he did not think much of assessments, which in the mainstream continue to be regarded as indispensable methods for selecting the right managers. As a result, he went to even greater trouble to obtain a reliable assessment. But you can only look in the eyes of people if they have been with a company long enough, because otherwise you have to rely on the files.

Maucher considers personality and character to be the most decisive factors. But how are these to be assessed in newcomers? Basically, that is not possible! The former successes of lateral hires in other companies can provide some indications, but nothing can replace the reliability of an assessment based on the long service of executives in the company and on the results achieved by an employee who time and again has been entrusted with increasingly important tasks and responsibility over the years and decades.

A corporate culture of credibility and trust

Perhaps more than anything else this personnel policy promoted the strong corporate culture of both credibility and trust, and truth and openness, which thrived at Nestlé under Maucher because people who are promoted as a result of having proved their worth and not as a result of coming from outside don't need to pull the wool over anyone's eyes. They are authentic. Cultural values such as trust, credibility, truth and openness are the basis for their authority.

Maucher was particularly careful and cautious when it came to matters of trust. He adopted the maxim by Peter Drucker, the doyen of 20th century management theory: » *It only takes a minute for trust to be lost but it takes ten years for it to be regained.*«

In addition to corporate culture in the strict sense of the word, Maucher also attaches great importance to the socio-cultural values which, as *Master Controls* also, provide a company with long-term fundamental orientation. It is his opinion that these major values include such attributes as freedom, equality, efficiency and solidarity.

Executives' attributes

In his lectures Maucher repeats, time and again, those traits which he considers to be necessary for good management and which he enumerates in detail. Depending on the purpose of the lecture, the number of important attributes varies: sometimes it is only eleven, and sometimes it can be as many as fifteen. The number of the attributes depends on the subject of the lecture and on rhetorical aspects.

Some of these attributes are courage, strong nerves and equanimity, learning ability, imagination, coherent thought, credibility, an ability to take decisions, a sense of responsibility, modesty, but also good manners and an exemplary presence.

Those who know my own publications will think that they can see a certain contradiction here between Maucher's views and my own in that I am less in favor of how executives are and attach more importance to what executives do.

However, this contradiction tends to be superficial and to result from using terms differently; it is not a matter of basic differences. In so far as anyone actually has attributes – and talents, too – he will doubtlessly have it easier than someone who does not have them.

For those people under someone's direction, attributes are mainly reflected in the way their boss acts. For that reason, my attention is directed more towards managers' actions and the principles they observe in the process than on the traits themselves, which you either have or have not. However one can learn certain kinds of action to a certain degree whereby – within limits – it is even possible to compensate for even weak or missing traits.

Charisma

Did Helmut Maucher have that charisma which is called for so frequently? It depends on what you mean by charisma and how you define it. Whether he had »the divine gift« which is the way the concept of »charisma« is defined from a religious point of view or whether he had »extraordinary revolutionary power« in the way the great sociologist Max Weber sees charismatic rule among other things, and whether Helmut Maucher was even born with it remains open to question.

For decades, however, Helmut Maucher acted in a way that was experienced as charismatic by many others and on whom it had this effect. Peter Drucker once said: »A leader is someone who has followers«. In this sense Maucher was, as already mentioned, a leader. But that is still not enough, for there can be many reasons why people follow others, at least for a time – curiosity, show, money, power and more besides.

People followed Helmut Maucher because he possessed a likeable and natural kind of leadership, because primarily they trusted and respected him and because under his leadership they achieved the right results. In this sense he was someone who genuinely led, unlike many who have misled.

An unusual person with unusual working methods, too

As has been seen, Nestlé's business success under Helmut Maucher's regime was consistently excellent in practically every respect. But what did Maucher himself do specifically to generate this success? What did his working methods look like? Or to put it differently: What does a man like him do when he arrives at his office in the mornings?

In our talks, Maucher said he needed few staff and hardly any consultants either, except when they were required for special tasks. Nor did he have personal assistants; one secretary had been enough for him, but he did emphasize that she had been with him for many years and had been very good. He was good at using a dictating machine. He had led the company through direct contact with the business lines at home and abroad because that was where the know-how and infrastructure were.

On account of his direct way of management he had travelled a lot, especially to the markets. How much of his time had he spent there? About 60 percent. There he would discuss business with the local managers and these discussions had frequently included their key employees. In particular they would talk about the features peculiar to the local markets and products, for although Nestlé was a global corporation with global markets, business tended to be mainly local.

Unlike many other companies, Nestlé did not keep a company aircraft even though the corporation is present in practically every country in the world and runs almost 500 factories in over 80 countries. Although he had spent 60 percent of his time in the markets, he had not really needed a company aircraft; he had always flown with an airline and if that had not been possible, he had been able to charter a plane at any time. Maucher says that they were modest at Nestlé but had style...

Maucher's preparation for launching Nestlé on the market in China is exemplary and unusual as far as working methods were concerned. He visited China in person no less than six times before Nestlé built its first factory there. As a consequence the plant was profitable from the very beginning and has remained so. En passant and with a smile, he compared this to other chairpersons who were not personally on the spot in the early stages, but sent their underlings. Consequently, these only met in China with the next best from there, which meant that they seldom get out of it what they required and certainly didn't get the necessary sturdy trust at the highest level or even lasting friendships such as Maucher had in top government circles and with Chinese Prime Ministers.

On my own numerous visits to China since the 1990s, I have frequently heard the name Nestlé mentioned at the highest levels, but I have heard the name Maucher even more often. Each time it was also mentioned with great respect that the CEO of Nestlé, Helmut Maucher, was a true friend of China. It also became of increasing significance for the Chinese that Maucher's presence and management were entirely different to that of most CEOs. As I myself had also advised the Chinese in business and in politics and repeatedly in the central party school over the years not to engage too one-sidedly in the Anglo-Saxon management approach, I was often asked how I, as an expert, rated Helmut Maucher's management.

No great words, but fine distinctions

Helmut Maucher is an astute thinker, who intellectually gets to the bottom of things. However, what strikes me even more is the fact that he has the art of communication at his finger tips.

His language is clear, unequivocal and powerful, enriched with expressive figures of speech, apt witticisms and delicious and even ironic wit. A selection of his aphorisms can be found at the end of this book. On the other hand, what makes a pleasant change is the fact that Maucher's language contains none of the euphoric expressions and buzz words that are so typical of management.

In interviews with the media, which are also printed in this book, it is striking how sovereign and skilful Helmut Maucher is in dealing with the ever so typical instances of linguistic polarity into which most executives blunder quite regularly. Maucher does not reply to the either-or questions which journalists like to ask with the usual, mostly meaningless »happy medium«; nor does he answer by taking divisive sides in favor of one of the mutually exclusive alternatives, He replies with skilful synthesis at a higher level of integration. For example, we hear him state categorically that companies require bank know-how but not a bank mentality; a good working climate but not a peaceful idyll; lateral thinkers but no oddballs....

This becomes particularly clear and meaningful when, for instance, journalists confronted him with questions on the aims of cuts in the workforce, as for example in the interview with *The Spiegel*, Germany's most important political magazine, which has also been included in the book. Job cuts for the sake of more return? – Definitely not; but on the other hand, job cuts are permissible in order to strengthen competitiveness; not in order to earn more money, but by improving the market position to make business even more sustainable, which as far as Maucher is concerned is not the same thing, even though so many others can only perceive it this way because they do not know, recognize or understand the fine nuances of management at Maucher's high standard.

Commonsense, pragmatism and wisdom

Maucher's mode of management, his long-term orientation, and his decision-making and actions geared toward the principles of corporate policy are grounded in his origins and family, his comprehensive world, his clear value structure, his remarkable knowledge of history and also in his love of music.

Unlike many top executives, Maucher is well-read. A small selection of authors, who Maucher is accustomed to quoting, include such great thinkers a sociologist Max Weber, the most significant management thinker in the 20th century Peter F. Drucker, Chancellor of the social market economy Ludwig Erhard; thinkers from the Freiburg School of Ordoliberalism as well as thinkers from antiquity such as Epictetus and Aristotle; and perhaps the greatest philosopher of science in the 20th century Karl R. Popper, as well as Schopenhauer, Descartes, Cicero, Thomas Hobbes, Goethe, Eduard Mörike to name but a few.

He is unusual among top executives in that he has a good grasp of macroeconomic and societal issues as a whole. He has an unusually profound knowledge of the economic order propounded by German ordoliberalism; he knows the advantages and disadvantages and the functioning of the market economy better than many an economics professor and he has a sound grasp of the most complex issues relating to economic policy. This is also a fundamental part of his credibility and his persuasiveness as a corporate leader. It only takes him to say a few sentences for you to know that here is someone who knows what he is talking about, who is broad minded and holistic in his thinking and therefore acts from a higher plane of wisdom and insight.

Thus, there were convincing and compelling reasons for inviting Helmut Maucher to play a decisive and leading role in top-level committees, as is described in detail in the appendix. Helmut Maucher has set a fine example by doing a lot for society and politics particularly through his commitment to associations and to politics at the highest level, which is also the subject of the final chapter on improvements in our democratic constitutions, which Maucher wrote expressly for this book. He has acted as Chairman of the International Chamber of Commerce (ICC, Paris) and as head of the European Round Table, a committee of some 50 top executives who bring expertise from the echelons of business to the integration process of the European Union.

However, he is not only committed to the really big issues, but also sets an example in his commitment to apparently smaller tasks, which are just as important, as for example opportunities for the area of Upper Swabia and the education of young people which was the subject of a lecture given before teachers at the commercial high school in Wangen in the Allgäu in Southern Germany – Helmut Maucher was born and grew up in the tiny village of Eisenharz in West Allgäu. It was there that he was shaped, formed and educated by his home and large family, by village life, school and by his early job in the local dairy, which was later taken over by Nestlé.

Numerous awards testify to Helmut Maucher's impact and the high esteem in which he is held. For example, he received three honorary doctorates from the universities of Munich, Guadalajara and Oestrich-Winkel, the Scopus Award from the Hebrew University of Jerusalem and the Appeal of Conscience Foundation Award, New York, and the highest awards from the International Institute for Management Development (IMD). He was also awarded the highest political orders of Germany, Austria and Mexico and of the Federal German State of Baden-Württemberg; he received the Fortune Magazine Gold Medal and the INTERNORGA Award and was elected to the Hall of Fame of the German *manager magazine*. He was awarded the *Preis Soziale Marktwirtschaft* (Prize for Social Market Economy) by the Konrad Adenauer Foundation for his entrepreneurial flair and social commitment in 2004. More recently, in April 2013, Maucher received the Hanns Martin Schleyer-Preis, the prestigious award for significant contributions to strengthening and promoting the principles of free and democratic policy.

One of his concerns has been having direct contact with people so that he could understand them and their social reality; he wished to experience for himself what and how men and women think. Market studies alone were not sufficient for his purpose. Another thing that was important to him was making the business world understandable to people and above all giving them insight into the realities of large-scale corporations, which were often regarded with skepticism, rejection and frequently with vague feelings of fear. The second part of Goethe's *Nature and Art*, one of Helmut Maucher's favorite poems, aptly expresses his being and strivings:

»[...] Such is the case with all forms of refinement:
In vain will spirits lacking due constraint
Seek the perfection of pure elevation.
He who'd do great things must display great restraint;
The master shows himself first in confinement,
And law alone can grant us liberation«

Part 2
From Helmut Maucher's Speeches, Publications and Interviews

Editorial Note

The following essays and interviews are each preceded by a brief introduction by Dr. Farsam Farschtschian in which he highlights the key arguments. These are in italics.

Corporate Policy, Corporate Management and Organization Policy

Walking a fine line

In the following newspaper column, Helmut Maucher writes about the key tasks of corporate management. In addition, he goes into detail about how corporate culture is greatly influenced by the style of management and how important it is for entrepreneurs' actions to be guided by long-term perspectives – despite the pressure from the financial world to act with a view to short-term profit maximization.

»Companies face the dilemma of increasingly opposing requirements«

Companies are constantly caught between diverse requirements and interests. Maintaining a balance is not easy and therefore all the more important.

In my opinion, the key tasks of corporate management consist in defining strategy and controlling its implementation, directly managing the departments assigned, coordinating the various divisions, and establishing organization structure, corporate governance and everything that has to do with human resources development.

When enumerating the tasks of a company, it frequently happens that something crucial is forgotten: we forget the impact that the style of management has on corporate culture. Moreover, tasks that have an impact externally are becoming more and more important. These include public relations as well as participation in the work of associations and other special interest groups in the business world.

In an over-regulated company bureaucracy needs to be tackled and its volume reduced. On the other hand, where nothing is regulated and sloppiness is the order of the day, systems and rules need to be created and there must be insistence that these are strictly observed.

At the same time, a company is constantly caught between diverse requirements and interests. Increasingly, the entrepreneur today finds himself facing a dilemma. On the one hand, he is confronted with the steadily growing requirements of ethics, ecology and social conduct and, on the other hand, he is subject to pressure from the financial world and global competition – a pressure which is geared towards short-term focus, orientation towards shareholder value and profit maximization. In this case, it is not easy to maintain the balance of long-term corporate policy – and yet it is of major importance.

There are other areas where corporate management has to achieve equilibrium between two opposing points of view and in the process it is necessary to take both long-term and short-term aspects into consideration. The task comprises centralizing or decentralizing; offensive marketing is rather up against defensive controlling and cost savings. When is diversification and when is focusing called for? Rules and regulations are necessary, but without individual scope nothing works either. The company has to be trimmed for performance and competitive acumen but at the same time its social responsibility should not be forgotten, and although it has its own national and cultural identity, it has to satisfy international demands if it intends to operate worldwide.

Besides, the company has to cope with the contrast between shareholder or stakeholder orientation whereby this contrast does not exist if corporate policy is geared towards the long-term and is thus sustainable. It arises principally if regarded from a short-term perspective. If shareholder value is to be optimized in the long term, the interests of various social groups – i. e. the stakeholders – are bound to be taken into consideration and measures have to be taken to strengthen the image of the company. If shareholders' interests are borne in mind in the long term, the views specific to the stakeholder are automatically included.

Source: Helmut Maucher, »Auf schmalem Grat« (Walking a fine line) in *Bilanz no.* 20/2010.

The fine art of managing a company

In the following interview Helmut Maucher addresses issues related to the concept of management. He talks about the role intuition plays in leadership tasks, reveals the three key management principles at Nestlé and illustrates what matters in the organization of a company.

»I see one of my key functions in keeping the company constantly alert to new trends, new issues ....« – is one of Helmut Maucher's maxims on corporate management, but otherwise the head of Nestlé favors apparently traditional values: trust, commitment and responsibility and that more than ever since it is difficult for them to become evident in modern corporate structures; when there are minimal hierarchical structures and decentralized organization.

EW: Mr. Maucher, you interpret the concept of management as the fine art of leadership. Moreover, you once said in this connection that this is one of the few instances where the word leadership is more appropriate.

Maucher: Leadership is more than mere technique: part of it is an art.

EW: Could you please explain that?

Maucher: A distinction is frequently made between the manager and the entrepreneur. The manager sees his tasks, the entrepreneur sees his opportunities. The manager is an administrator and optimizer, the entrepreneur is a strategist and business developer. The manager has expertise, the entrepreneur has charisma. The manager makes forecasts and long-term plans and even believes in them. In contrast, the entrepreneur simply has more ideas, more perception of the future and has long-term views. The manager works with statistics and checklists, hedges the risks, and defines targets and measures in the light of the pros and cons. The entrepreneur is prepared to take risks and he has the strength to weather them out. It is not unknown for him to have almost brutally simple concepts, which he follows with great persistence. Often, the entrepreneur also faces difficult issues, difficult decisions, which cannot be taken clearly from a rational point of view or on the basis of analyses.

EW: You play off skills and talents against each other. Does the business world need more artists, then; more instinct in the boardrooms?

Maucher: Now and again when I no longer know what is right or not, I say: Now, I'm just going to rely on my compass. Once I was asked: Do you apply the theories of business administration or use your intuition? I don't really know. I think both are important in my case.

EW: What do you mean by intuition?

Maucher: As far as I am concerned, intuition is the creative utilization of information, for even when we think something is purely intuitive, it is influenced by the sum of our experience and knowledge. However, it is not everyone who knows how to exploit information creatively. They have experiences without benefiting from them. However, I don't want to detract from the value of both functions. I think that today one needs to be both manager and entrepreneur, and combining both is perhaps the very essence of the art of leadership.

EW: That sounds very ideal-typical, and especially in comparison to the conspicuously large amount of literature offering practical advice, which wants to tell managers what really matters in corporate management and which range from management and self-management to management by chaos; from customer focus to the Japanese Kaizen Principles.

Maucher: If management by chaos were actually such a good concept, far more companies would be successful. These are all terribly big words and of course there is an element of truth in all of them. But, as a rule, for people who have always managed properly, there is nothing entirely new about it.

Take »consumer focus«, for example – someone comes up with the fantastically new idea of recommending businessmen to turn their attention to the customers. And there are large enterprises that then say, we will have to do that too. But what do they do? Instead of engaging three new sales staff to look after the customers they establish a department for customer-orientated marketing. Is that the way to solve the problem? I have just read the latest piece of wisdom in »Fortune«: »Future of Success – Neglect your Customer«, but this, too, contains an element of truth.

EW: Neglecting customers?

Maucher: If I focus solely on the customer – just like the rabbit gazes hypnotized at the snake – and I no longer make use of my skills, my ideas, my technology and research to produce something new about which the customer may know absolutely nothing, then that can't work either.

Or let's take »self-management«. That is another one of these brilliant ideas that are tried out somewhere or other every ten years as a mixture of early Christianity and Cultural Revolution. Of course, there is some truth in that, too. We don't need watchdogs and supervisors everywhere; there are many people who could perform tasks autonomously. My advice is to be more careful and not to tackle such things naïvely and illusorily.

EW: And the manager as a coach?

Maucher: Of course, management is considerably more than mere coaching. It requires, for example, leadership skills and the ability to take decisions. Tasks relating purely to care and support should be safely left to a psychiatrist – that's his job, after all. What is true, however, is that you really have to take care of people.

My advice, in view of all these buzz words and concepts, is to learn to distinguish between genuine, innovative ideas and mere trends and fads that are of more use to the authors of such theories than to us. Apart from that, it is sometimes not a bad idea to wait for them all to blow over. I nearly have a heart attack when I see what PR departments, designers, self-styled gurus and HR departments, for example, try to talk good, sound companies into believing. It is up to us to decide for ourselves what is right, what is suitable for our company and what makes sense.

EW: How are things done at Nestlé?

Maucher: We have three key management principles:

1. We are a company that focuses more on people and products than on systems.
2. To a large extent Nestlé has a decentralized management.
3. We think long-term.

EW: Could you explain that, please?

Maucher: Well, take focusing on people and products. Naturally we need systems in a complex company that operates globally. However, it is all a question of priority and besides systems should never become a target as such. Systems are a means to an end to help us run the company better.

As far as decentralization is concerned: we all know that it creates flexibility and means that employees can identify more with their own company.

That is why we go to great lengths in our company to find the right balance of cooperation and decentralization between headquarters and our subsidiaries. We are working on the idea of a world-wide networking system and use »centers of excellence« wherever we can find them. That is a somewhat different philosophy to the traditional thinking in terms of the parent company and the subsidiaries.

In my opinion, some of the key aspects of organization are decentralizing, delegating responsibility, minimal hierarchical structures and the ability to communicate laterally.

EW: »Minimal hierarchical structures« – but that is a term that is also in fashion. How can these be implemented in the company?

Maucher: Minimal hierarchical structures are naturally part of decentralization. That leads to a greater range of control so that automatically bosses have less time every day to tread on everyone's toes.

Decentralizing also means delegating. But that doesn't mean not having to bother any more about what has been delegated. If I have delegated the choice of a hat to the reception clerk, that doesn't mean that I can't grouse if it turns out to be a hat suitable for carnival.

Decentralization fails when you don't realize what it automatically entails: first of all, you need to give very careful thought to selecting the people to whom you are going to assign authority far away from headquarters; secondly, you need a corporate policy so that the people will know what the company wants in principle and what attitude it adopts. A corporate culture supported by everyone is a help because automatically the people will act more correctly without constantly needing detailed regulations.

EW: How do you define corporate culture in connection with decentralization?

Maucher: Someone once said:
»Corporate culture is the sum of everything that is taken for granted in a company«.

The problem isn't just saying: »We are going to decentralize«. Part of a corporate culture is that we understand other cultures. We can mesh with the mentality of the Japanese and with the Brazilians. Moreover, there are some basic essentials that fit everywhere. It is accepted everywhere that we don't put up with lazybones; that we tend to be pragmatic rather than dogmatic; that we attach great importance to trust and not to the fact that everyone covers his back by always writing umpteen notes, and that one has a personal style of leadership instead of only communicating in writing.

We need both the will to understand others and to integrate into their culture, and in addition we need the skill to form a general cohesion. It seems to me that this combination is crucial in a large international company.

Finally, you have to be prepared to take the necessary steps if the executive is no longer up to scratch or if trust has been betrayed. In a huge decentralized system an abuse of confidence is the one point where you have to be brutal and hard. For me, betraying trust is one of the cardinal sins and is unforgivable. However, I tend to be in favor of giving people the benefit of the doubt.

EW: Control is good, but trust is better?

Maucher: I think we can afford to be trusting otherwise people won't develop. Lenin said it the other way round. To a certain degree, we may well need control mechanisms but I tend to agree more with Goethe's statement which is:

»If you treat an individual as he is, he will remain as he is; if you treat him as if he were what he ought to be and could be, he will become what he ought to be and could be«.

EW: Is that part of the long-term thinking at Nestlé?

Maucher: In view of short-term pressure, stiff competition and the many demands, it isn't easy always to think in long-term categories and to include this thinking in reaching decisions. Of course, long-term thinking functions better if I know that my next profit and loss statement will be more or less correct – hence the importance of short-term statements, too. On the other hand, long-term thinking ought not to be an excuse for short-term failures. However, it cannot be denied that only long-term thinking leads to the sustainable development of companies – over years and decades in fact.

[...]

EW: A plea for feelings in management?

Maucher: And for sensitivity, too. We know meanwhile that such things are much more important than the beliefs we have held since Descartes' times. You need sensitivity if you are to feel anything and to know what is happening. But you shouldn't be soft either. We need strength, nerves, courage and sometimes toughness even for corporate management. But one thing is certain: no one will succeed if he is cold, has no heart and is inhuman.

Moreover, what we don't need are people who have lost the balance between their own hedonistic optimization of life and their commitment to the company; people who start to think about their pensions immediately after being hired. I would like to have employees who are committed to us; if they are successful, they should also have a better life. But I can't win future competition with people who spend more time thinking about themselves than about their tasks and the business.

EW: Nestlé competes globally. Perhaps that applies less to the management of decentralized companies and more to management in headquarters. How is it still possible to manage a company of this size?

Maucher: In my opinion it's possible to manage a company of any size. It depends on the style of leadership, the management and the organization. There are people who fail when turnover grows from one million to two million. Mostly they haven't understood that growth means changes in organization and the style of leadership. I'm all in favor of a team with a leader and I'm not in favor of a team of leaders. That means, I really am in favor of the team, too; for a collegial management style, but I am not in favor of responsibilities being blurred. I don't think we can afford that in competition nowadays. From time to time a company simply has to think somehow or other about which forms of organization it needs.

EW: When was the last time that Nestlé thought about its organization?

Maucher: We were faced with this question a few years ago after expanding so much subsequent to the last reorganization. As a result, we had to deal with new market structures; new product lines were added to our product range; global communication had increased; the globalization of the markets had continued to intensify and common economic areas had developed. We had to reconsider whether in view of all these changes we were still properly organized. One problem we had, for example, was that we were active in very many food areas and were competing to some extent with companies that were large and powerful but only covered one or two food areas. Our answer to the problem was to retain the regional concept, but to develop and establish strategic units for products and product lines at general-director level. So then it is more than just marketing.

EW: But surely that isn't everything that has to be done when a company wants to change?

Maucher: Change requires more than logical, technocratic decision-making. It's a real leadership task. And there is no doubt that leadership coupled with charisma can cope with the change better than when this attribute is missing. In this connection I would like to recall one aspect that is crucial and that is trust.

If all in all, people trust the management and the company, they are much more ready to listen and then together they are prepared to lend their support to what has to be done. If this trust is missing, the people say: What have they come up with this time? – A trick; an absolute mess? Only if we have their trust, can we create a culture of change and promote those people who are prepared to adjust continually to new things and are capable of managing the change. I see one of my key functions in keeping the business alert to new trends, to new issues etc. Some firms have gone bust because they were too sluggish. However, the time factor is every bit as important. You can't be inactive for ten years and then try to change.

EW: There are quite a few companies that apparently wait until the last opportunity, until the life cycle of their best products has been exhausted.

Maucher: Change is a daily task. Anyone not doing that constantly will find himself at some point or other in situations where only the greatest of efforts can help and this usually involves dire consequences for the employees – which is what has happened in some large-scale enterprises in recent years.

I think that rather pessimistic people have talked us into believing the theory of the »life cycles« of products: sales increase at first and then they decline. I just don't believe in »life cycles«.

EW: Instead?

Maucher: Innovation is – like marketing – a management issue. I believe in the constant change of products on the basis on new technological developments. There is nothing worse for a company than people failing to consider constantly how they might change a product and what the new things are which could be used to improve a product before they abandon it once and for all.

[...]

EW: Finally: Entrepreneurship and optimism are mostly mentioned in the same breath. Are you optimistic?

Maucher: You can't operate a business without having optimism and, to some extent, a positive attitude towards taking risks. Anyone who can't take a risk ends up taking the biggest risk of all. However, optimism shouldn't be mistaken for »wishful thinking«.

Source: »The fine art of leading a company« in *Ernährungswirtschaft* no. 1/1996 on February 5, 1996.

»I don't yearn for simple solutions
but I do see things more simply«

In the following interview, Helmut Maucher talks about the complexity of a top manager's career. Furthermore, he addresses the activities of non-government organizations, disputes with activists and strategies for conflict management.

[...]

brand eins: To the outsider the career of top manager seems to be either over-taxing or to be so challenging that only the extraordinary talented make it. How immense is the complexity really?

Maucher: Well, first of all we need to distinguish between two levels: the one is the complexity of the company a manager runs and the other is the complexity of the job itself.

Let's start with the job.

One thing's for sure: in the last few years it has become more and more complex and this is due to competition, modern techniques, internationality and everything that impacts on the company. But today the biggest dilemma every manager faces is the conflict between the short-term goals of share-holder value fetishists on the one hand and the requirements of society on the other hand; that is the ethical and social requirements to which a manager is committed.

Didn't these exist in your day, too?

Oh, yes! In the mid-90s there was a real shareholder value wave, when every CEO had to decide how much time he wanted to spend on the numerous financial analysts and financial journalists. At that time, I had an interview with one of your colleagues, who accused me of only meeting financial analysts twice a year whereas my own colleagues did that more often. He asked whether I didn't take the shareholder seriously. I replied that I did my duty. I would see the analysts twice a year and would give him an interview here. Furthermore, I was of the opinion that it was in the interest of the share-holders if I spent more time on my actual business and delegated the tasks concerning investor relations to my colleague in charge of finance, who could explain things just as well as I, but that I was in a position to run the business better than he could. That, in turn, would help the figures and the shareholder value and was called long-term success. [...]

That sounds plausible. Did he get the point?

I don't know. Considered from a short-term point of view, opinions are more important than facts – but from a long-term point of view, facts are more important than opinions. I've always stuck to that and accordingly I've tried to divide up my time as fairly as possible.

Of course, as the number one in a company you have certain obligations: we have to belong to associations, express our opinions, make our points of view heard, make the company transparent of course, and serve all those groups that are interested in us as a company. However, if we only concern ourselves with this, then we have a real regional disadvantage compared with countries like China, where you don't have to do all this.

Presumably the Chinese worry perceptibly less about all the non-government organizations (NGOs) that have targeted Nestlé since the 70s....

... and which have increased almost exponentially since then. I used to have dealings with a maximum of 10,000 of these organizations and I was perhaps directly involved with 300 of them. Meanwhile, there are a good 30,000 such organizations, who are always thinking up something or other. But there are all kinds of NGOs and many of them are useful. What I would ask is that NGOs address their criticism openly on the market place, that they are transparent, that their financing is not kept secret and that they don't use violence. After all, these are all things that are demanded of us.

A tribunal has just been formed and awarded Nestlé the Public Eye Award – for its anti-union and anti-employee policy in Columbia among other things.

We can refute it all, but it takes a lot of time.

When you were appointed to the Board of Directors of Nestlé, Switzerland in 1981, the famous powdered milk scandal was at its height. Nestlé was accused of preventing mothers in Africa from breast-feeding so that it could sell its powdered milk. That can't have been very pleasant.

It all started before I came to Vevey, in the mid-70s. »Nestlé is killing Babies!« it was claimed. The Swiss were absolutely shocked and treated it as a legal case. I asked if I might be allowed to settle the matter myself as far as Germany was concerned. Next day I wrote a letter to around 13,000 employees and contacted UNICEF and other welfare groups. Compared with the Anglo-Saxon countries, we, in Germany, got off lightly.

However, the accusation persisted a long time and was still hovering over the company when you came to Vevey in 1980.

I met people there who felt that they had been accused unjustly and who had retreated behind the barricades – which is the worst thing you can do in such a case.

Why's that?

Displaying such a mentality means reinforcing the barricades, defending oneself against the world outside and uniting everyone inside in the conviction that »we« don't make mistakes. That's nonsense, of course. First of all, you need to look and see what the matter really is; you need to find out where the problems are – problems which may not be your fault but which look like it in view of the situation in an undeveloped country. You have to ask yourself whether you might have made a mistake after all, and if so, where it might be. But no company is perfect. We employ 250,000 people – something can always go wrong.

And what was your strategy?

I had to separate those activists who were using this accusation against the multinationals for their own purposes from those who meant well, who were genuinely worried and wondered: »Are they killing babies? That's impossible! What kind of company does something like that? «. We wanted to convince those who were genuinely worried by giving them the facts and in the end we finally succeeded after very tough negotiations and a lengthy process.

Why didn't you just stop selling the powdered milk? Powdered milk in Africa – it doesn't sound like big business, does it?

We are talking about 1.5 percent of our total business – that means that our annual growth rate was three times higher than sales of baby milk. But that wasn't the point; it was a matter of principle. I was convinced that the product was needed. What would have happened if we hadn't delivered any more baby milk? Women not able to breast-feed would have had to give their infants starchy manioc like they used to – that's like giving them potatoes to eat. I was sure I was doing the right thing and didn't quit simply because a few activists wanted to stop me.

Have you any explanation why you were never really able to convince the NGOs with this stance and why it is that Nestlé has remained one of the favorite enemies of Attac and other groups up to the present day?

We are a large, successful company; we are the prototype of the multinational company and we have products everyone knows. There is a strong temptation to want to annoy Nestlé now and again. And any efforts to clear up any misunderstandings are useless!

But the world is complex; the attacks don't actually seem to have harmed business, do they?

At that time, I was convinced that this story had caused us considerable harm in America where the boycott was at its fiercest, but the financial statement at the end of the year showed no signs of this. Those products that sold badly sold badly anyway – and all the others sold well. But unfortunately you cannot rely on such things: if you do nothing about it, then you can be hit by the long-term effect.

How do you prioritize in such situations? Does all your energy go on dealing with conflicts?

Well, you do have to spend considerable time and effort on such matters at first, but then they can be steered quickly into calmer waters. That, by the way, is another problem that the manager's job entails: the fact that in general, you can never prioritize. Events occur every day that require me to alter my priorities and in that case I have to know how much time I need to devote to them myself and what I can delegate. That is an important aspect of the job and it's where most mistakes are made. Many managers can't take it: when their nerves are bad, their health isn't good and when they get annoyed about everybody and everything, they suffer from burnout quite quickly. (...) I just can't afford to be surprised at how bad humanity is – and certainly not every day!

And how much of his capacity should a manager spend on open dialogue with the public when things are normal and not for example when Greenpeace is in the middle of staging a protest by climbing up the smokestacks?

With regard to transparency and all that entails, I would set aside about 25 percent of the entire capacity. Naturally, the remaining 75 percent wouldn't ›only‹ be taken up by mere management. As a manager I need time for the employees, no matter who they are. Moreover, when I run a company like Nestlé, which comprises 500 factories, I don't have any option but to travel all over the world. I traveled a lot looking at the factories, having talks with the management, looking at the sales locations, the products, advertising etc. but there were no charts. They can be looked at on the plane.

I was interested in people and wanted to have contact to the people in the factories as far as I could; and whenever possible, I wanted to spend an evening with major representatives from the business world or with people who knew the country. That way I had a good overview after two days.

And when does the top manager, who gives the most talks and travels the most, think about major strategy?

Actually, you are always doing that because you are constantly stimulated by information. You're obliged to keep yourself informed – that's part of the complexity of the job. If you keep your eyes and ears open while going through life, you take in an enormous amount of information. The important question is whether and how you can process it in the shortest possible time. I have always been asked whether I work intuitively or academically, but no one really knows exactly which roles the brain or intuition play. As far as I am concerned, intuition is the creative exploitation of information. But I'm not just talking about statistics and the results of market research, by the way; you also get information when you talk to people and see how they live.

Is it possible to learn to digest such information correctly?

I don't think so. It's a talent or is genetically determined. Naturally, that doesn't mean that education doesn't matter; I would say that selecting information is more important. I was always eager to learn; inquisitive about life. But I never possessed that form of motivation that sometimes can be observed in very well brought-up children from good families, who are entirely driven by the question of when they will get the next pip on their shoulders ... I never thought of that.

It would appear that you were scarcely less relaxed when you were working than you are now in your retirement.

That's true. From my point of view, it isn't difficult to run a company like that.

Then why do many people seem to find it difficult?

I can't answer that question. If I look at myself, I find that I am no Einstein, but by chance I happen to have those 15 attributes* that are essential for such a job. Surely it cannot be that among 80 million Germans there aren't at least 500 who likewise possess this combination of various attributes. I assume the wrong choice was made; I've no idea; it's a mystery to me.

Perhaps other companies are simply more complex – Nestlé has always stuck to its core business, food.

That brings us to the second level, the complexity of the company, although this also has a lot to do with the way someone does his job. In times when great emphasis was placed on diversification, I did not buy a bicycle factory and that's why I didn't have to sell it again when core business came back into fashion. I have always believed that you are most successful at the things you know something about.

And yet, Nestlé expanded enormously in the 80s and 90s.

We were too dependent on Nescafé; we had concentrated too much on Europe and had invested in restaurants and other business fields where we didn't have anything special to offer. So we added new products: pet food, water, ice-cream, chocolate bars etc. Then we turned our attention first to

---

* Please refer to »Human Resources and Management Policy – Challenges for future corporate management« for elaboration on these attributes.

America and then to lots of other countries. All in all, we sold companies worth CHF 6 billion and bought some for CHF 35 billion.

That sounds very much like real portfolio management, which is generally considered to be complex.

No, it isn't. It's more a matter of its strategic focus. When making the acquisitions in America, for example, I had a look at the mistakes the Europeans had made there and vice versa. Then I went to the trouble of trying to understand the Americans. I employed Americans as bosses, talked to them and promised them that I'd see to it that our staff didn't descend on them. I assured them that we trusted their efficiency because they knew themselves what they wanted and that we could still learn from them.
    [...]

One of the distinctive features of your management is the fact that in time of crises, as in Russia or Asia, you didn't pull out but remained there.

That's the difference between short-term and long-term thinking. The Americans backpedal when the three-month statement doesn't look good – even though establishing business is never as favorable as in times of crises. That has two advantages: you can buy additional companies at favorable prices and the people in the region hit by the crisis appreciate you because you didn't go away.

That sounds so simple – and yet it is rarely done.

The reason for that is that managers often think of the short term and are afraid of the next financial statement.

Perhaps of all the 15 attributes you mentioned they don't have the one that is needed to understand a complex world. After all, you have said yourself that the environment is becoming more and more complex. And if we add all the technical developments to the NGOs, it can easily become unmanageable.

You're right of course. The development of technology is such that people don't understand it anymore and that's why they feel insecure. They think that dangers are lying in wait which they cannot grasp. The facts need to be explained to them but who's to do it? Companies can only do so in a limited way because they are tied to certain interests. Then people would say: All they're interested in doing is talking about their own business.

But in the case of gene technology, you did give it a try ...

... and after my interview with »Stern« nine years ago I was trounced by my own people. I said the process was irreversible, but that in Germany it would take 10 years longer than anywhere else. Moreover, the rejectionist front is slowly crumbling because they simply can't find anything detrimental about gene technology.

Your opponents in the NGOs see it differently.

The fact is that 70 percent of the German population is contra and 99 percent of the scientists are pro. What was counterproductive, however, was the conduct of Monsanto at the time, who believed they could solve the problem with American PR methods.

And Nestlé?

In principle we don't mind whether gene technology comes to stay or not because we sell to consumers what they want from us. However, what we should not do is resign ourselves to the fact that 800 million people are starving and yet we hardly use one percent of the plants that could be used as food for people. Gene technology could be used to reduce water consumption by half. We still produce far too much food using animals in the process. I advocate a solution to this problem; but it has nothing to do with Nestlé.

Have you ever actually felt overtaxed?

No, never.

Not once in the whole of your long management career?

I know, no one believes it, but it's true. On the other hand, I have never experienced a real catastrophe. Of course it would have depressed me no end if I had run the company into the ground. Fortunately, it never happened to me.

Perhaps one of your 15 talents is that you don't immediately regard crises as catastrophes. After all, things didn't always go well when you were at Nestlé; there were setbacks and difficult situations, too.

When I took over Findus at the age of 35, we recorded a loss of DM 24 million. I worked night and day for two whole years, exploited every avenue, and phoned every warehouse every Monday morning until I had re-established a system in the organization. Sure, you have to be able to stand the pace – and that was what I did.

Does coping with complexity also have anything to do with the way you perceive things?

Yes, it definitely does. If I look at things nowadays, I often have the feeling that everything is analyzed over and over again. I think I was somewhat more easy-going. Of course a company like Nestlé is complex. The following saying was a great help in dealing with things in the early days: »System frees, bureaucracy hampers«.

You have been married for 52 years. Which task is more complex – such a long marriage or running Nestlé well?

Oh, what a difficult question! Well then ... Being a husband is quite easy and wonderful or it goes wrong.

Is being a CEO different?

No, it isn't; except that marriage is much more intimate and personal.

Source: Fischer, Gabriele: »I don't yearn for simple solutions but I do see things more simply« in *brand eins* no. 1/2006.

Corporate management in a global economy – Thoughts on future leadership requirements and requisite leadership attributes

The following lecture addresses the difficulty of corporate management, especially in times of increasing globalization. Helmut Maucher discusses the key attributes which executives ought to have in these tougher conditions if they are to be successful. In addition, he gives details on the principles of corporate policy such as social responsibility, organizational policy and the human resources policy of a company. He deals with the question of what a company ought to do at global and local levels and finishes with comments on marketing strategies and the communication policy of a company.

Today the subject of my talk is not going to be management in general but rather I am going to address what changes there have been and what will be the main focus of management with regard to globalization in the future.

Changes in the future or new focal points are not only the result of globalization but are the result of other changes, too; some of them are related to globalization and some are magnified by it.

In this context I would like to mention some points which I have summarized in the following keywords:

- Increasing mobility of people, capital, and ideas and opinions.
- Accelerated growth of knowledge (double the amount every three to five years) as well as technological progress and its circulation internationally.
- Increase in free trade (WTO and market economy – i. e. free-market elements).
- Greater international cooperation (G8 to G15) despite many persisting problems, opposing interests and despite continuing regional conflicts. (We will have to live with terrorism for some time to come.)
- Issues concerning the integration of foreigners and future migration.
- Emergence or boosting of regional economic areas (EU, Mercusor – the Southern American common market, Asia etc.)
- Demographic developments.
- Shifts in the importance of individual countries and regions with regard to population, gross national product and political significance (China, India, and Asia in general, Russia, Brazil, Mexico, USA, and Africa).
- Issues such as climate protection and other ecological themes.

- Imminent shortages in the world (energy, water, grain).
- Increase in critical and well-informed consumers and citizens – and in this connection the demand for more democracy and the increasing key role of the media.
- Increase in the importance of capital markets, the financial world, and investor relations etc.

All these changes result in demands on and requests to general government and economic policy, in other words to framework directives, on the one hand; and demands on corporate policy on the other hand.

Even though it is not exactly related to my subject today, I would like to say, especially in this circle, something about framework conditions.

Speaking generally, we need to return more and more to a really social market economy, which is also deserving of this name.

In this connection, let me remind you of its origins: the Freiburg School, ordoliberalism and Erhard, too.

We are all aware that part of this social market economy has been denatured today, due to a bureaucratic straitjacket and due to the expansion of the welfare net into a welfare hammock. We know that there are too many obstructions and impediments to pushing economically viable matters through. (We need only think of the motorway between Lindau and Munich, the extension of Munich Airport and the like).

Moreover, we need a balanced policy between the economy and ecology. Many things may be ecologically sensible; if, however, these things are only done in Germany, we lose competitiveness compared with the other European countries; and the same applies to global competition, too.

Currently climate protection is topic number one and from my point of view – despite the necessity to do something in this direction – the emphasis being placed on it is much too one-sided.

But we all aware that many things, even in scientific discussions, are controversial. For example, it is almost difficult to understand why, under our present coalition, an extended use of nuclear energy is not possible.

As far as the one-sidedness of the discussion is concerned, I would only like to mention that in the discussion other things are being ignored which will be exceedingly vital in future. I would only remind you of the future shortage of the three major resources – water, energy and grain.

A few words on the subject of labor legislation

What is certainly required, in view of the numerous individual legal requirements, is appropriate labor legislation. In this context, we need to press for
more flexibility, more flexible age limits, and some modifications in the right
of co-determination and in the Industrial Constitution Act. There has been
an initial easing of legislation with the creation of the Europa AG, the European public limited company.

In addition, there ought to be an increase in the annual working time, too.
Admittedly we have made progress in labor costs, but they are still too high.

Finally, we need an immigration policy which is geared more towards our
interests and less towards social aspects.

We have made progress in fiscal policy, too, but we need further measures
towards heavier taxation of consumption and a reduction in the high taxation
of performance and assets; apart from that, state intervention and linked to
this the ratio of government expenditure to gross national product need to
be reduced; that means that a decrease in the total tax burden is necessary.
Public debt is still rising; unemployment figures are dropping but they are
still too high.

From an industrial point of view, Prime Minister Koch of the State of
Hesse has triggered a crucial debate: to what extent do we need to consider
how we deal with investments and the acquisition of foreign companies that
are state-owned and have strategic importance beyond mere economic considerations.

Many who have spoken out critically are either too fundamentally committed or they didn't understand Mr. Koch properly.

Finally, I would like to point out that these essential changes in the framework conditions as part of increasing globalization assume increased significance for our competitiveness and need to be discussed from this point of
view.

A few words on the subject of European
and international framework conditions

In the EU we have again made moderate progress and a gridlock has at least
been avoided. As far as international importance and our competitiveness
are concerned, it is, apart from anything else, particularly important that
we speak with one voice, that we extend majority decisions and that no one

is given an opportunity to obstruct initiatives. Moreover, European bureaucracy needs to be reduced and more attention must be paid to the principle of subsidiarity again.

The steady increase in globalization will require a strengthening of international commonalities in the direction of G8 or perhaps even G15 at some stage. The UN needs to be aware of certain tasks so that, for example, what we originally established as ordoliberalism in our country becomes applicable internationally.

In this respect I would like to point out something which is very difficult but whose importance ought not to be underestimated. I'm talking about the need for changes in mindsets. Thankfully, there have been changes in the awareness of the population, but we have still a long way to go. As long as trade unions organize strikes when working time is to be raised from 35 to 38 hours and, in addition, oppose any modification with respect to the Works Constitution and the law on co-determination (which is known to be unique worldwide) and such like, we are still a long way from where we should be. What we need is a new balance between the necessary cross-territorial planning and decisions on the one hand and the likely protests on the other. At some stage we will have to give up our irrational stance in green genetic engineering – a stance which persists in the face of all scientific evidence.

In general, our mentality of focusing on our own demands and desires needs to be supplemented again with an attitude where conscientiousness and responsibility have top priority.

Position for Europe and Germany: the real »Middle Kingdom«

This brings me to issues of corporate policy within the framework of increasing globalization and the other changes mentioned. In general, I would like to say that as far as the requisite leadership attributes for top managers are concerned, aspects of personality and character are becoming more and more significant compared with education and professional expertise and experience.

Some of these I would like to refer to especially in connection with globalization and the changes in the world.

Undoubtedly courage, strong nerves and equanimity are required; likewise a capacity to learn, openness to anything new, and an ability to imagine the future; and finally a willingness to change constantly, the skill to manage change and the willingness to acquire international experience or at least an understanding of other countries and cultures.

I would particularly like to emphasize credibility which, in my opinion, is perhaps the major leadership attribute in the future; to emphasize it in view of today's peculiar attitude towards truth and on account of the importance of credibility for establishing long-term trust internally and externally.

Moreover, I always say: » *Anyone lacking sensitivity cannot lead, nor can anyone who is only sensitive*«.

One of my dearest wishes is for entrepreneurs to again voice their views more often and more perceptibly on all social, political and economic issues. We cannot just leave the debate to other social groups.

Some of our political opponents or perhaps I should say in this meeting some of my political opponents no longer seem to be used to entrepreneurs speaking out clearly and saying what they think.

Where has the courage got to that I have demanded of every entrepreneur? (We all have a spinal column but only a few of us have a backbone).

In view of globalization and the increasing number of international companies from all parts of the world, we need to ask ourselves which priorities our corporate leaders set. Unfortunately, the heads of our companies are forced nowadays to deal more and more with things which have actually nothing to do with business management. Investor relations and all the issues related to this are taking up more and more time. Into the bargain, there are issues of corporate governance and many critical issues to be dealt with – justified or not – that are the result of the current strength of the media or the fact that we have more than 30,000 NGOs nowadays. That is, without a doubt, a competitive disadvantage compared with companies from emerging economies or other parts of the world that don't have to address these issues to the same extent.

Let me mention some of the principles of corporate policy which I developed for Nestlé in those days and that have assumed more and more importance today in view of increasing globalization, the increasing importance of computers and technocracy and the steadily rising pressure towards short-term aspects – whether it is financial pressure and pressure from analysts or whether it is from competition. These principles are:

a) We focus on people and products rather than on systems
b) Thinking and acting are long-term
c) Decentralization: In cases of doubt, I am more in favor of decentralization than centralization.

In this context let me say something about social responsibility, which is the subject of a great deal of discussion nowadays.

The entrepreneur's major social and ethical responsibility is to be successful in the market and in competition, thus ensuring the company's income in the long term. In this way, a significant contribution is made to affluence and to the thriving of the economy, from which we all benefit in the end. A good company pays the taxes needed for the joint tasks in the community and finally due to successful corporate management, jobs are ensured, retained and their number increased. These fundamental tasks of a company, therefore, constitute its major social and ethical responsibility.

Moreover, companies today find themselves in a real dilemma: on the one hand they feel the increasing squeeze from financial pressures and the demands for short-term maximization of profits, and on the other hand they try to satisfy increasing demands, social responsibility and obligations.

In fact, business managers often have to take into account two diametrically opposite things that are both important. For example:

1. Long-term and short-term aspects
2. Centralization versus decentralization
3. Marketing versus controlling (spending or saving)
4. Diversity (diversification) versus focusing
5. The need for rules and regulations versus preserving individual scope
6. Performance and focus on competition (especially in human resources and wages policy) versus social responsibility and social protection
7. The national and cultural identity of a company versus international claims and worldwide activities

Achieving an optimal balance between these aspects is one of the key factors of success for a company. They need bearing in mind when decisions, above all decisions on strategy, are being taken.

And now some issues concerning organizational policy in a globally operating company

Speed is becoming increasingly important and that entails many difficulties in today's complexity and also in view of the mentality of large-scale organizations. It is essential to find the correct balance between the ability to take decisions and leadership skills on the one hand and a thorough discussion in committees and with the people involved on the other hand.

My motto in this case is:

»More pepper, less paper«.

Moreover, I prefer something which has always proved successful in practice: a team with a leader is preferable to a team of leaders.

Besides it is important to adjust the structure of the organization to the specific circumstances and magnitudes. The central question has to be: »What needs to be done globally; what needs to be done locally?« (»Global strategy, local action«, and »local commitment«).

Another fundamental question is whether a company should be organized according to regions, product divisions or functions. This depends on the structure of the company and whether the individual product divisions are very heterogeneous or strongly linked together. Outsourcing often makes sense, but my warning is that it should be kept within bounds.

Another issue at this point is sound corporate governance and I would just like to say this: a clear division of responsibilities, fewer rules and the correct appointment of suitable persons to the Board of Directors and the Supervisory Board are naturally important. The Annual General Meeting has important tasks to fulfill, but grass-roots democracy ought to be reduced to prevent abuse by individual shareholders. It is important for the Supervisory Board to place greater emphasis on the long term in their dealings with the Chairman as the latter sometimes tends more towards the short term as a result of daily pressures.

Further business policy issues in view of globalization

a) Human resources policy

Within the framework of the subject of my talk, I would like to make a few observations on human resources policy. I have summarized these in the following keywords:

- Selection is more important than education and training. Check lists by the HR department are useful in making a selection but over and above that, my advice is always to: »Look more in the eyes than in the files«.
- Developing a professional international management and striking a bal-

ance between the necessary rotation principle and continuity in individual posts are both crucial.

Globalization and tougher competition mean a greater reward for those who really achieve something, and greater penalization for those who underachieve.

In general, internationalization is a process that has to encompass the entire company. At the same time, you don't need to renounce your origins, your traditions and certain elements of your corporate culture. Maintaining a balance between these factors constitutes a key factor of success. In a global context, corporate culture has to be created in such a way that it can be applied in every region of the world without violating local traditions and mindsets. On the other hand, it must be specific and not so tentative that it is impossible, for example, to differentiate between the corporate cultures at Siemens, Shell, Unilever and Nestlé.

b) The question as to what ought to be done globally and what should be done locally

Due to globalization new questions are arising about production locations.

There is a general tendency to relocate production to those places where manufacturing is most advantageous. But it pays to be careful because it is not the personnel costs alone that set the benchmark but the quality of the personnel and the quality of the location (infrastructure, legal security etc.) that also play a role. In addition, it must be remembered that some locations change with the increasing development of the economy (see Japan 20 years ago).

Partial solutions (outsourcing etc.) can make sense, as long as the original location is kept to deal with core tasks. Thanks to relocation and additional economic success these also create additional jobs.

c) Questions relating to marketing and communication policy

I just want to say this much about marketing: Marketing is more an attitude focusing on the consumer and the customer and less the application of particular marketing techniques. As I see it, the following applies despite the constant intellectual marketing talk:

Back to basics: what counts is developing a product in line with the market, advertising it and selling it.

In spite of all the strategies, the selling aspect remains crucial – something that is sometimes neglected by so-called marketing experts.

Apart from that, marketing shouldn't just be delegated to one department; the basic attitude must encompass the entire company.

I once read the following sentence somewhere: »The sales department is not the entire company, but the entire company ought to be a sales department«.

A concerted effort is needed internationally to rethink strategies in the face of competitors who likewise operate internationally. These are multi-oligopolies or part-oligopolies. In future, we are going to have more competitors from the current developing countries, which is already evident in the activities of Japanese, Chinese and Indian companies.

Apart from that, it must be apparent to everyone that the innovative strength of a company and research are crucial for sustainable international competitiveness.

Today's world, as it presents itself with the force of its media, its numerous social groups and increasing international communication, naturally requires a professional PR and communications department. But apart from that, the head of the company needs to remain its major communicator because every message coming from him attracts greater attention. Moreover, a professional corporate affairs and PR department today entails the constant surveillance – and the management – of all issues which concern the company in any way.

Today, a so-called pre-warning system is of prime importance to avoid being constantly caught out by some information or other.

Ladies and Gentlemen, I would now like to close with the following two remarks:

1) Despite all technological developments, the famous process orientation and the computerizing of our world and our companies, we ought not to forget the following:

> »Be close to your people, be close to your customers
> and be close to your products«.

If that's done properly, then it's no longer possible to do everything wrong.

2) It is well known that the word *Angst* is typically German; and we also coined the word ›*Bedenkenträger*‹ to denote doubters and worriers. In this context I would like to remind you of Edward Harriman, the constructor of the American railway, who said 200 years ago:

»It is never safe to look into the future with eyes of fear.«

Source: Helmut Maucher, »Corporate management in a global economy – Thoughts on future leadership requirements and requisite leadership attributes«; a lecture given before the Frankfurt Association of Trade, Industry and Science in September 2007.

Human Resources and Management Policy

Challenges for future corporate management

In this speech, Helmut Maucher talks of key leadership attributes in the light of his own experience. He discusses the future trends arising from globalization and elaborates on the demands made on corporate management which will be even more crucial in future. In this lecture, he also addresses the human resources, communication and organizational policy of a company. Finally, he emphasizes the ethical and social responsibility of a company.

Professor Wieselhuber,
Ladies and Gentlemen,

Describing his life, Confucius said: » At sixty I could follow all my heart's desires without transgressing the norm«.

As we will all grow at least 20 years older, this doesn't yet apply to Professor Wieselhuber; on his 60th birthday I would like to wish him continued dynamism and creative energy – naturally, without transgressing the norm.

Ladies and gentlemen, before saying something about the demands on the entrepreneur in the future, I would like to talk about some demands on corporate management that always apply.

But first of all a truism: The quality of management is decisive for the success of a company; in the end it is the management that creates momentum and decides on all further strategies, on human resources policy and other measures that lead to the success of a company.

My experience has shown that in addition to education and professional experience the following qualifications – i. e. leadership attributes – are important:

1) Courage, strong nerves and equanimity
2) A capacity to learn, openness to anything new, an ability to imagine the future or as they say today: vision
3) Communication and motivation skills internally and externally
4) Ability to create an innovative climate (the meaning of innovations)
5) Coherent thought (despite – i. e. contrary to – too much specialization).
6) Credibility (crucial!)
7) A willingness to take decisions coupled with a sense of responsibility
8) A willingness to change constantly and the skill to manage change
9) International experience and understanding of other cultures (crucial with regard to our subject)

And finally:

10) Modesty is particularly important in view of some of the excesses which prevail, even though it is mostly a question of isolated cases that have been exaggerated in the media), but modesty with style.
11) Moreover, nothing should be done that promotes a degeneration of morals. Today, this point is all the more important because other institutions have failed in this respect. (Consider the appearance and conduct of certain people, which is not what you would expect from them).

Besides, courage and the strength to make decisions – despite all the committees and analyses – remain key attributes. By the way, my definition of a committee can be expressed as follows:

>>A group of men who keep minutes and waste hours<<.

I also mean the courage to take a stand on specific issues in public; something, unfortunately, that not enough people do. By neglecting this, we too often leave the discussion to our opponents and to specific media. Courage requires having the necessary backbone. It's not for nothing that is it said:

>>Men all have a spinal column but only a few have a backbone<<.

Moreover, the question often arises whether it is intuition or analytical-scientific corporate management which is required more. (I think that both attributes are necessary; for me, intuition is a creative utilization of information).

In the following, I would like to elaborate on some of the demands on corporate management that are new or which will have greater significance in the future.

To that end we need to ask ourselves the question: What is changing today and what will change in the future? For this purpose I have summarized these changes as follows:

- Even greater globalization, internationalization and an increase in free trade – and particularly the globalization of the financial world – can be expected.
- The world will be completely captured by computerization and the Internet etc.
- A demographic development is taking place: firstly, towards increasing population ageing; secondly, towards the shift of the global population to other regions (to Asia in particular) and towards a steady increase in the world population.
- Geopolitical changes can be expected due to the growing importance of other regions outside America (for example China, Russia, India, Brazil etc.), whereby the question arises as to how important Europe will be in future and what role it will play.

Linked to these geopolitical changes is the fact that we are marching from a G7 towards a G20, whereby it is to be hoped that this will be accompanied by an improvement in global co-operation.

- For some considerable time we have experienced – and this can also be expected in the future, too – global peace especially between the Great Powers such as has never been experienced before, although local wars and terrorism continue to abound.
- We observe certain trends in society mainly in the direction of more democracy – even outside the United States, Japan and Europe.
- Despite local and isolated setbacks, we are moving more in the direction of market economy systems. These are linked to an ordoliberalism as it is defined in our latitudes.
- In spite of the current crisis we are moving towards more social and ecological responsibility and this includes the issue of climate protection.
- This whole field also includes the increasing water shortage, as well as the growing discrepancy between the supply and demand of agricultural products.
- In view of the further growth of the world population and the increase in affluence, we are also faced with the question of how the increasing demand for energy can be met. However, it is not just a matter of the total amount of energy. We need to address research into and the mar-

keting of alternative energy sources over and above oil, gas and nuclear power.

- In the same connection, there is also the issue relating to the provision of additional food to meet demand.
- In the case of developing countries, it is primarily a matter of additional quantities of grain and animal products and also of a better quality of these foods. This is a huge problem because the price of meat (i. e. foods using animals in the process) is seven times higher than the price of crops.
- In industrialized countries, on the other hand, it is a matter of additional consumer trends towards more convenience food, taste and nutrition.
- At present the trend all over the world is towards more regional co-operation, also beyond the EU. It is to be hoped that we will achieve a strengthening of institutions and regulations which will be valid world-wide so that globalization can be allowed to take effect without negative spin-offs.

What does all this mean for a company?

First of all, it must be emphasized quite succinctly that more globalization also leads to more competition. That also means that performing well on the market meets with substantial rewards and that failure is penalized severely. I have always held that leadership consisting of a team of colleagues doesn't work in difficult times and this is particularly relevant in view of this tougher competition. That's why I am in favor of *a team with a leader and not a team of leaders.*

In my opinion appointing two people for the job is likewise problematic. The same applies to the solution often to be found in German companies of a Chairman with technical know-how and a Chairman with business acumen. To that end I quote a Turkish proverb:

»A ship with two captains sinks.«

Furthermore, the world is revolving faster and faster especially in the field of technological changes and scientific knowledge (findings double almost every three years). In such a situation the time factor – speed – plays an even more significant role. That is why I say:

»Be first, be daring, be different«.

Anyone who is first – and therefore ahead of the others – to recognize trends and developments, who decides on requisite changes in good time and who implements them quickly and consistently will be successful. (Frequently such a process is handicapped by planning bureaucracy, objections and long licensing procedures that result in disadvantages in global competition).

The increasing importance of capital markets, institutional investors, and financial analysts etc. is something of which the management must be fully aware. Moreover, the necessary know-how is needed to be able to deal with such matters, and that includes investor relations. But there is a danger today of managers spending too much time on these, allowing themselves to be influenced excessively by these and not having enough time to carry out their real business.

That also applies to the subject of corporate governance, extensive reporting and much more besides. These are real disadvantages, by the way, compared to the multi-national companies being established in emerging economies (in India, in China etc.), which don't have to deal with such matters to the same extent. As far as I am concerned, we need fewer regulations and more good people (with the necessary attributes; something which unfortunately has been neglected at times).

Another disadvantage we face compared with companies in these countries is the fact that absolute safety – starting with the production process through to the workplace – is a must. And besides, it is well known that the last percentage of safety is the most costly.

Moreover, today the management is stuck in a dilemma between the requirements of the capital market, the financial world which tends to be geared towards the short term and pressures from investors and shareholders on the one hand and the increasing demands with regards to ethically and socially responsible management on the other hand. In this respect finding and maintaining a happy medium and balance in terms of long-term corporate policy is not easy but it is absolutely crucial.

Besides, as multi-national companies in an increasingly globalized world, we need to redefine priorities with regard to what can be organized and controlled centrally and what can be decentralized. In cases of doubt I am, in general, more in favor of decentralization and a delegation of responsibility right to the place where the action is. (That promotes greater motivation of employees, a stronger identification with their tasks, more flexibility and greater proximity to events on the market).

On the other hand, in a global world, global strategies such as research and development, information technology, the world-wide exchange of information, and the selection and development of staff are gaining greater significance. But the organization also needs to become more flexible, with more networking, wider ranges of control, projects etc. Moreover, I am not just in favor of the adage: »*Global strategy, local action*«. I even amend it with »*local commitment*«.

Therefore the motto should be: don't do anything that is not, in the long term, in the interests of the country in which we operate.

Another difficulty is that of having to make adaptations locally without endangering the entire corporate policy. I only have to think of human relations and staff requirements as well as unions in totally different worlds, the different demands on ecology, safety, and issues of child labor or corruption.

It is also imperative to pay attention to making the necessary adaptations in marketing with respect to consumers, trade structures, competition and legislation, which differ to varying degrees.

Within the framework of internationalization and globalization global brands have a greater role to play. Behind the global brands are global products, of course, and the quality of these often needs to be adapted locally to suit the varying consumer habits. This applies particularly to the food industry because eating habits and taste vary considerably.

In the context of the shortage of energy, water, agricultural commodities and agricultural products, companies need to increase their efforts with regards to economies on the one hand and improving production efficiency on the other. In this respect, green gene technology will play a significant role.

One success factor comprises the geographical optimizing of production locations – a further field which I cannot amplify today. It is here that differences in costs, flexibility, economies of scale and consumer proximity play a significant role, but it pays to be decidedly cautious.

Further questions on human resources policy

Within the framework of globalization it is particularly important to answer the question as to how much uniformity and international differentiation are necessary.

Naturally, human resources policy in general, strategies and principles all need to be standardized; but otherwise, adaptations to the situation in the individual countries are required (for example, with regards to the various wage levels, different mentalities, and different labor legislation, also with regard to co-determination and the Industrial Constitution Act).

Nowadays, there is a lot of talk about the importance of further education, training, and staff development. In principle, this is absolutely okay because improving the motivation and quality of our employees makes a decisive contribution to our competitiveness. But selection is more important than training courses and apart from making use of the check list provided by the HR department when selecting staff the following should also be observed:

»Look more in the eyes than in the files«.

A word about organizational structure and organizational policy

I have already talked about the importance of decentralization and of delegating responsibility. Nowadays, modern information technology also offers the opportunity to standardize methods and information.

On the whole, I also think that there should be no excess of departments at headquarters – for this automatically reduces decentralization. After all, there is the saying:

»The business lines know everything but staff units know everything better«.

Such staff units need to be asked: »Are you helping us to find a solution or are you part of the problem? «

Specifying the general basic structure of an organization also needs to be addressed – whether it is to be organized on the basis of central divisions, regions or functions. However, I can't enlarge on this field any further today.

Further demands on corporate policy

In the following I would like to describe some demands on management – demands which have emerged since the global crisis.

The reasons for the crisis are known to be companies thinking and acting in the short term, excessive greed for quick returns and linked to this the willingness to take terrible risks, and a considerable amount of stupidity, too. All of these have contributed to the fact that confidence placed in companies has suffered considerably. That is why it is particularly crucial to regain confidence by adopting an appropriate corporate policy. That isn't easy and won't happen from one day to the next. Peter Drucker, the well-known professor and management consultant, once said: »It only takes a minute for trust to be lost but it takes ten years for it to be regained«.

Today there is a lot of talk about value-oriented management. In this context I would like to make two comments:

1) We live in a market and competitive economy, and in this respect value-oriented management can only be shaped by values that can guarantee the existence and development of the company in the long term and that contribute to the sustainable success of the company.
2) The selection of executives and the attributes that are expected from top employees are priorities in value-based corporate management right from the start. No one can lead with values that he doesn't personify himself!

I have already talked about the requisite attributes for leadership.

[…]

As far as value-oriented management is concerned, issues such as co-determination and employees' involvement etc. – irrespective of the legal situation at present – are also pertinent here.

In a multi-national company, we have to consider of course that various regions of the world have different moral values and we have to take these into consideration provided they do not violate our own prevailing values.

[…]

More generally, I would like to mention, in connection with this subject, a principle of corporate policy that I made into a guiding principle at Nestlé:

>*We at Nestlé are a company that focuses more on people and products than on systems*«.

Of course, we need systems to lead a complex company, but systems should not be a goal as such. Besides, it is a question of priority.

In this context, I would also like to say something about the ethical and social responsibility of companies, a responsibility which is frequently quoted and called for. Not to beat about the bush: the entrepreneurs' key social and ethical responsibility is being successful on the market and in competition in the long term thus ensuring the company's earnings for years to come. In this way a significant contribution is made to affluence and the flourishing of the economy, from which we all benefit in the end. A good company pays the taxes needed for the joint tasks in the community and finally due to successful corporate management jobs are ensured, retained and their number increased. Consequently, these fundamental tasks of a company constitute its major social and ethical responsibility.

I regard it as self-evident that, over and above this, responsible and ethical conduct is necessary, generally and that we practice social responsibility. Besides, it is in the long term interests of the company because a company cannot be successful in the long term if it does not have a good image and highly motivated employees.

In summary, Ladies and Gentlemen, I would say:

Value-based leadership, in the proper sense of the word, can contribute to the success of a company in the long term because such leadership creates a better working atmosphere, more security, greater trust and confidence and higher motivation and linked to these a higher commitment.

Naturally, we have to weigh up and find the correct balance between direct, operative efficiency and measures focusing on values. You can't manage a company with fundamentalism or rigorous moral rectitude. In this context I would refer you to economist and sociologist Max Weber, who analyzed the problem of the correct balance and the difference between the *Ethics of Conviction* (the intentions to act and the principles of action; acting out of principle and not from utilitarian considerations) and *Ethics of Responsibility* (which focuses primarily on the results of actions by society and not on ideological objectives).

Concluding remarks

Apart from all the demands on corporate leadership that have been described, there remains in the end, as ever, the key factors of success: the quality of management and the motivation of employees. After all, it is on these that everything else depends. That is why management and human resources policy are so important. But I don't mean by that the administrative and other systems that are connected to them but the following two things:

1) Greater importance should be attached to personality and character rather than to purely professional attributes when selecting an executive.
2) Linked to that is the following maxim:

    »*More attention to people and less bureaucracy with people*«.

Ladies and Gentlemen, as I do not wish to repeat the demands on management and companies in an increasingly global world, I would like to add two remarks which I consider to be crucial and which concern the demands on corporate management:

1) No matter what developments there are in technology and in so-called modern scientific corporate management we should bear one thing in mind:

*»Be close to your people, be close to your products
and be close to your customers«.*

2) If I wish to reduce management features to a common denominator, I
always say that the following is required:

- Heart and mind
- Mens sana in corpore sano
- Stick to the main philosophy: do what is right and don't shun anyone.

Mr. Wieselhuber, I would like to offer my heartiest congratulations on your
60th birthday and to wish you all the best, good health, success and continued creative power. Ad multos annos!

Source: Helmut Maucher, »Demands on future corporate management«, a speech given
on the occasion of Professor Dr. Norbert Wieselhuber's 60th birthday in October 2009.

»Courage is needed«

In the following conversation Helmut Maucher talks about the requirements profile for top managers and about fundamental aspects with respect to the fine art of corporate management.

mm: Mr. Maucher, you have been managing the largest food company in the world for the past 15 years. Have you ever experienced a real crisis within the company while in office?

Maucher: No, I haven't. Not even a leadership crisis. In the early stages I parted with two managing directors – i. e. members of the Board. That was unusual enough for Nestlé. I had to ensure that everyone acted in concert.

mm: No crises, no disruptions, and successful into the bargain. What do you do that's different; what do you do better than your competitors?

Maucher: It's quite simple: you have to lead well and that requires the courage to take decisions. You have to say what you want. You have to be open and be convincing. And you have to be open to conviction and to admit: »Goodness, I should have thought of that! «

mm: Anyone unable to communicate can't lead either. Would you agree?

Maucher: Yes, I would! The ability to communicate is more important today than it used to be. And there's something else that I firmly believe: it's easier to make changes if there is a climate of trust and confidence in the company.

mm: But if you don't have controls, nothing will work either.

Maucher: I'd rather accept the fact that I might be cheated twice in a 100 cases. If employees have the feeling that there is a trick behind every measure taken by the management, any changes will meet with resistance. Anyway, one of people's basic attributes is that they can't be bothered changing.

mm: And how does the manager create trust and confidence?

Maucher: I have to tell the truth. I have to practice what I preach. And if we are restructuring, I have to tell the employee what the alterations mean for him and that we won't cause him misery and hardship. Personal catastrophes have to be headed off.

mm: But it is the very principle of needing to create trust that is violated so often.

Maucher: That's true. There's a lot of fancy talk. Empty phrases are written in the corporate directives on the basis of the motto: The employee occupies center stage. What it really means is: He's a nuisance. And next day things are dealt with differently and speedily. People just won't put up with that.

mm: Do you bank on appeasement?

Maucher: I bank on a good working climate, but not on a peaceful idyll. We have to expect more from the employees than we used to because things are changing faster and because competition forces us to do so. But we can't do with cynical, brutal action or with cowardice when it comes to changing things. In the end, both of them would lead to disaster.

mm: Obviously you are not one to favor putting things abruptly into effect.

Maucher: No, I'm not. I prefer to take one, two years longer for the entire process of reorganization and to spend ten million more on it instead of radically axing jobs. This policy is much more successful than anything in human relations brochures. The people simply develop a greater sense of trust.

mm: You can't please everyone.

Maucher: Of course I can't. We have always done well with our way of managing. I'll give you another example. In Switzerland, employers' contributions to insurances are low. Our employees were hard hit when insurance premiums were increased considerably a year ago. That's when I said: our people are in trouble, so we'll pay half.

mm: Of your own free will?

Maucher: Yes. And it's hard to believe the effect it had. The employees said:

That Maucher thinks about us. It might be banal: everyone knows that we make a profit, that we are developing the company in the long term, that we have to rationalize and that we don't tolerate slackers – that is the one side. The other side is: when anyone has a problem, he knows that Nestlé will probably help him.

mm: That sounds like a patriarchal system.

Maucher: You can call it what you like.

mm: Of course, a company is always changing. Are there moments where clear signals have to be given, where changes turn out differently?

Maucher: Sometimes changes are put into operation quite brutally – especially when nothing has been done for 10 years. Or a calamity strikes from outside! And it is then that the management has to react at all costs. But we try to avoid that by constantly making a profit, by solving problems in good time and continually making changes and improvements. We don't wait until a catastrophe strikes.

I'm convinced that the so-called reforms that are sometimes carried out with brute force under the label of re-engineering have permanently damaged the working atmosphere and motivation.

mm: Why do many companies react so late?

Maucher: Partly because they couldn't be bothered; the name of the game is: Perhaps we'll be spared. And secondly: despite all the market analyses and early-warning systems – whether anyone really notices what is happening is another matter.

And yet having a feeling in good time for what is going on and what that can mean is one of the major management attributes. And the man at the top needs to be in a position, too, to distinguish between passing fads and genuine trends.

mm: Are there too many passing fads?

Maucher: Yes, there are! Things come and go with ever increasing rapidity. A consultant creates a new method; a professor favors us with a new theory. And these will be believed until something else comes along. That's part of the game. But only if you're at the top, do you have to be able to sort them out.

mm: But you can't do that merely with gut instinct, can you?

Maucher: I'm so glad that there's such a thing as the *manager magazin*; it's great that there are consultants and professors; I learn an incredible amount of things every day. I have to constantly take new things on board, but then I have to sort them out. For me, intuition is a creative utilization of information.

mm: What attributes do your top people have to have?

Maucher: Apart from intelligence, education and experience, personality counts more the higher you go. However, you can't expect deeds and solutions from narcissistic intellectuals who dissect and analyze everything to the last detail.

mm: How do find such personalities?

Maucher: I prefer to look an applicant in the eye and not at his credentials. I said once that I am no Einstein, but I happen to have the 17 skills or so that are more or less requisite for managing a company.

mm: It would be enough if you list half of them.

Maucher: You need courage, strong nerves and equanimity. You need the ability to communicate and motivate both internally and externally. You certainly need the skill to create an innovative climate in a company. You need people who can think in context; who don't get completely bogged down in a thing. You need the skill of change management. You need the ability to remain true to yourself; in other words, to stand by what you are. At the same time, you need to be able to put yourself in someone else's place and be able to understand other cultures. And finally, there is credibility, which is the most important of all.

mm: Where can one find such universal genii?

Maucher (laughs): One of them is sitting in front of you. But seriously: we do have such top people at Nestlé. I regret to say that one of them, my deputy Ramón Masip, died recently.

mm: You can also increase the willingness to embrace change if you persistently rejuvenate the management.

Maucher: Unfortunately, experience can only be handed on to a limited extent and young ones just don't have the experience. That's why I am all for the complementation theory: a mixture of old and young, of skills and temperaments, and of local and international know-how.

mm: Do you give young people management responsibility early on?

Maucher: What is crucial is securing management in the long term through constant recruitment and the development of trainees, who can then assume management tasks after 10 to 15 years; at the same time we attach importance to having a third of them willing to work abroad.

mm: Does team-playing count more than the performance of the individual?

Maucher: I'm all for a collegial, open style of management, but – and that's important -– with a clear leader at each level. We don't think much of a management where there are no clear demarcations of responsibility, of management consisting purely of a team of colleagues. I'm in favor of a »team with a leader« and not »a team of leaders«.

mm: Does that mean that basically you are of the opinion that in the end everything depends on the man at the top?

Maucher: A good man at the top gets hold of the right colleagues. He gets strong people; he gets the people who like working for him and develops and trains future leaders. At this stage of my career I am particularly proud of the fact that I have succeeded in creating a strong management board and of having in Peter Brabeck a man who is really capable of managing Nestlé further.

mm: The problem arises when the man at the top is weak, as can be seen from lots of examples in Germany.

Maucher: We don't need new laws on corporate governance and Supervisory Boards. What we need are people who react immediately in cases of doubt and take the appropriate steps if things don't work. And another thing: Anyone at the top has to accept that he hasn't tenure on the job.

mm: Well, it seems to work with you. At 69 you are well past the age of retirement and are still in office as Chairman and CEO. Do you find it so difficult to step down?

Maucher: I'm healthy and the Board of Directors is of the opinion that things are going well with me in charge.

mm: Does Nestlé not have a statute that stipulates the age of retirement?

Maucher: In the Board of Directors the age limit for stepping down is 72 and I'll make the most of it until 2000. Until that time, I'll remain in office as Chairman of the Board of Directors. Next summer, I'll be handing over my office of CEO to my colleague Peter Brabeck.

mm: There are many companies, like Bertelsmann for example, where the retirement age for top managers is 60. Do you think that is too schematic?

Maucher: I would consider Bertelsmann and Reinhard Mohn to be an exception. They are an exceptional case. I think rigid age limits are wrong. They are only good in the case of weak Supervisory Boards and managers who need rules to get rid of people. Besides, rigid age limits are a competitive disadvantage. I have to be able to get rid of someone at 45 if he is no use. But I also have to have the sangfroid or the strength to keep someone of 65 if he is still full of sap.

mm: That sounds too good to be true.

Maucher: I pushed through this flexibility for the management board and we settled on a retirement age between 58 and 68. And I'll avail myself of the same right. However, that should never result in neglecting to establish a successor. I have a successor.

mm: How did you select your successor?

Maucher: Mr. Brabeck, who is Austrian by birth, has been with the company for 28 years. He's now 52. We've had years to observe how he acts in difficult situations; whether he has the strength to survive turbulences. Mr. Brabeck speaks four languages and as a former country manager he knows the world.

mm: How much of management can be learned and how much is due so to speak to one's genes?

Maucher: That's something no one really knows. But from my own experience I would say that selection is decisive. If you select the right type who, just let's say, has quite a lot to offer genetically, then every training course, every experience that is passed on to him will give a return of 1,000 percent. If he doesn't have what it takes, an employee can be sent to training courses for hours, days and years and the return will be 0.3 percent. That's an unfortunate fact.

mm: Jack Welch, the head of General-Electric and one of the most successful managers in the world, considers vision is the be-all and the end-all. Well, Germans' experiences with visionaries haven't been exactly positive. Where is the right mix of the visionary and a grip on reality?

Maucher: I never use the word vision. I think I must be too down-to -earth. But, it is of course a question of terminology.

mm: Don't you like the word?

Maucher: No, I don't, because it symbolizes aspects of fantasy and bright eyes, and when eyes light up I always get chary. But if you mean the ability to anticipate future trends and to develop a concept and call that vision, then I agree entirely.

mm: Charisma is a word that has become hackneyed, too. In this context we found a quotation by Fredmund Malik, Professor of Management at St. Gallen. He says: »I prefer boring chairpersons because they worry about their own tasks and are not obsessed with personality cults«. Is Mr. Malik right?

Maucher: No, he isn't. I discussed this subject with the people in St. Gallen in a different context and they thought that we need professional technicians for decision-making, for all the analyses etc. My reply to that was: Whether you like it or not – if someone has charisma as well, it's easier for him to convince people. I also told the professor: What do you think would happen if you got up in front of my staff and presented them with your finely honed analyses?

mm: How did the argument end?

Maucher: At the end the students stood on their chairs and applauded me.

mm: Charisma frequently means seduction and not leadership. That could easily turn into a personality cult.

Maucher: Most attributes have positive and negative aspects. If someone ends a speech in a welter of euphoria and thinks he's the greatest or if he doesn't notice what is really going on, it becomes dangerous.

mm: Do you see danger in the media's excessive enhancement of leading characters?

Maucher: It is certainly a danger. The media concentrate all their attention on those at the top, on the bosses. The dilemma is that what interests us is that Nestlé is trustworthy, receives recognition as a company and that the image is right, but we also know that this image transfer works best via a person; namely via the person who's at the top; no one else can do it.

mm: Nestlé, c'est moi?

Maucher: No, that's not true. Although in many respects I am Mr. Nestlé today, I have kept both feet firmly on the ground. No one can accuse me of airs and graces. Moreover: the Board members at Nestlé are re-appointed every year. I don't even have a contract because as far as I am concerned, the Board of Directors must be free every year to decide on my position. Into the bargain, the post is too important.

mm: Mr. Maucher, what would you advise a young person wanting to get to the top in a company?

Maucher: First of all, he should have a close look at himself and decide whether the goal is realistic. And secondly, apart from education, languages, and an understanding of other cultures, he needs inward assurance and the ability to concentrate on his work. Anyone thinking only in terms of his own career will never make it to the top.

Source: Wolfgang Kaden/ Winfried Wilhelm, »Courage is needed«, in *manager magazin* no. 12/1996.

»Don't do anything that can't appear in the press tomorrow«

In this interview with a reporter from the German newspaper Die Welt, *Helmut Maucher discusses the demands on the executives of tomorrow: »They need courage to accept responsibility and to think globally«.*

[...]

DIE WELT: What will the leader of the future look like?

Helmut Maucher: Well, for a start, he needs all the attributes which have been needed in the last thousand years: personality, responsibility, intelligence, especially emotional intelligence. In future there will be two components which will be in greater demand: firstly, courage, strong nerves and equanimity, and secondly communication skills internally and externally.

DIE WELT: Emotional intelligence?

Maucher: The courage to bear responsibility that is apparent to the outside world has become important. You cannot use tricks. As long as we don't do anything that needs to be kept secret, we can manage a company transparently, and that's just as well. I once applied Kant's categorical imperative to communication and said: »*Don't do anything that can't appear in the press tomorrow*«. That doesn't mean that I always want everything to be in the press tomorrow. We can live very well with that as long as we pursue a proper policy.

DIE WELT: Is it necessary to know the world?

Maucher: Anyone who has no understanding of other cultures, who cannot think globally, who is not open to the world and who only moves in his own national or regional environment has a problem.

DIE WELT: What does global thinking mean to you?

Maucher: The world is growing together, not just economically but in every respect; that's modern communication. Anyone who doesn't have a certain feeling for it and who doesn't understand the world and know what is happening will never understand the global consumer in his various facets and will draw the wrong conclusions. That, by the way, is one of the problems of the Americans, who dominate and lead the market. Their country is so vast that they have difficulty understanding people who have a different way of life, a different culture or other consumer habits.

DIE WELT: A new role for the boss?

Maucher: Of course he has to concentrate on the management of his company. But he has to show commitment in society and in associations and to take a stand on his views. If we don't have the courage to call a spade a spade, who's going to do it? Otherwise the scene will be dominated by others who are not our friends. Courage, responsibility, self-confidence – these are the things, as far as I'm concerned, that will play a major role in future.

DIE WELT: What counts more: character or intellect?

Maucher: You need both. If a person only has intellect, things can come to a bad end. If he only has character, he's »Mr. Nice Guy«, but he won't get by on that. He needs those 12 or 15 talents which combined result in someone becoming the successful head of a company. I'm no Einstein in any field, but I happen to have a combination of talents that is necessary for managing a company.

DIE WELT: What is the difference between an industrial, a political and an intellectual leader?

Maucher: I have problems with the concept. If someone is only an intellectual, he is no leader. Perhaps he is a person of influence because by dint of his intelligence, his work and his scholarship he can influence a debate or further scientific matters and thus exert a direct influence on society. I think that the attributes displayed by an industrial or political leader, in the case of both these concepts, are 80 to 90 percent the same. Perhaps the industrial leader is literally more geared towards pragmatism, efficiency and leadership when he makes decisions himself and influences matters. He is surrounded by less democracy and for that reason has to accept more personal responsibility. The political leader has to be sensitive to trends around him. He has parties, he has a cabinet, and despite many difficulties he has to be able to create a forum and convince others with his arguments. However, this also applies to an industrial leader in so far as consumers and trends beyond his sphere of responsibility are concerned. But internally he still has more opportunities to say after a two-hour debate: That's enough for now.

[...]

DIE WELT: Were you ever tempted to go into politics? Do politicians take advice from you?

Maucher: I've always been interested in politics and I assume I would have achieved a great deal in politics. But I've always had so many new and interesting tasks in the company that I've always thought that that was worth something, too. And so in the end I stayed in the company. But I did feel tempted, and now and again there were others who also thought I should go into politics.

[...]

DIE WELT: It used to be that the mortality rate in childhood was high. Few people reached old age; there were fat years and lean years, and that was often the difference between life and death. Today, the First World lives in abundance. But that has its price. People worry.

Maucher: Yes, I know these moods of *Angst*. On the whole, the situation is such that people live longer due to modern medicine, food and affluence and they certainly don't want to change places with their ancestors. But of course nothing has only positive sides. The modern world is complex and anonymous. Technology, which isn't easy to understand any more, overtaxes people. Mankind is over one million years old, but all these technical developments have only been achieved in the last 150 years. Everything before that was readily comprehensible and straightforward. The products that were manufactured could be understood more or less by anyone. The modern division of labor, complex mechanisms and modern technology are things for which mankind was not programmed. That creates problems and it is a question of whether we're capable of adapting. People have a problem if they are anxious, and don't have the courage, optimism or strength to cope with it all. But there isn't any other way. On the other hand, they have much more social security and more protection against illness and diseases. The positive outweighs the negative and as for the rest, we will just have to put up with the fact that we don't understand everything and that we can only make our contribution according to our intelligence. As for the rest, I need a certain trust in God, but it shouldn't be carried too far. There are always charlatans in science and in politics and we should always ensure by democratic controls that no one can make use of modern methods to cause destruction.

DIE WELT: IT and globalization are changing every industry. What impact does that have on human relationships?

Maucher: Nestlé' has always had leanings towards a global corporation – first of all, due to its origins in Switzerland and secondly due to some pioneers at the beginning who very early in the company's history went to Australia and built factories there. Nestlé hasn't just become an international company today. Less than two percent of our sales are generated in the home country. Our approach has always been of an international and multi-national nature. When I came to Vevey 20 years ago, my whole concern was about understanding the new times and new opportunities and leading the company into this new dimension: developing a global presence. Modern communication technology has helped – plus the development of world-wide co-operation and common markets. After the end of the »Iron Curtain«, the former communist countries have become stronger.

DIE WELT: How is management changing?

Maucher: It is absolutely clear that the more we work with computers, with Intranet and Internet, the greater the danger becomes that the whole thing will become abstract and will stop being »human«. By the way, that started already with the introduction of the Dictaphone. But personal contact to employees is a question of attitude. We can't avoid or prevent modern ways and means. That's always the wrong way. But we can overcome the weaknesses that they entail. Despite all modernity, we want to maintain a personal style of management. I think it is very important that executives' efforts are directed towards maintaining a personal approach. Moreover, when executives are being selected, one of the criteria is an interest in people and the ability to deal with people. If these are observed, technical aids become a marvelous thing. But if people crouching in front of their computers and forgetting the world are cut off from each other – that won't lead a company to success because the human elements – motivation, commitment, security and the right atmosphere – will always be crucial to what happens in a company.

DIE WELT: What had a decided impact on you as a child?

Maucher: I come from a very simple background; I grew up in a village. I had a happy youth. We never starved, we were never freezing cold and we were always nicely dressed. I was 12 or 13 when the war began. But it didn't have much of an effect on a little village in the Allgäu, in the south, as it did in other areas.

DIE WELT: Who are your friends?

Maucher: I have many friends, some of them since my youth. I have always had various degrees of friendship: very close ones, where we know each other thoroughly; or such that were interesting for their conversation or for other reasons.

DIE WELT: What is your idea of a happy life?

Maucher: What kind of ideas do people have? At one time they would have been happy sitting outside their hut eating a piece of bread. But the more people's expectations are raised and they are promised paradise on earth, the more problems they have being happy. Happiness is a mixture of expectation and reality. Absolute affluence isn't an issue.

DIE WELT: What annoys you?

Maucher: Practically nothing. I know in the meantime what people are like, what their life is like and I can't be continually surprised when I find myself faced with something irritating. I certainly get annoyed if someone is stupid and yet pretends that he's terribly clever.

DIE WELT: What's your greatest weakness?

Maucher: I never answer this question which originates in America and is always asked in questionnaires.

DIE WELT: What would you have liked to be if you hadn't been Helmut Maucher from Nestlé?

Maucher: I've never asked myself that question because I've always been happy. But I could envisage myself as a politician. In my youth I wanted to be the District Administrator in the Allgäu. I've always been interested in having a multi-faceted task which involves people and organizations and where you try to achieve something.

DIE WELT: At Nestlé you expect a good deal of personal loyalty. Is that a gift from heaven?

Maucher: That's one of the things that have changed, too. It used to be that people were loyal because it was considered a virtue. Today, this natural loyalty is called into question. Today, you have to do something to get loyalty in return. You have to motivate people, pay them a decent wage, and give them a feeling of security and the feeling that if they are in trouble you will help them. Today, people go more for options. That can be seen in the way people change jobs and change their minds. It is a change that liberates people on the one hand, but taken generally, it is more difficult to hold society together.

DIE WELT: In the Middle Ages loyalty was the bond between the two poles in society.

Maucher: Loyalty has to come from both sides. Today, management side is called on to create loyalty because it isn't given automatically any more. It used to be in feudal societies in particular that there was loyalty if the lord fulfilled his obligations to a reasonable extent, didn't leave his vassals in the lurch and took care of them.

DIE WELT: In your life, what was luck and what was hard work?

Maucher: I don't know. I've always worked hard. I was committed to the company and didn't just make use of its instruments to optimize my own life. But of course there were lucky circumstances as well! That'll always be the case. But I think I can also say with a certain degree of self-confidence that if this or that lucky circumstance hadn't occurred, something else would have turned up. But it's up to you yourself in the main.

DIE WELT: Have you ever been disappointed?

Maucher: Generally speaking, no, but I have been taken in by a person once or twice. That can always happen, but it wasn't often. When deciding on pure business matters – on which business is good and which isn't – I've actually made few serious mistakes.

DIE WELT: Can you reach the top without making enemies?

Maucher: No one sets out to make enemies intentionally. I don't think that a sustainable career and rising to the top of the company should be based on making use of your elbows or getting rid of others. That was never my way. I've always tried to get on by dint of my performance and by obtaining recognition among those who had a say in things. I have never promoted that disgraceful competition between one or two people as to who would get the top job. Nor have I ever been prepared to take on such a fight. That's not the type of person I am. Either I was selected or I wasn't.

DIE WELT: If you could recreate yourself, what would you do differently?

Maucher: I don't know. Firstly I would say that I would be happy if things went the same way again. I've no reason to complain.

DIE WELT: Do you like yourself?

Maucher: Yes, I think so.

DIE WELT: One last question: What advice would you give to the younger generation that now bears responsibility?

Maucher: I've no intention of leaving a legacy that people should adhere to. Times change and that means we change, too. But three things are crucial to success, irrespective of all the maxims and techniques, computers and communication methods:

» *Be close to your people, be close to your customers and be close to your products*«.

If these three things are done properly – and it's here that a lot of mistakes are being made currently – then success is more likely than if you follow new maxims and new buzz words.

Source: Dorit Brandwein, » *Don't do anything that can't appear in the press tomorrow* « in *Die Welt*, on Sept. 23, 1999.

Sustainability and Value Orientation

Are morals worthwhile in business?
The importance of morals for sustainable success

In the following lecture Helmut Maucher gives his views on the financial crisis and especially on the influence from America. He lectures, on the occasion of the symposium ›Bayreuther Dialoge‹, on the management attributes of the last generation compared with today, on the social and ethical responsibility which a company has to bear, on principles of business policy at Nestlé and finally on the importance of focusing corporate policy on the long term and on values.

Introduction

While preparing the theme for this year's symposium (»Raising the Moral Standards of the Markets«) the organizers were certainly not aware of how relevant this subject would be in view of the current financial crisis and of the extent to which action without morals can be harmful to business in the end.

Thus we have a striking example today of the importance morals also have in business. I don't think anyone believed that this financial crisis would ever become so disastrous; nor could anyone guess how badly some of those involved would behave. From my point of view this development can only really be explained by the attitude of some of the participants – an attitude that testifies to exaggerated short-term orientation, excessive greed and a tremendous amount of stupidity.

In this context, an observation on the side: I think that in the last five years there has never been so much talk of focusing on values, of sustainability and ethics and yet at the same time these principles have never been compromised to such an extent. We have to ask ourselves how such a development was possible. Without a doubt, increasing globalization and linked to this tougher competition play a major role. Added to that, there is the increase, to a certain extent, in the Anglo-Saxon influence of pure capitalism both in Europe and Germany. I would call to mind the increasing influence exerted by analysts, some institutional investors and quarterly reports in addition to an over-emphasizing of short-term shareholder values. I term these people shareholder-value fetishists.

Then there are also changes in mindset, which I would like to mention with considerable caution. It is never correct to make generalizations, but I would like to state briefly and in general terms that earlier generations of executives were people who had commitments. Today, we are dealing increasingly with people who merely look at options. In our day certain things, as far as we were concerned, were non-negotiable. However, I have to admit that I have noticed, especially in today's younger generation, many positive attributes that are again more related to commitment and performance. To some extent we have probably used the wrong criteria in selecting Supervisory Board members and executives in the past 20 to 30 years. Professional skills, knowledge and cleverness were sometimes more important than character, personality and values.

Ladies and Gentlemen, I hope, however, that we have learned from this financial crisis and from other scandals such as excessive remuneration. I hope that we have recognized that the behavior of some hedge-fund managers, excessive relocation abroad with the short-term in view and an immoderate outsourcing mentality, but also the frequently brutal behavior of purchasers and the increase in corruption and slush fund accounts are not ultimately in the interest of the company and its long-term success.

Actually, that is the answer to the question whether morals are worthwhile in the long term or not. Nevertheless, on the basis of individual aspects of management and corporate policy, I would like to look into the importance of morals and their benefit for sustainable success by making the following observations.

In this connection I do not quite agree with the basic subject of this year's symposium. I find that the concept »Raising the Moral Standards of the Markets« is too moralizing and can easily lead to hypocrisy and untruthfulness and nothing could be more deadly to real and specific moral behavior in business practice.

In this context, let us address the much-vaunted and often quoted ethical and social behavior of the company. There aren't many business reports or

PR brochures which don't state: »We are conscious of our corporate and social responsibility and needless to say human beings take centre stage« but in practice things often look quite different.

Put clearly, Ladies and Gentlemen, the entrepreneurs' most important social and ethical responsibility is to be present on the market in the long term, to be successful in competition and thus to ensure sustainable earnings, thereby making a major contribution to affluence and the flourishing of the economy from which we all benefit in the end. A good company pays the taxes needed for the joint tasks in the community and finally, due to successful corporate management, jobs are ensured, retained and their number increased. Thus these fundamental tasks of a company constitute its major social and ethical responsibility.

Apart from that, we naturally take our social and ethical responsibility seriously. Besides, such an attitude is in the long term interests of the company, promotes the corporate image and preserves the long-term motivation of the employees. However, such attitudes, if they lead to additional expenditure, reach their limits when we endanger our competitiveness if competitors do not behave in the same way.

In this connection, the question is often asked about our attitude to the necessary streamlining and restructuring of a company that often entails job cuts. To be quite clear: in order to remain competitive and thus to be successful in the long term in the interests of the employees, too, we need to exhaust every possibility to rationalize and lower costs. But it depends on how it is done and how it is handled. Measures accompanied by a social component and spread over several years etc. are often the best investment in employees and their motivation and also in the corporate image which nowadays makes a major contribution to survival on the market.

I also think that with such a policy, redundancies for operational reasons can be avoided if all possibilities are exhausted and if the streamlining goal doesn't have to be achieved within the shortest possible time. For example, it's sensible to make use of age limits for retirement and of normal fluctuation, and to try to place employees in new jobs by means of training programs.

But nowadays the real dilemma is that the entrepreneur is confronted on the one hand with a constant increase in social demands with regards to ethics, ecology, social behavior, sponsoring, the support of charitable organizations, and on other the hand – due to the increase in financial pressures – with short-term orientation, shareholder value and profit maximization.

In terms of the interest of the company which is directed towards a long-term timeframe, it is important for the head of the company to find the correct balance. That isn't easy but it's very important.

At the start I said that long-term, successful corporate management and the attention to moral aspects, too, depend primarily on the correct selection of executives.

As far as courage is concerned you need backbone; think of the saying: »Men all have a spinal column but only a few have a backbone«. Of all things, courage and strong nerves are required when it comes to keeping the company's long-term objectives in sight despite short-term pressures.

When emphasis is placed on the long-term orientation of a large company, the members of the Supervisory Board have to assume an important responsibility. In particular, they have to examine whether the measures and decisions will be good for the company. They can do that more easily because they are not directly involved in short-term, operative events and therefore they can place greater emphasis on long-term orientation.

Apart from that many family-owned companies have the advantage of automatically thinking in the long term because they think in terms of generations.

Long-term thinking and acting must be embedded in the principles of business policy, which aren't changed every day. At Nestlé I developed the following three principles:

1) We think and act long-term.
2) In cases of doubt we are more in favor of decentralization.
3) We focus on people and products rather than on systems.

With regard to the principle of long-term focus, it must also be said that due to today's pressure from increased global competition and the financial world it isn't always easy to maintain action geared towards the long-term. Moreover, this isn't helped by the vanity of bosses wanting to show short-term success. Often wages policies, too, can lead to short-term action because bonuses and incentives are linked too closely to the annual results and less on long-term development.

Furthermore, too many changes at management level endanger the long-term focus of the company because after being in office a short time the new bosses want to show what heroes they are. In my twenty years of office at the head of Nestlé I have done many things with sustainability in mind – for example, accessing new countries, certain acquisitions which needed time to become profitable, long-term human resources development and human resources policy etc. Some of it only took effect properly when my successor had long taken over the running of the business. He now does the same and therefore he will undertake and decide many things which will extend far beyond his period of office.

Of course it's easier to persist with a long-term policy if I also make short-term profits and the shareholder value develops very satisfactorily. But if you're up to your neck in it in the short term, then that's the end of long-term policy and morals.

In summary: anyone who thinks in the long term is also interested in developing and motivating his employees; he avoids short-term streamlining measures that make employees insecure and he does nothing that could damage the long-term image of the company. In the end such a policy is also interesting to shareholders because then they also remain loyal to the company in the long term. In this context I always say: *»I prefer shareholders to share traders«.* We cannot pursue a corporate policy that addresses short-term yo-yo shareholders. An entrepreneur should not allow himself to be influenced by quarterly reports, short-term demands from some analysts and brokers or similar things. A long-term policy is also better in the market situation. Of course, that requires really strong nerves.

A few remarks about human resources policy

Apart from what has been said already, long-term development of managerial staff and investment in training are very important. However, selecting the right managerial staff is almost more important. If you have the wrong people, you can train them as much as you like, the result will be minimal.

As far as so-called assessment centers for selecting executives are concerned, I don't think much of the idea. I'm certain that the reliable judgment of experienced staff in your own company is indispensible. Of course it is crucial that long-term human resources policy does everything to encourage motivation in employees. I have always followed the motto: *»Look in the eyes and not in the files«.*

As an illustration of how to treat employees I would like to share with you a story about handling horses from my book *»Management Brevier«*. Taking up some interesting ideas from Jürgen Fuchs' book *»Lust auf Deutschland – Ein märchenhafter Roman für Menschen mit Mut«* (A Yen for Germany – a Magical Novel for People with Courage) I quote as follows:

» [...] in the folklore of many primitive peoples there are tips on how human beings can live successfully with their oldest companion:

- The horse accepts leadership if a person radiates authority but not if leadership is authoritarian.
- The horse respects leadership if it is clear and unequivocal but not if the hand that leads trembles.
- The horse never forgets who helped him in a dangerous situation but he doesn't forget either who injured him.
- The horse delights in performance but not if he is forced into it.
- The horse allows a person to ride him but only if he has had time to become familiar with that person.
- The horse is capable of incredible achievements but only if he trusts his rider. Literally, he would go through fire for him but without his rider he would panic«.

What is said about the horse here can be applied to people without further ado.

However, the lowest management level is often forgotten when it comes to developing and cultivating managerial staff. Although at times this level is the least suitable for management, it should be remembered that the people at this level are those who deal with the majority of the employees.

On the subject of value orientation

Sustainable and morally irreproachable behavior is often promoted by long-term value orientation.

In emphasizing value orientation we have to ask ourselves what values we mean.

To start with, this requires returning to the main roots of our values, the Christian-Jewish and the Greek-Roman developments. Finally, at the beginning of modern times and the Renaissance, these values were complemented by the development of materialism, individualism, democracy and human rights etc.

Of course, as executives and managers we need to know something about this if we are to be in a position to give our companies orientation. Finally, it is important in value orientation to constantly weigh up four properties which have been assessed and weighted differently by various people, by various social systems and in different eras: liberty, equality, efficiency and community. Depending on the emphasis placed on these four aspects we have different socio-political solutions, constitutions, political programs and legislation and finally different value-oriented management systems. Moreover, value-oriented management cannot be removed from the current socio-political situation, from the current spectrum of opinion and zeitgeist.

On the other hand, value orientation should not only reflect the *zeitgeist;* it also goes beyond the current *zeitgeist.* Somehow, management always finds itself between the need for tolerance on the one hand and the exercise of authority and orientation on the other hand.

Naturally in modern and developed societies, especially in Germany, we also need to ask ourselves how we deal with co-determination, with employees' participation and with their rights. Although employees have every right to co-determination in a modern industrial society, I think that we have gone to extremes in our country. There are no such far-reaching regulations and rights to co-determination in any other European country.

Of course we also need to know in many other instances what values we mean. For example:

- Should remuneration increasingly correspond to services rendered or should a smaller differentiation of wage scales and more equality be to the fore?
- Should top performers be developed or should more time and effort be spent on helping the less able to keep up.
- Should we direct our attention solely towards active employees or should we also take care of those who have retired thus honoring age and merit? A difference in the regard for young and old is important here.
- Should the length of service and loyalty be taken into consideration or should it be the current performance that counts?
- Are we more in favor of a co-operative management style, a team of colleagues and coaching or for a greater emphasis on leadership? (Remember my motto: »A team with a leader«).

Part of value orientation is how we treat suppliers. I've always told my employees: »Treat our suppliers in the way you want your customers to treat you«.

Therefore, we always need to weigh up and find the right balance. You can't manage a company with fundamentalism or rigorous moral rectitude. Max Weber has already pointed out: »We need to distinguish between an ethic of opinion and one of responsibility«. According to Weber, a proponent of the ethic of responsibility is someone who considers the consequences of an action in their entirety and uses his assessment of these consequences as a standard for his decision. A proponent of the ethic of opinion is someone who qualifies certain actions as moral or immoral irrespective of the context – he does what he considers to be morally right irrespective of the consequences of certain actions or omissions.

You can afford to be a proponent of the ethic of opinion if you don't bear any responsibility.

Concluding remarks

And so, Ladies and Gentlemen, I come to a close and would like to summarize my remarks as follows:

Moral conduct in the sense that I have defined is not only a question of ethics and morals in terms of our general perceptions and fundamental values and perhaps religious views, but affords a major contribution to the sustainable success of a company.

Epictetus in his theory of »utilitarianism« pointed out that ethical conduct is in the interest of the entrepreneur. Anyway, I am of the opinion that morals are important in themselves irrespective of how they affect the interests of a company. Moreover, economist Wilhelm Röpke, too, addressed this subject in his book »Jenseits von Angebot and Nachfrage« (Beyond Supply and Demand).

Finally, let me mention Aristotle's cardinal virtues which have accompanied me as principle all my life; these are:

- Courage,
- Wisdom,
- Moderation and humility,
- and Justice.

Source: Helmut Maucher, »Are morals worthwhile in business? The importance of morals for sustainable success«, a lecture on the occasion of the symposium Bayreuther Dialoge on October 24 and 25, 2008 (printed in the brochure of the Bayreuther Dialoge and entitled ›Raising the moral standards of the markets; the new »powerlessness« of the consumer‹).

Value orientation as an important constituent of modern corporate management – Experiences in the management of an international corporation

The following speech deals with the fact that in Mr. Maucher's opinion value-oriented management is successful. A corporate policy characterized by principles, a proper corporate culture and corporate governance are just as fundamental as a well-functioning communication policy. In conclusion Mr. Maucher mentions how important it is for companies to be aware of their ethical and social responsibility.

A)

The key topic of today's lecture is »Integral and Authentic Leadership«. By »integral« management I mean holistic and credible leadership. I would like to add »leadership with integrity« to this »integral leadership«. In view of the many scandals and the decline in morals and manners, which are frequently to be observed, this kind of leadership is again acquiring new and important significance.

With regard to the word »authentic«, I would say that it means nothing other than being true to oneself, never becoming corrupt and never being dishonest or hypocritical. It is only thus that the confidence and the credibility can arise that is so important for a company.

B)

Now, I would like to address the topic of »value-oriented leadership«.

As an entrepreneur, I would like to stress first of all that we live in a market and competitive economy and that value-oriented leadership can only occur if we focus on values which guarantee the continued existence and the development of the company in the long term. If we don't do that, the continuity of a company is at risk – with all the implications such as the loss of jobs and tangible assets that are linked to this.

My lecture consists of two parts:

1) Evidence that value-oriented corporate management can contribute to the company's success and is in no way detrimental to its success.

2) Some deliberations on the values I mean in this context.

Part 1):

Value-oriented corporate management starts with selecting managerial staff and determining the attributes we expect from top people.
[...]
After all, we can do without career opportunists with their focus on the short term and job hoppers who only think of themselves and never the company. We need a good balance between effort on behalf of and commitment to the company and a sensible organization of one's private life.

Generalizing is always a problem, but I would say generally that my generation tended to be a generation of commitment whereas today's generation tends to be one of options.
[...]
Leadership in terms of merely exercising the authority conferred on you does not suffice. I always speak of added-value leadership, which means as good as: »Don't lead by virtue of the office conferred on you but from the point of view of how you can make your contribution to sustaining the value of the company«. That is also why I speak of employee involvement – i. e., informing the employees and incorporating them in necessary developments and measures as far as possible.

My own behavior is guided by the principle of the cardinal virtues which I often quote in this connection; these are courage, justice, wisdom and humility.
[...]
I have deliberately addressed the qualification of executives and the business elite in great detail because that is where value-oriented leadership begins.

However, I would stress once again that we should pay more attention again to character, reliability and responsibility than to whether someone has top grades in Math. That would be conducive to the acceptance of the elite. What follows are some aspects of corporate culture which were once defined as the sum of all self-evident truths.

Within the framework of the principles of management and leadership at Nestlé as defined by me I have also defined the major principles of corporate culture. On the one hand they have to be kept so general that they can be adopted all over Nestlé's world; that they apply from China to Alaska; on the other hand, they have to be specific so that they are not mere platitudes such as »Man should be noble, helpful and good«.

One of the key principles is respect for other cultures and traditions (this is absolutely essential in a multi-national company), but without relinquishing certain principles which can be valid in every culture.

Elements of the Nestlé culture are, moreover, a pragmatic rather than a dogmatic approach to business activities; a realistic attitude as well as decision-making that is based on facts and not on dreams or illusions; work ethics, integrity, honesty and quality; relations based on trust and confidence, whereby mutual frankness is expected and intrigues are rejected; and a personal, direct approach in dealing with others so that bureaucratic procedures can be reduced to a minimum.

Nestlé employees do not show off, but they are aware of their value and the positive image of their company. In principle, they are modest but they have style and appreciate quality.

Nestlé employees are open to dynamic and forward-looking trends in the field of technology, changes in consumer habits and also to business ideas and opportunities; but they retain respect for fundamental human values and conduct. Nestlé is skeptical of passing fads and self-appointed »gurus«. Nestlé is a humane company, which is evident in its relations to its employees and in the esteem in which employees hold the company.

And finally, the members of Nestlé's management at all levels show strong commitment to the company, its development, its culture and the leadership principles described above. Apart from professional efficiency and experience, the ability and the will to apply these principles are the most important criteria for promotion and not a person's passport or his/her ethical or national origin.

At meetings and seminars with Nestlé employees I've always told the participants from all over the world: »Keep your own traditions and don't deck yourself out in false clothing because that won't make you successful. Moreover, you should take the following to heart:

1) Affirm and accept the general basic rules of Nestlé's culture that have been created so that your own culture is not violated in any way, but keep your own traditions and customs.
2) Develop an understanding of other cultures, otherwise we at Nestlé will not be able to co-operate.

[...]

Just a word about corporate governance, top salaries and some scandals! It is impossible to understand someone pocketing a salary in the two-digit million euro range and at the same time announcing that thousands of employees will be made redundant. Members of the Board of Directors and the Supervisory Board have a clear duty to see to it that remuneration is not excessive and doesn't get out of control; to select executives accordingly and to take social aspects into account. These fundamental things are more important than the current trend of furnishing the entire corporate governance with a comprehensive set of rules.

On the subject of streamlining and restructuring: Remaining competitive means exploiting every opportunity. But it depends on how this is done and how it's handled. Here are two examples from my own company: In co-operation with a team of consultants and on account of certain organizational changes, there was an opportunity to reduce the number of employees at our headquarters in Switzerland by about 10 %. My formula was: open information (employee involvement), a transitional period of two to three years by fully exploiting the implementation potentialities etc. and the inclusion of the voluntary leaving of personnel – i. e. retirement – so that in principle no one would have to be made redundant. The delay in the rationalization effect coupled with the costs incurred during that time was the best investment in motivating the employees. Sayings like »Our focus is on human beings« or human relations brochures are no use at all if you don't practice what you preach. In my second example, I gave away a factory in the British town of Grimsby in order to acquire a ›purchaser‹ who was prepared to take over most of the workforce.

On communication policy: There is frequent talk of transparency and in principle rightly so, but once again it pays to be careful. After all, we also have competitors and we don't exactly have to let them in on everything.

[...]

We shouldn't leave all the other information solely to the financiers because they only address the investors and don't take the opinions of the public, the press and the personnel into consideration.

On the subject of internal communication: Today employees are often inundated with information. Mostly they only hear the hymns of praise issued by the company and the real problems aren't broached. Employees frequently say that they would like to be better informed: what they really mean is that they should be shown more honesty and trust.

Part 2 – Definition of values:

Former Asko and Coop CEO Wiegand founded a responsibility forum. During its last conference this forum discussed the topic »The cultural values of Europe«. (The contributions have been published by Fischer in a paperback edition; it's a book I can thoroughly recommend.)

According to Professor Joas, values are strongly emotional perceptions of what is desirable. Our moral values are rooted initially in Christian-Jewish and Greek-Roman moral values. The development of the modern era and the Renaissance brought additions to these values, of course. I can only sum it all up in keywords.

In the course of the Enlightenment a greater emphasis was placed on rationality (see Descartes' »Cogito ergo sum«), and there was a greater emphasis on individuality and self-realization, that even goes as far as narcissism. The outbreak of the French Revolution saw the end of absolutism and an increase in the importance of materialism. At the same time earthly thinking spread at the expense of religiousness and transcendence (see Nietzsche: »God is dead«).

Finally a stronger development and manifestation of democracy and human rights have developed on the one hand and – during the last century – two totalitarian ideologies have arisen on the other hand. (This brief outline illustrates how fragile everything can be.)

At present it can be ascertained again that the enormous significance of the right half – i. e. the emotional half of the brain – is receiving greater recognition. Knowledge about genetic substances is gaining in significance and in its train brain research, too, with its new determinism. As I said, these are only headwords but they are important when we discuss the question as to what values form the basis of our actions in general but above all our actions as executives.

[…]

I don't wish to go into the topic today but I would like to mention something I said to the members of the Supervisory Board and the members of the Works Council and unions who were involved when qualified co-determination was introduced at the time:

»I 'm like the leaning tower of Pisa I might incline to your point of view but I stand firm.«

Therefore we need to weigh up things again and again and find the right balance. We cannot lead with fundamentalism or rigorous moral rectitude.

(Refer also to Max Weber's distinction between the ethic of opinion and the ethic of responsibility).

Concluding remarks

1) Value-oriented leadership in the normally accepted sense brings a company success in the long term because such leadership creates a better work climate, greater security, greater trust and confidence and a higher level of motivation which is linked to higher performance. Leadership which is focused on values is also of value to the company externally because thanks to a better image the company is held in higher regard in society and in public. That is a key success factor today, particularly since customers and consumers want to know more and more about where the goods come from.
2) No two values are the same. We always have to make a choice which corresponds to our own perceptions but which doesn't differ entirely from the *zeitgeist*.
3) No one can lead a company with values which he doesn't epitomize himself – which brings us back to today's topic of authenticity.

I'd like to close with a little story.

A few years ago I gave a lecture before the Association of Private Bankers in Switzerland. It was an evening event which was attended by both wives and husbands. A lively discussion about the topic of shareholder value broke out and at the end of my remarks I said:

>*»And by the way, ladies and gentlemen,*
>*I do hope that we share more values than just the share-value«.*

Source: Helmut Maucher, »Value orientation as an important constituent of modern corporate management – Experiences in the management of an international corporation«; a lecture on the occasion of the Personnel Symposium »Authentic and integral management« in September 2005.

»Backbone is required«

»Even if a company records a profit, it can be perfectly legitimate to part with employees« – In the following interview with the German newspaper Die Zeit *Helmut Maucher talks about how companies can maintain their competitiveness and what long-term corporate policy looks like.*

[...]

DIE ZEIT: Mr. Maucher, many companies report record earnings and yet they make employees redundant. Do managers have no sense of decency?

Helmut Maucher: That has nothing to do with decency. A company always has to endeavor to be as competitive as possible. In a market economy it isn't possible to ensure that the earnings generated today will continue forever. At some stage, a competitor will come along who offers the same product at a much lower price or can even supply a much better one. As a manager I have to guard against such things. I have to rationalize; I have to make my company more efficient – even though our earnings are high. And if that means having to part with some employees, that is hard but still better than having to close up shop in the long term because a competitor comes along and sweeps you from the market.

ZEIT: You mean, then, that job cuts are a legitimate means of increasing returns?

Maucher: No, that's not what I mean and that's where the misunderstanding lies. I'm talking about maintaining competitiveness. It can quite definitely mean the management investing money in new machines or acquiring another company – i. e. undertaking something that reduces profit – and thus returns- in the short term. What I do condemn are the returns fetishists among company leaders, who only think of doing everything in their power in the short term to drive up their own share price. They don't part with employees because it benefits the company in the long term, but because that's what the stock market likes.

ZEIT: Is there an upper limit for returns?

Maucher: As long as I manage money from external sources – the money provided by investors – I am of course obliged to offer them something in return. Good returns are important to shareholders; they have to be at least higher than the interest that can be achieved with long-term and comparatively secure investments, and if shareholders think that we do a reasonable job that also attracts new shareholders. If managers today propagate increasingly higher returns, it has either something to do with their own vanity or with their share options and they possibly want to conceal the fact that they cannot offer their shareholders a sensible, long-term business strategy.

ZEIT: Many managers claim they need to force up returns because otherwise the company could be subject to a hostile takeover.

Maucher: Well, I can understand that in part. But, as long as we have a free market economy, companies can always be taken over, but preventing a takeover shouldn't be the primary goal of the management.

ZEIT: Well then, is long-term based corporate policy acknowledged by the financial market at all? After all, investment bankers and analysts have quite different perspectives, which are geared much more to the short term.

Maucher: That's partly true. However, as long as a company makes good profits and I see to it, as manager, that the share price is all right in the long run, I can cope with the short-term fluctuations. But then I need the necessary backbone and that's what some of my colleagues in office seem to lack today. Failing to make a sensible investment because it could lower profits in the short term – and consequently the share price – is not acting in the best interests of the company.

ZEIT: You say that job cuts are not reprehensible if a company wants to remain competitive. Explain that to people who lose their jobs.

Maucher: If a company generating profits axes jobs, it depends on how they do it. It can be spread over a number of years and you can make use of natural fluctuation. If you're not up to your neck in it, you don't have to go to extremes. The most important thing is for managers to explain to their employees what's going on; to explain that ensuring the long-term survival of the company is behind it all. After all, refraining entirely from such measures is not in employees' interests either. Everyone has a great time for a further year or two and then comes the crunch – the moment when the entire company will suffer for it.

ZEIT: Do managers and the workers still speak the same language?

Maucher: A manger getting a salary in the two-digit million euro range and then making people redundant isn't accepted and rightly so. A good company sets a good example by showing moderation. I don't object to high salaries, but that ought to mean that in good years the employees and not just the shareholders are given a share of the profits. A few career opportunists who think only of the short term and change companies every few years can discredit the entire market economy.

ZEIT: Is the social responsibility of companies that many managers love to emphasize today only a marketing gimmick?

Maucher: No, it isn't. It's also in the long-term interest of the company because it has a positive impact on the company image and employees are motivated quite differently. At one time, I actually gave away an entire factory. At that time Nestlé had an unprofitable factory where fish were filleted. In the end we would have had to close and then 500 people would have lost their jobs and that in an area where there was high unemployment. Besides, you can't sell a factory running at a loss. So I gave it away on condition that some of the staff would retain their jobs.

ZEIT: If returns continue to spiral upwards, will capitalism lose its legitimacy?

Maucher: No, it won't. If competition functions, returns won't spiral forever. Moreover, there are only a few cases which have given rise to criticism. Most entrepreneurs act in a socially responsible way.

Source: Marc Brost/ Arne Storn, »Backbone is needed« in *Die Zeit*, issued on Dec. 1, 2005.

»Our generation had more staying power«

In the following interview Mr. Maucher talks about the opportunism displayed by many of today's managers, shareholders' power and why the Salzburg Festival is a must.

[...]

Mr. Maucher, why aren't you in Salzburg at the festival?

Don't worry. I'll be flying there. We go every year.

Managers like Salzburg, do they?

Well, we are interested in music. My wife studied music and I used to play the violin and the clarinet. Besides, Nestlé is one of the Festival's sponsors.

Did you arrange that?

Yes, I did, but I didn't do it to finance my own hobby.

That's what all the Board members say.

That's true. There are plenty of bad examples. But my conscience is clear. It gives us an opportunity to reach a target group that we wouldn't otherwise reach. It suits Nestlé, enhances its image and is much cheaper than sponsoring football.

Are we right in thinking that notable businessmen prefer to go to Salzburg and notable politicians prefer to go to the Wagner Festival in Bayreuth?

Bayreuth has a promenade which acts as a showcase for politicians. Personalities like Angela Merkel or Edmund Stoiber have to put in an appearance there. The standard is excellent in both places.

Are Bayreuth and Salzburg major social events that are a must for top managers?

There may be a few top managers who think they have to put in an appearance so that they get a mention in the newspapers afterwards. However, most of us do go for cultural reasons.

Is it important for top managers to be in the newspaper?

If they've got nothing else to offer ...

... it's not so important, then.

This inclination to put oneself on exhibition is on the increase. It is excessive. I mean, although a reputation depends on how someone presents himself, it's the results that count in the end.

If you look at Dieter Zetsche at Daimler or Klaus Kleinfeld at Siemens – are both of them representative of a new generation of managers?

Quite by chance, you have mentioned two very good CEOs. However, all in all, I think that the new generation has become a bit more opportunistic and are more strongly influenced by short-term events. My generation had more staying power. Perhaps we had more leeway.

Where does short-term thinking come from?

The influence exerted by Anglo-Saxon capitalism has grown and linked to that there is the pressure on managers to produce good earnings figures in the short term. Moreover, the power of the financial analysts and fund managers, who tend to think in the short term and want to play yo-yo with shares, has risen considerably.

Can we learn anything from analysts?

What is there to learn? In my last years in office I was always being accused of not speaking with analysts often enough. I admit I was arrogant enough to say that a 25-year-old analyst straight from university who had never seen the inside of a factory was hardly in a position to make useful proposals. But in general, it must be said that analysts have improved over the past few years.

That sounds as if you longed for the old days when shareholders didn't have a say.

117

No, I don't. In fact the opposite is true. There used to be too many managers who had lost touch with reality and didn't perform their duties. Pressure of the Anglo-Saxon kind would have done them good.

Nowadays, managers are fired more quickly than they used to be. Is that a good thing?

Yes, it definitely is. In that respect we were much too dilatory about taking action. The members of the Supervisory Board were either too gentlemanly or were friends of the Management Board. There were some terrible instances. The fact that members of the Supervisory Board and shareholders can exert more pressure is decidedly more positive. America showed us the way.

How do managers today differ from former corporate leaders?

On the occasion of the retirement of Reiner Gut, the longstanding head of Credit-Suisse, I made a claim before 800 young bankers that we old hands were managers of commitment and the new managers formed a generation of options.

That is something we don't understand.

As far as we were concerned, there were values and attitudes that were not negotiable. Our successors seem to be more flexible in this respect, but of course it's wrong to make generalizations.

Have managers become more conceited and for that reason chase after the zeitgeist, or are they the ones being driven?

They are driven by the money market, but they are also more strongly influenced by the *zeitgeist*. A good manager needs to follow a long-term strategy despite short-term pressure. We need managers who think beyond today; who remain steadfast when the going gets tough and who don't think only of the quarterly figures.

What's bad about good quarterly figures?

Usually they lead to short-term thinking and they are often achieved by dispensing with development and research, advertising, investments or acquisitions. I know of some recent examples of acquisition opportunities that were turned down because it would have meant endangering the targeted returns that had already been announced.

Who was it?

I don't wish to mention any names.

Are the CEOs of Allianz, Siemens or Daimler, who have hit the headlines because of their plans to reduce the workforce, harder, more anti-social, and colder than the managers of the old school?

We could be hard, too. Anyone wanting to survive in the global economy needs to make use of rationalization opportunities. If he doesn't, he doesn't last too long. Managers are under greater compulsion to solve problems quickly. Many of them simply have a different attitude.

And that is?

The CEO of a company that earns a great deal of money should spread restructuring measures over a long period instead of undertaking cutbacks in one fell swoop. That reduces earnings in the short term but benefits the company in the long term. Employees remain motivated, customers remain faithful and the image is not impaired. You can print thousands of brochures on the subject of »Our focus is on human beings« but they aren't much use if you set the employees of today on the street tomorrow.

You're talking about Allianz intending to reduce the staff drastically despite earnings of € 4.5 billion.

I mention no names. I think basically that it pays a company to have a social attitude. This is not my contention as an altruist but as a person wanting to improve the value of the company in the long term.

Would you say that employees are the losers in the new economic world?

Perhaps they are in the short term because the rationalization measures that are necessary are usually carried out at the expense of the people. That's why I'm convinced that both the state and the companies need to cushion these effects. In the long term rationalization also benefits the employees because the competitiveness of the company is preserved.

Where was your social attitude formed?

I don't know exactly. I hope that some of it is in my genes. I grew up in a Catholic village in the Allgäu where everyone knows everyone else. I think that in a small environment the ability to think socially and to show consideration to others is much better developed than in anonymous cities.

Were you never worried that power could make you lonely and aloof?

No, I wasn't. Anyone attaining a leading executive position has to take care that power and responsibility are reasonably congruent. When selecting our management elite, we don't merely have to make sure that they have top grades in Math. It's more important that they're decent guys.

On average, management board executives leave their companies at the age of 54. Is that a good thing?

I think this mania for rejuvenating is an immensely undesirable development. Arbitrary age limits in particular never add up. There are people who need to be retired at 55 because they can't keep up any longer, but anyone who's still bursting with energy at 65 shouldn't be sent packing. Currently good managers are retiring non-stop in Germany – on grounds of age. A recent example is at BMW. What a loss for the economy! 40-year-old managers thought that up just so that they could get rid of their older superiors.

But Supervisory Boards find it easier to rejuvenate the management board because of retirement age regulations.

That's true. If you don't have such regulations, you need courage as a Supervisory Board if you want to get rid of someone. That's what's lacking.

How did you manage to avoid falling into a sort of limbo when you retired?

I was Chairman of Nestlé until I turned 73 years of age and until then I had always worked full-time. Today, I sit on eight to ten Supervisory Boards,

Boards of Trustees or booster clubs. I enjoy working and as a 78-year-old I work six hours a day – which is what the trade unions always wanted.

Research and Innovation

The significance of research and innovation for long-term European competitiveness

In this lecture Helmut Maucher elucidates the importance of research and innovation. He explains that the influence exerted by the Anglo-Saxon philosophy of economics leads principally to short-term actions in companies. However, long-term investments in research and development are decisive for achieving sustainable success. Furthermore, Mr. Maucher emphasizes the importance of global cooperation in order to strengthen the benefit of research for society.

First of all I would like to express my thanks for the conferment of the title of Doctor and for the laudation; it is very gratifying that the doctorate comes from Bavaria, from Munich and from a university with whom we, from the food industry, have numerous connections.

With regard to my topic, there is probably no one present in this auditorium who is not convinced that research and innovation are crucial to European competitiveness in the long term. Consequently, I would like to address a few aspects only.

We find ourselves in a unique situation today; the acceleration of globalization and liberalization means that companies and states are experiencing an increase in competition and in competition between business locations.

There are opportunities for transferring technologies such as have never been known heretofore – which is what we do daily. The differences in costs are huge.

These circumstances illustrate how much our competitiveness in Europe is contingent on our quality, our technological standards, our innovative capacity and thus on our standard of research and education.

Currently, one of our primary concerns is unemployment. Here, too, it needs to be brought to mind repeatedly that competitiveness, in addition to structural shifts and adaptations, is the major factor in the future creation of jobs.

Minister of Finance Erwin Huber once said that anyone cutting back on research today axes the jobs of tomorrow.

Due to all these problems and discussions, we constantly find ourselves in an area of tension between and in conflict with long-term policy and short-term pressures and behavior.

This applies to politics, which in a democracy frequently inclines towards short-term opportunistic thinking and tends to neglect longer-term objectives and aspects that are not immediately appreciated by the electorate.

Moreover, there are obvious trends in business which bear witness to the strong influence exerted by the Anglo-Saxon philosophy of economics, which can be paraphrased polemically as the »Wall Street mentality« and »share-value fetishism«. This leads to behavior in business that is increasingly geared towards short-term orientation. It cannot be denied that shareholders' interests are of prime importance to the private sector and take precedence. Nevertheless, it is unacceptable that a short-term policy, with focus on profit maximization, is pursued at the expense of long-term development, which is also in the interest of the shareholders.

The significance of pursuing a long-term policy can be observed to an even larger degree in research, where very long periods of time are often required to produce viable results. For example, the development of a new pharmaceutical product requiring an expenditure of 500 million or long starting-up periods in a new market are things that just have to be accepted. For that reason, it is absolutely vital that the promotion of basic research is not neglected either at the universities or in industry. That's a far cry from saying we should pursue art for art's sake; it is imperative to set clear targets even for long-term projects and to couch them in precise terms.

Nowadays, even more co-operation is required to increase the benefits which research affords society, innovations and our competitiveness; and this is essential world-wide, within Europe, between universities, between universities and industry, and within a sector. We, at Nestlé, have also opened up considerably as far as co-operation and collaboration are concerned.

Our former tendency to keep everything to ourselves because of competition has changed. With the exception of some specific research findings in our laboratories, we benefit more in the long term if we co-operate more intensely, create more transparency and collaborate.

Despite more intensified collaboration with universities and institutes, we have not neglected basic research because we believe that it is here that we can maintain our competitive edge in the long run. There is also the fact that basic research and applied research are becoming more and more integrated. There is greater inter-dependence.

It certainly will not harm research either if the competitive spirit takes a greater hold. This applies both to research in companies and at universities. Resources can be allocated according to excellence rather than according to traditional public finance accounting.

In general the following applies: the climate for promoting research and thus the will on the part of the state and of industry to free the necessary resources depend to a large extent on how prosperous the country is; whether its productivity and GNP are rising; whether public finances are in good order and whether companies are generating profits. For that reason, it is also vital that the framework conditions in a country permit efficient companies to make profits so that some of this money can also be invested in research and development in the long term.

It is often said that Germany or Europe needs to be more innovative. I believe that this depends mainly on two things:

Firstly, we must do everything within in our power to ensure that our employees regain a more positive and optimistic attitude and they are less plagued by irrational fears. An innovative culture is what we require.

Secondly, the capacity for innovation especially in small and medium sized businesses depends largely on the tax burden and the amount of red tape. In no respect does it encourage the capacity for innovation if the first profits are immediately swallowed up by taxes and people are discouraged in the face of so many laws.

Indirectly these issues are also linked to a still prevalent hostility towards technology. I well remember the very topical issue of bio-genetics at the time, where the manipulation of plants in particular was not accepted by large sections of the population. It is here that we must make a concerted effort to promote greater awareness. Science and technology in particular need to be aware of this task because greater objectivity and authority are attributed to it in this area. Sometimes we would wish for somewhat more commitment and courage, although there are many good instances meanwhile of science and technology making it clear where they stand in these matters.

Naturally, the more seriously and reliably scientific research is undertaken, the greater its authority becomes. Unfortunately there are also negative examples. Needless to say, self-control is in the interest of industry and science both.

Ladies and Gentlemen, we have evolved the concept of »sustainable development« in the field of ecology. I would most assuredly welcome it were this policy to be applied to the development of the economy and society. If we strive for long-term positive development in every respect – i. e. »sustainable development« – more and more people will become aware of how crucial and necessary investments are in education, the quality of people and in research. Only in this way can Europe's location be ensured, can competitiveness be preserved and a positive and better future be guaranteed for all.

Source: Helmut Maucher, »The significance of research and innovation for Europe's long-term competitiveness«; a lecture given on the occasion of the Doctoral Conferment Ceremony in February 1998.

The significance of innovation and research for the future development of the food industry

In this speech Helmut Maucher addresses the needs of the consumer. In addition to the importance of trends and needs, and innovation and research in general, the paper primarily addresses the research areas involved in the development of products in order to be able to guarantee optimal nutrition in developing countries.

1.

In order to fully appreciate the significance of innovation and research for the food industry, it is first of all important to know and explore the trends and needs of the consumer of today and tomorrow so that the strategies and plans of the food industry and investments in research can be focused accordingly. I would therefore like to start with an outline of these developments.

According to recent estimations by the United Nations, the world population will grow by an annual average of just over 1%. That means an annual increase of 74 million people, which is almost the population of the Federal Republic of Germany. The gross world product is growing by 1% to 3% depending on the economic situation (last year it was 5%) whereby growth in the developing economies is higher. Therefore, aggregate output is growing more strongly than the population, which is leading to a steady increase in per capita income. It is only natural that developing countries are striving for the same standard of living enjoyed by the industrialized world. There is little doubt that in addition to the distribution of the population the aggregate output, too, will shift considerably in the direction of developing countries and to Asia in particular. Currently, the wealthiest fifth of the world population possesses 86% of the gross world product while the poorest fifth has just about 1%.

According to the »World Watch Institute«, the number of overweight people, which is put at 1.1 billion, exceeds the number of hungry people, which is put at 800 million at present.

Increasing globalization, the increase in free world trade, the creation of common markets in major regions, the constant transfer of technology and information technology, and general technological progress are bound to accelerate these trends and lead to an increase in affluence in the developing economies. In the past few years, 500 to 600 million people have left the poverty threshold behind – due to globalization alone.

In developing countries, there is a steady rise in the number of people who are able to afford more. We know for a fact that the increase of the food industry and its sales is highest among people with a pro capita income of between US$ 1,000 and US$ 15,000.

Thus the increase in population and income in developing countries provides the food industry with immense opportunities.

2.

Now I would like to turn my attention to global consumer trends.

On the one hand there has been an increase in the number of global segments (like Coca Cola, McDonald's, and Nescafé etc.) and, on the other hand, there is a trend towards regionalization and preserving one's own identity, regional tastes and consumption habits.

Whereas improvements in the quality of products are generally of importance in developed countries, the provision of additional quantities including a better supply of nutrients such as proteins and the like play a more significant role in developing countries. But in these countries, too, there is a larger segment of the population daily that appreciates the consumer habits of developed countries.

Furthermore, we have ascertained that attractive products originating in a particular country or region are becoming popular globally. We need only think of pasta, for example, Asian dishes or even ethnic food.

In the industrialized world, moreover, convenience, quality, health etc. are gaining noticeably in importance. An increase in the number of one-or two-person households means that there is a growing demand for small packs. Eating out in canteens, restaurants and schools etc. is on the increase. A certain trend towards vegetarian food can be observed – i. e. meat consumption is falling – and that is not just due to the recent BSE events.

A significant indicator of affluence is beverage consumption, which amounts to approximately 600 liters per capita. We have observed considerable movement within this consumption: the consumption of spirits and beer has fallen perceptibly in the last 10 years, the consumption of wine has remained constant – i. e. it has risen slightly – and the consumption of coffee has remained more or less the same whereas the consumption of mineral water has risen considerably.

Even if the developing countries have adapted to our consumer habits in many respects, it is inconceivable for example that they could ever achieve a consumption intake of ca. 50–60 kilos of meat per capita. (This is entirely out of the question due to costs and prices, due to energy and water consumption and for ecological reasons). The trend towards foods which don't use animals in the process needs to be continued as it is common knowledge that such foods are seven times cheaper.

In recent times there has been a growing trend in developed countries towards a healthy diet (i. e. nutrition). I'll come back to that later. This also includes the increasing popularity of so-called natural foods – of organic foods (whatever that means) – and fish.

From a general point of view, price awareness has escalated in the last few years. At the same time, however, the demand for quality and brand name products remains. The safety of food also looms large and an increasing number of consumers inquire about the producer of the product, which means that the image of the producer is assuming greater significance. I would also like to comment on a certain albeit modest trend towards fair trade where consumers are prepared to pay for a particular product in order to improve the living conditions of farmers in developing countries.

Generally speaking we need to bid farewell to the idea that there is a so-called average consumer. Consumption differs more and more according to tastes and lifestyle, which is why we need to adapt to the specific needs of the consumer.

3.

Where is the starting point for research and innovation?

Basically everything must be done to increase the quality of products produced by industry. By quality, we mean mainly taste, convenience and nutritional values.

Another aspect is the durability of the products without the taste being impaired in any way. Food safety plays an increasingly vital role which is why research needs to be concerned, beyond their own plant, with the obtaining of raw materials and their quality. In future green genetic engineering can make a considerable contribution, which is why we need to do everything feasible to reduce the aversion to genetic engineering that prevails in some areas of the world. It is not possible for me to enlarge on this theme today, but I would like to mention that the three major shortages in future are likely to be grain, water and energy. Genetic engineering and other research, particularly in the field of energy, could do much to solve many of these problems.

In order to satisfy certain specific needs of developing countries to a greater degree, we need to develop a larger number of products whose raw materials are available in these developing countries; these products could perhaps contain less sophistication and convenience etc. but could be produced more cheaply, which would fit in well with the lower purchasing power in these countries.

A further area of research which ought not to be forgotten is packaging: safe packaging, less use of materials in packaging, degradable packing material, easy to handle packaging and of course the cost of the packaging.

In general, the cost aspect ought not to be forgotten in research. Research can also be used to make a contribution to lowering costs by means of more efficient production processes, also with respect to the entire supply chain from the raw material to logistics and distribution.

I would now like to enlarge on some specific demands on research from the nutrition sector.

One of the major demands is the production of products with fewer calories without impairing the consumer's taste experience. With this in mind, there are some developments in progress at Nestlé focusing on producing products with fewer calories that do not impair the so-called »mouth feel«.

However, there should be more general efforts made to reduce the percentage of salt, sugar, glutamates and fat in the products, but at the same time there should be no impairment to the taste experience. This could be achieved by using new seasonings. For lower calorie foods to be successful, the feeling of satiety and the retention period in the stomach are important because that way hunger is stilled earlier and a new feeling of hunger only sets in later.

From our research into optimal nutrition we know that in many cases (especially in older people) food supplements such as calcium, vitamins, minerals etc. are necessary.

We are increasingly indentifying groups in the population (whether for physiological or age reasons), who have specific nutritional needs. We need to adapt to these and to increase bio-availability in particular.

The rise in the number of diabetics, for example, means that we need to make great efforts to serve this group in a more optimal way.

A further aspect is research into food with the aim of strengthening the immune system. Here too there are many interesting approaches.

I would also like to refer briefly to the specific need for clinical nutrition for post-operative patients etc. (an area in which Nestlé, too, has recently become more strongly engaged).

New findings indicate a connection between the function of the brain and nutrition and so Nestlé has launched comprehensive research and collaboration into improving cognitive skills and memory etc. by means of nutrition and into counteracting or delaying dementia, Alzheimer's and similar illnesses.

4.

Just some general remarks on research: It needs to be stressed repeatedly that it is absolutely essential that research is fine-tuned to the real needs of the consumer and that there is extremely close contact to marketing departments and market research.

Furthermore, the research carried out by a company needs to open up to a greater extent. There needs to be collaboration with other companies or even with universities and institutes. Thank God, the fear of internal knowledge sharing is decreasing. Research often needs long-term staying power, which is what short-term thinking share-value optimizers ought to remember. Long-term thinking in research doesn't mean haphazard research; it means working with an objective in mind. However, a further problem in research can be that the research process is accelerated to achieve early results.

As far as organizing research is concerned, a sensible solution has proved to be a combination of research facilities in different parts of the world in addition to a basic research and co-ordination center in order to be closer to specific market conditions and to be able to collaborate better with regional universities and institutes.

5.

And now a few particular remarks which will certainly not make life easier for the food industry:

I'm thinking here of the frequent aversion to so-called industrial food, in other words the use of chemical additives – food additives among other things. Naturally the various scandals of late have done nothing to weaken these aversions. People need to be better informed and the food industry needs to adopt a more responsible attitude. But research can also make a contribution to improving the situation with a responsible attitude to its work and by providing clear and understandable scientific explanations. If science and research give people information about and explain the facts about genetic engineering and the like, that will have more impact than the food industry doing it because without making any attempt to differentiate people would accuse us of self-interest.

6. Closing remarks

All in all, the future developments of consumer trends and needs such as I have described, the growth of the world population and purchasing power mean huge opportunities and potentialities for the food industry. In this respect, the development of innovation potential and of research assumes enormous significance. We need to increase the innovative climate in industry and science and to promote creativity if innovation potential is to be developed.

The areas where research needs to set in or develop further have already been mentioned by me. What is crucial is increasing the efficiency of research through opening up, co-operation and objectives, and promoting employees and scientists who are innovative and show a decided talent for research projects.

Finally we cannot just take make use of such occasions to talk about the importance of research and innovation; we need to ensure in companies and in universities and scientific institutes that the requisite financial means are made available.

Source: Helmut Maucher, »The significance of innovations and research for the future development of the food industry«, a lecture on the occasion of the »Forum Life Science 2007« in February 2007

Acquisitions

Growth through takeovers, acquisitions, co-operation, joint ventures and mergers – The practical experience of prominent captains of industry

In the following lecture Helmut Maucher expresses his thoughts on and his recommendations for acquisitions: what ought to be done and what ought to be left undone.

Five hypotheses

1) Due to the fact that challenges have changed fundamentally, we find ourselves currently in a wave of restructuring the entire industrial machine across all departments and corporate boundaries. New technologies (information technology in particular), new perceptions in corporate management, the opening of previously inaccessible markets, the creation of regional markets, but above all globalization (fiercer competition, confrontation with new dimensions and market positions) require a redefinition of corporate strategy. Takeovers and mergers are an important means of achieving these targets.

2) In the long term, there is probably no alternative to takeovers and mergers. It is they alone which lead to unequivocal responsibility and clear leadership. Strategic alliances, partnerships or joint ventures can be beneficial depending on the situation. At a certain point in time they are the only realistic possibility. However, as a rule they only function for a limited period. In the long run it is impossible to manage strategically important parts of a company in tandem with another company that frequently has a different culture and other interests. Here the principle of

general corporate management applies: *A team with a leader, not a team of leaders.*

3) Today – although the relative position is constant – mergers inevitably have different dimensions to twenty years ago because both the business world and with that the markets are becoming increasingly globalized. Once the proper structures are in position and the right personalities have been entrusted with corporate management (leadership mindset and management structures, organizational structures, corresponding forms of decentralization, flexibility, etc.), it is possible in principle to manage a company of any size.

4) Even with takeovers in the food and beverage industry, an answer to new opportunities and challenges is essential. In addition to the general points in my first hypothesis the food industry has to address the increase in the high-quality requirements and the new needs of consumers as well as the creation and development of new technologies. In this respect I am thinking of genetic engineering for example.

Moreover, the establishment of world-wide positions is of major importance today, as are the economic benefits from increased expenditure on research and the exploitation of existing market potential and marketing organizations. In addition, there are other structures in the retail trade (concentration and internationalization) to be considered.

5) Successful acquisition policy requires clear objectives. At Nestlé in the period between 1984 and the early 90s, when acquisition activity for developing the company was particularly intense, three main strategic axes were decisive in the takeovers:

   1) Gaining access to new business segments and innovations
   2) Increasing general market presence in major regions and countries
   3) Reducing the period required to establish a position and the chance to keep risks within readily comprehensible and straightforward bounds.

In this respect I would like to give some general recommendations about what ought to be done and what should be left undone, if possible.

What ought to be done

1) To a large extent the permanent success of mergers depends on management leadership. The caution exercised there is one of the major conditions for success. It is not only our own experiences that show that a long-term

increase in competitiveness can only be achieved with good strategy, clear corporate objectives, and the correct execution of mergers and takeovers. In general, qualitative aspects (leadership potential, know-how, brands, and the quality of research, etc.) are more important in decision-making than the analyses in quantitative terms and figures that are so frequently overestimated.

2) A decisive element is the right timing, embedded in entrepreneurial far-sightedness: it is important to introduce all the restructuring measures early enough – i. e. to introduce those measures that are to be effected by means of takeovers. The costs – i. e. the price of the takeover – are usually lower with forward-thinking strategies, and there is more time for reappraisal and for a comprehensive integration of the newly acquired company divisions – including integration into the common corporate culture.

3) Human resources and psychological aspects subsequent to the acquisition are ultimately decisive for the success of the acquisition. From the very first day we at Nestlé pay attention to equal opportunities for the management of the company acquired; we pay heed to keeping promises and pay attention to an altogether speedy but psychologically skilled integration. Many managers affected by acquisitions have been given important positions at Nestlé. Everyone has the opportunity to get on in the company.

Furthermore, a great deal of attention needs to be given to the different cultures and »the way of doing business«.

Things to be avoided

1) Mergers and takeovers should not unite weaknesses but combine strengths; size is not a cure-all for problems; size and growth ought never to become an end as such or a matter of prestige.

2) For similar reasons the formation of conglomerates should also be avoided. Instead, clear priorities should be set around core competencies. In today's globalization, the international expansion of businesses is more important than the frequently heterogeneous expansion of portfolios.

3) Often those acquisitions which in terms of sheer figures are »cheapest« prove to be the most expensive in the end.

4) Communication: One of today's problems is the often one-sided, sometimes one-dimensional perspective when takeovers and mergers are announced by the management – for example, by those who are geared too

much towards financial analysts, investors and short-term profits. I'm thinking here of official press releases promising additional profits of billions of euro in connection with redimensioning without even mentioning the securing of jobs or long-term competitiveness and thus the continued existence of the company.

Source: Maucher, Helmut: »Growth through takeovers, co-operation, joint ventures and mergers- The practical experience of prominent captains of industry«, a lecture on the occasion of the Goldmann Congress on »Managing Change« in February 1998.

»The frosty winds of change«

»The quality of management is what matters in corporate success« – In the following interview Helmut Maucher discusses the implications of globalization, bad management and overrated management consultants.

[...]

DIE WELT: You too, have now written a book on proper management. Aren't there enough of them already? Were you bored?

Helmut Maucher: No, it wasn't that. In fact, I, too, had always thought that everything had been written on the subject. I didn't actually intend to write a book; not even an autobiography – I prefer to keep my vanities to myself. But then it struck me that no one has ever written a clear, plain and simple guidebook depicting the experiences of an old helmsman in industry. There is nothing revolutionary or new in it, nor is it a collection of scientific opinions.

WELT: Did you also do some market research beforehand – as is usual at Nestlé? Who is going to read the book?

Maucher: I never really thought about it. I simply sat down and dictated twelve chapters into a Dictaphone on twelve weekends. It was only afterwards that I wondered about who might find it interesting: the book is certainly of interest to lay people who are interested in the subject and to students and managers who would like to find out what Maucher thinks about such matters.

WELT: Could you please give a synopsis of the book: What matters in corporate success?

Maucher: It has been my experience that ultimately it is the quality of management, the character, the courage, the reliability and steadfastness of the individuals involved. Corporate governance or reporting may be of significance, but in my experience 98 % of all management problems can be solved with the pre-conditions I've just mentioned and with common sense.

WELT: You have written that the importance of management consultants, law firms and investment bankers are perceptibly overestimated.

Maucher: In some cases they are indispensable, but I think they should be employed as little as possible. It is unbelievable how many millions are spent on consultants and studies even though the lawyers in the company could deal with 80 percent of the issues that arise.

WELT: Do managers, in the case of mergers for example, hide behind studies and consultants?

Maucher: In many cases, they certainly do. If an acquisition goes wrong, they can always claim afterwards: »But it was the experts with the big names who advised me«. When I embarked on my first takeover, I collected all the vital aspects on 13 sheets of DIN A4 paper. That was more than enough. I more or less kept to this method ever after and it always worked well. What's the point of making pages of lists of sales trends in the last 15 years and derive extrapolations for the future, when due to developments on the market, everything is going to be obsolete after three months anyway.

WELT: Would fewer mergers fail – if ›Maucher's law‹ was taken to heart more often?

Maucher: Maybe. Most mergers fail afterwards because financial experts have too much say in things and the real reasons and values (i. e. business experience and brands etc.) are not taken sufficiently into consideration. To start with, a good manager focuses mainly on psychology. The people in the acquired company shouldn't feel that they have been taken over in the negative sense of the word. I was always to be found in such a company the very next day, talking to the people and entrusting competent employees from the company we had acquired with important executive positions in the whole company. After a takeover a good manager primarily takes care of the psychological issues, too.

WELT: So the new colleagues didn't feel in any way that they had been taken over?

Maucher: Well, at least that was my intention. I also kept my own people – I always called this particular type the ›ants‹ – out of the integration process as far as possible, if there was any danger of them wanting to incorporate the acquired company immediately, according to their own ideas. I only involved three or four reliable people at the most. That way, not everyone could interfere. That creates trust. That isn't a matter of witchcraft; it's quite simply a matter of everyday psychology. If it is used incorrectly, however, which happens now and then, the motivation of the employees is destroyed. In that case it's no wonder that even promising- looking mergers don't work.

[...]

WELT: Companies from emerging economies and aspiring states like India, Russia or China acquire companies in Europe or the United States. What changes does this entail for the corporate culture?

Maucher: The winds of change are becoming frostier, for these guys are anything but softies; they'll teach Western consensus-thinking managers a thing or two. We even have problems if we have to transfer an employee from Frankfurt to Munich. That is something that's entirely foreign to them; they've got a different combative spirit and identification with their company. But I don't think that'll last long because with increasing success, the managers from emerging economies will also become calmer and more mature. Nevertheless, we'll always have problems if we don't develop strengths of our own and adapt to new competition impartially.

Source: Seidel, Hagen: »The frosty winds of change; Helmut Maucher, former CEO of the Nestlé food company, on the implications of globalization for managers, on bad management and overestimated management consultants« in ›Die Welt‹ September 3, 2007.

»Some players are conquering the markets«

The appetite of Nestlé, the multi-national food company, appeared to be insatiable: under the leadership of Helmut Maucher, Nestlé bought up one company after the other. Maucher was one of the first to see that a new global international competition was emerging. In the following interview Mr. Maucher speaks about the backgrounds to his strategy.

[...]

SPIEGEL: Mr. Maucher, in the last few years your appetite for foreign countries has been almost voracious. Your first mega deal was at the end of 1984 when you acquired Carnation, the American food company, for the record sum of around DM 9 billion. In the last two months alone, you have engineered two more billion-DM deals: you intend to purchase Buitoni, the Italian Food Company, and Rowntree, the English confectionery company, for a total of almost DM 9 billion. Are you a megalomaniac?

Maucher: Anyone thinking and having to think in these dimensions has to expect this question. But the whole thing has nothing to do with delusions of grandeur, for there were and are strong reasons for each transaction.

SPIEGEL: And these are?

Maucher: Take Carnation for example. The strategy was clear: we wanted to improve our position in America; we wanted to enter some new areas, such as pet foods; and we wanted to expand our bulk-consumer business where our position was relatively weak. The purchase of Carnation meant that we acquired, at the same time, the Contadina brand, which sounds Italian and is of considerable importance in the culinary business. That way we killed a number of birds with one stone – particularly since we were able to incorporate Carnation's international business into our own global operations. If we had wanted to achieve this with internal growth, the process would have taken 20 or 30 years, even supposing it had been possible.

SPIEGEL: You don't have that much time?

Maucher: Well, we don't have that much time. Above all, we wouldn't achieve our objective of also being a successful, internationally operating company in the future. There were others after us who tried similar transactions. Everyone saw – we perhaps a bit earlier than others – that a new kind of global international competition was emerging; that the world was converging; that there was more collaboration and that there were some major players on the market who were conquering the markets internationally. Apart from that, internal growth still has priority in our company. Last year it amounted to five percent. I consider this to be paramount for the internal dynamic and the esprit de corps of the company.

SPIEGEL: Apparently that isn't enough. What are you buying – market shares, production capacities, or brands?

Maucher: Well, not production capacities, that's for sure. We can build those ourselves. At some stage we had to decide, and that applied to Carnation, whether we wanted to sell some nice brands of chocolate in America or whether we wanted to try to keep up with Unilever, Procter & Gamble and General Foods in strategic competition.

SPIEGEL: Is size a value as such?

Maucher: I have neither the delusions of grandeur you quoted nor do I become ecstatic over size. But there happen to be some dimensions in the world that we need to address with our strategies. Nestlé operates in all sectors of our industry. I need to look at product group upon product group and ask questions like: Am I strong enough? Am I competitive? What new areas are there which I would like to deal with because that's where consumer trends appear to be heading?

SPIEGEL: The *Wall Street Journal* wrote that you had »a hoard of gold the size of the Alps« – CHF 7 billion. Is the pressure exerted by this cash box so large that you need to go for it time and again?

Maucher: No, it isn't. There isn't any pressure at all. We attach importance to having certain financial means at our disposal because if a good opportunity presents itself, we want to get in on the act without causing problems to our moderately conservative financial policy.

SPIEGEL: How do you identify good opportunities? Do you have specialists for that?

Maucher: I work with few staff; I can read newspapers for myself. I spend a lot of time travelling around. Some of my colleagues at headquarters in Switzerland do that, too.

SPIEGEL: Have you been travelling around Europe more frequently of late?

Maucher: Recently we have been considering the subject: the European home market in 1992 –- what is its significance and what is growing together in Europe? Are we prepared for this situation? Where are the product areas where we are weak? Are there countries where we are too weak? And it was in the course of these deliberations that Italian food company Buitoni approached us.

SPIEGEL: Because the former owner, Italy's prodigy entrepreneur Carlo De Benedetti, needed money.

Maucher: Certainly, Benedetti wanted money. But what hit him hardest was the fact that he didn't achieve his objective – the establishment of a food company in Europe.

SPIEGEL: And that fitted into your concept.

Maucher: We reached a decision in a matter of hours ...

SPIEGEL: ... more than DM 2 billion?

Maucher: There was a waiting list of interested parties. Do you know, what is actually needed to be able to assess an acquisition isn't what is after the decimal point; it isn't what has been calculated by some controller or other.

SPIEGEL: But presumably what is in front of the decimal point is of importance to you, too.

Maucher: Yes, indeed. We can see that relatively quickly. Everything at Buitoni was analyzed within ten days. Then we made a grab for it because the advantages were obvious: we could improve our position in Italy in one go; the chocolate brand Perugina provided us with an area that was of interest to us as far as expanding Nestlé was concerned. Above all, we are now present in a new sector, the pasta sector, and in a few other culinary specialties.

SPIEGEL: Nestlé as a pasta company?

Maucher: For me that is also a qualitative-psychological aspect. I think that as a food company, Nestlé also has the task of spreading the ways of life and nutritional habits that exist somewhere else in the world.

SPIEGEL: To make money ...

Maucher: ... to do business. At present there is a very clear trend in Europe that »the way of life« – cooking, in other words the cuisine, is developing from the south to the north.

SPIEGEL: And you want to industrialize this Mediterranean cuisine. You want to produce the usual packaged, canned mass products.

Maucher: Yes, we do. We are talking of products that taste good and are interesting.

SPIEGEL: Do you really believe that the industrial production of food can convey something of the character, of the quality of cooking, or, as you said, the cuisine?

Maucher: The food industry produces a whole range of excellent products, whether you are talking about sauces, soups, frozen foods, canned food ...

SPIEGEL: ... if you like that sort of thing ...

Maucher: Canned food tastes quite different to 30 years ago. You should give it another try, and without any intellectual and culinary bias and arrogance. Small portions are important to consumers; safety is also a factor; health factors are also important if we can provide dishes with many more vitamins or whatever else is necessary. Regrettably »food additives« or supplements added to food are something that has acquired unfortunate overtones.

SPIEGEL: Do you want to pour even more chemicals into food?

Maucher: That's a separate issue. I think that in the next few years the food industry needs to work hard at making it clear to people that what we add is a whole range of natural substances which serve to make the products durable.

No one wants to have anything to do with the bad chemicals you are talking about.

SPIEGEL: I'm sure you will understand that in this respect, we are particularly careful when it comes to the name Nestlé. It's well known that you manage a company that makes huge profits, but it is equally certain that your name is still closely linked to the famous baby milk scandal in the developing countries that in the 70s was said to have been responsible for the deaths of so many babies. Your company spent huge sums on advertising to push the powder onto the market but without being able to ensure that the hygiene regulations were observed.

Maucher: We conducted discussions with the groups affected and with activists and we applied and actively supported the code of the World Trade Organization which, for example, forbids advertising these products in the Third World and in principle we were able to clear up the story of the babies – even though the controversy somehow continues to flare up somewhere or other. Apart from that, there is no doubt among experts that these products are needed and are the best alternative if a baby's mother doesn't have enough milk or there is no milk for the baby at all.

SPIEGEL: Let's come back to the present. The attempt to take over Rowntree seems to be proving difficult. Jacobs Suchard, another Swiss food company, already holds 30 percent of the share whereas you only have around 10 percent.

Maucher: In the meantime we have around 15 percent. At present we are buying up what is on the market.

SPIEGEL: How on earth do you hope to absorb a company with such a small share especially when the management doesn't even want you?

Maucher: The situation is such that Jacobs has 30 percent meanwhile. We have made the shareholders an offer that from our point of view is very attractive.

SPIEGEL: Apparently this opinion isn't shared by many of the shareholders.

Maucher: A few months ago the price was 400 pence a share. Today we are offering 900p or 22 times the annual profit. I think that is more than fair.

SPIEGEL: In the case of Carnation you were fastest. In the case of Rowntree your competitor Jacobs appears to have been quicker off the mark.

Maucher: It's not a question of speed but of behavior. Last year I negotiated with the Chairman of Rowntree myself and expressed our interest in the company, whereupon he informed me that the company wanted to remain independent; the company was not for sale. I respected that and inquired if there were other opportunities for collaboration because the two companies were an ideal match. Together we could achieve more if, for example, we combined our sales organizations in certain countries. The Rowntree management took a long time to reach a decision, but they didn't close the door in our faces. We respected that and didn't buy any shares. Meanwhile Jacobs started buying. Our restraint has cost us, at a guess, CHF 200 million.

SPIEGEL: How come it has cost you so much?

Maucher: During that period we, too, could have acquired 15 percent at a price of 450 to 600 pence. That would have been no problem for us. We didn't do it. We didn't buy a single share because it is against our principle to attempt a takeover bid against the wishes of the management.

SPIEGEL: You appear to dispense with this principle quickly – see Rowntree – as required ...

Maucher: ... not quickly and not as required but under quite definite circumstances. Jacobs' attempt to gain access to Rowntree is one such exception. From that point on, it was no longer a question of whether Rowntree would be taken over but rather a question of who would take it over. And in this case we felt justified, also from the point of view of competitive strategy, in acting so.

SPIEGEL: Jacobs has a lead that you will hardly be able to overtake.

Maucher: No, that's not correct. Jacobs has 30 percent now. According to English law, Jacobs can only buy more than 30 percent if they make a public offer to all the shareholders. They would have to outbid us ...

SPIEGEL: Can they afford to?

Maucher: It's considerably more difficult for Jacobs than for Nestlé. Jacobs has equity of approx. CHF 1.5 billion. We have roughly ten times that. And we have CHF 7 billion in cash. Jacobs has 600 to 700 million. That means: we are in a financial position to make a transaction. What Jacobs are planning, I can't say.

SPIEGEL: Perhaps they'll sell their share to you with a hefty premium. Would you be interested?

Maucher: From a logical point of view, we could live with a minority shareholder, even à la Jacobs. But of course we are open to an offer for their shares – but only at a reasonable price. Apart from that, Rowntree's product range goes well with ours and geographically we complement each other, too. That is ideal in every respect.

SPIEGEL: Do you fear there will be resistance from the government?

Maucher: Yes, I do; particularly for national reasons. English politicians are demanding that the takeover of Rowntree be forbidden because British companies are not in a position to purchase Swiss companies to the same extent.

SPIEGEL: Swiss companies fence themselves off with registered shares with restricted transferability; their shareholders are more or less hand- picked.

Maucher: But that's not a political issue. Registered shares are based on civil-law agreements between the particular company and its shareholders, who are prepared to put up with a disadvantage because the price of the registered shares is perceptibly lower on account of the narrower market.

SPIEGEL: But it's unfair practice all the same.

Maucher: You must try to understand the Swiss, too. The whole world wants to work here; everyone wants to buy a house here. And that in a country where the population is smaller than London's! The need for protection that the Swiss feel is correspondingly large.

SPIEGEL: That's not likely to move the British politicians. Do you expect a refusal?

Maucher: No, I don't. Anyone who refuses has to consider the consequences such an action might have for the British multinationals that buy companies all over the world. Besides, the politicians know that jobs at Rowntree will be safer due to Nestlé. With our marketing department we can sell more Rowntree's products than Rowntree can.

SPIEGEL: No matter how the battle for Rowntree turns out – it will be one of the most spectacular deals of the year. Will mega deals like Nestlé-Rowntree, which are almost commonplace in the USA, be in store for Europeans, too?

Maucher: It's impossible to predict that clearly. To be sure, there are other structures here. Just think of the influence banks have in Germany. But generally speaking, acquisitions among the big companies are a more and more popular means of realizing strategies.

SPIEGEL: Do you think there is a disreputable boundary beyond which a company should not go in its urge to expand?

Maucher: As far as I'm concerned the boundaries are reached if competition is impaired.

SPIEGEL: Do you expect us to believe that you are interested in fierce competition?

Maucher: In the long term we are interested in maintaining competition because that is the breeding ground for a free market economy to flourish. If, as responsible entrepreneurs, we are not in favor of it, we'll be digging our own graves.

SPIEGEL: But competition would benefit most if you brought your own innovations onto the market instead of buying up foreign companies

Maucher: But we do that, too. We launch hundreds of products on the market every year.

SPIEGEL: Can you give some examples?

Maucher: In the confectionery division alone we have launched products like »Yes«. Today that already has a considerable market share in Germany;

almost as big as Rowntree's »Quality Street«. We have launched »Choclait Chips« which is a really excellent product, innovative in its combination as a snack ...

SPIEGEL: ... if you like that sort of thing!

Maucher: Do you like »Choclait Chips«?

SPIEGEL: No, we can't try everything.

Maucher: (laughing) Why are you talking about things you know nothing about?

SPIEGEL: Potato crisps are bad enough but Chocolate Chips ...

Maucher: ... taste great!

SPIEGEL: Let's be serious. You mentioned that you preferred takeovers which were endorsed by the management of the company you wished to acquire. But even those managers who are well-disposed towards you have to be integrated into Nestlé. Can you actually accomplish that at your present rate of acquisition?

Maucher: We've coped well with this task so far. In our company, the work of an acquisition doesn't stop with the takeover. After an acquisition, the questions of management, integration, and co-operation are tackled carefully and intensely.

SPIEGEL: Do you run these companies mainly as independent units? How does the top-heavy administration at headquarters in Vevey cope with all the acquisitions?

Maucher: That is why we have one of the smallest top-heavy administrations in relation to our sales and to other companies. We have a very pronounced philosophy of decentralization. That applies both to our existing companies and to the new ones.

SPIEGEL: And how do you monitor these companies?

Maucher: They don't need so much monitoring. For me, the people themselves are the most important control. I look at the CEOs of these companies very closely. I talk to them; I visit them; I get an impression and can combine this impression with market shares, sales, profits or other data. And if I see that it won't work, it's much cheaper and more efficient to change the people than to intensify controls or interventions by headquarters. It doesn't only depend on figures.

[...]

Source: Werner Funk/Armin Mahler, »*Some players are conquering the markets*«, in *Der Spiegel*, issue 20/1988

Interview with Helmut Maucher about his highly successful acquisition policy at Nestlé

The following text is an excerpt from an elaborate discussion with Helmut Maucher in connection with Farsam Farschtschian's research at the University of St. Gallen. It addresses why Nestlé, under Maucher's leadership, was so successful with his long-term acquisition strategy over the years. In addition, it illustrates the quality of Maucher's management and his confident co-operation with the Board of Management.

Farsam Farschtschian: Mr. Maucher, how would you describe the way you undertook acquisitions at Nestlé?

Helmut Maucher: As far as this subject is concerned, it is important to note one thing: as you know, the Board of Directors exercises overall management control according to Swiss law and that means that it is they who normally run the business.

In practice, this is naturally not realistic because in a large company the Board cannot possibly run the business with 15 members. As a rule, the Board delegates the actual management to the CEO, the so-called »Delegate of the Board of Directors«. When that is the case, the CEO has relatively full power and the Board of Directors is almost but not quite downgraded to the equivalent of the Supervisory Board in Germany by dint of the fact that it has delegated its rights. However, that never goes as far as they do in Germany for there the Management Board can for example buy a company for 10 billion without asking the Supervisory Board.

That is not the case in Switzerland: not only does the Board of Directors nominate the General Directors but it is involved in everything to do with the management, with key strategies and acquisitions. As a rule that is stipulated. At Nestlé I specified that the Board of Directors had to take a joint decision if an acquisition was to cost more than CHF 500 million. But the Committee of the Board of Directors had to give permission for acquisitions exceeding CHF 150 million. After all, we invest billions – you can't involve the Board of Directors in everything every day.

To summarize: Firstly, the power of the CEO ceases as soon as acquisitions reach a certain limit. Secondly, it ceases if the acquisition were to lead to a change of strategy; for example, if we were to go into pharmaceutics or travel that would be a strategic issue.

At Nestlé, the powers of the CEO and the Committee were far-reaching but only within the stipulated strategy. This was set out in a lengthy document and discussed by the Board of Directors at least once a year. Then it could be said: »On the basis of this strategy we are going to buy a pet food company«.

The functions of the Board of Directors consist in having a say in important matters and determining strategy beforehand. The CEO – i. e. the Committee – can act within these two parameters. You need to know that otherwise you won't understand the rest.

Farsam Farschtschian: Let's assume that acquisitions exceed the limit – i. e. they are more than 150 or 500 million. What happens then?

Helmut Maucher: Obviously the initiative comes from the CEO. He is also a member of the Board of Directors and having determined the strategy with them he now says: »Within the framework of this strategy I'm now going to by a pet food company or nutrition company«.

The CEO studies the project with his employees and if he thinks the idea makes sense, he will present it to the Board of Directors and they have to take a decision. If they decide against it, then the project is finished. In my case, if the Board of Directors vetoes my proposal three times, I would step down because then I assume that they have a problem with me and not with the project.

The CEO's position is therefore quite strong. As long as he is successful, the Board of Directors will find it difficult to say »No«. I have always had 100 % consent – but then I always provided the Board of Directors with all the necessary information. The members of the Board of Directors always knew the facts. They trusted me. But if I had abused this trust, they would have had every opportunity to take action.

After the decision is taken by the Board of Directors the plans for the acquisitions are set in motion and carried out. After that the management has an obligation to report. We have to keep the Board of Directors informed about everything: how the project will continue; how things are going with the new acquisition; whether it is going well or whether it is going badly; whether it is what we have planned; and whether there are any problems. That is all part of the normal obligation to report to the Board of Directors. Of course, in deciding about acquisitions it is not just a matter of whether you do something or not but generally about the financing concept; whether we issue new shares, or whether we try it with commercial papers, and then try it with self-financing; or whether we take out a major long-term credit. As a rule these questions are part of the decision-making concept.

In general, I would like to say the following about acquisitions: At Nestlé we have never made acquisitions which never proved successful. That is certainly due to the fact that we never engaged in risky ventures. We always knew what we were buying.

The Board of Directors is always interested in how far the profit will be affected in the short term. It might happen that I would like to make an investment that is strategically right but would lead to a short-term dilution of the profit per share. If I have to pay out a huge sum of money momentarily, this might affect the net profit because for 2–3 years the new profit margins will be somewhat smaller than the new interest charges until the acquisition begins to be profitable. Then of course such matters need to be discussed.

We had practically no failures at Nestlé. Firstly, we always looked at things realistically and soberly and secondly, we only acquired companies in our own sector because that is what we knew about. McKinsey claims that two-thirds of all acquisitions go wrong – but that was never the case with us.

When it comes to acquisitions, it is important what your decision about an acquisition is based on. Nowadays, investment bankers produce tons of paper in reaching such decisions. We, on the other hand, rarely made use of investment bankers. We were very selective in using them: only if they had a better knowledge of the legislation in a country or when the other company had called them in, for example. We didn't spend billions and billions on them. We always told ourselves that we had to know what we were doing. We were very careful in our dealings with investment bankers. Today, documents are produced by the ton but so many of them are not really needed.

I can give you an example. Buying »Carnation« was the first-ever big acquisition by a European company in the United States. We're talking about US$ 3.5 billion. That was an enormous sum of money over twenty years ago. At that time, I presented the Board of Directors with exactly thirteen pages. They contained all the necessary information and it was on the strength of these thirteen pages that the Board of Directors made their decision.

What I would like to stress is that it's better to take decisions using fewer documents and studies because as a rule details aren't correct anyway. Anyhow, the world always moves in a different way to what people imagine and an excessively large number of studies feign an accuracy that doesn't exist. Naturally my thirteen pages contained all the essentials: why we were making this acquisition; whether we were strengthening our position in America; whether we were strengthening »Pet Food«; how much it would cost and how we would finance it. That was all.

What is even more crucial and is, in my opinion, the reason why many acquisitions go wrong, are the measures taken after the acquisition. It is there that many people make mistakes. Frequently a number of staff from head headquarters is sent into the acquired companies; and they always know everything better and frustrate the entire company with psychological mistakes. It often happens that the management isn't involved sufficiently and a climate is created that leads to people losing their motivation or even that the entire management is dismissed. These are all aspects that lead ultimately to an acquisition failing.

In this respect we made no mistakes and I'm very proud of that. I was to be found in the new company on the very next day after the acquisition talking with the people and the management, too. If they were any good, I left every squad in their positions or I gave them the opportunity to take up a new position within Nestlé. After all, they weren't bad people. I deployed the staff from our headquarters with the greatest of care. If these descend on such a company like a hoard of ants, then it will go bust.

I think that from a psychological point of view and as far as involving new people were concerned, we didn't make any mistakes. Many of those making an acquisition think they're the clever ones and the others are the fools. I listened to the people because they were not fools by any means. For example I acquired the »Stouffer« company. The head of »Stouffer« became head of American business for a period after the takeover. Later I bought »Carnation« where I had to inform the CEO – he was over 70 – he would have to go. He had a successor who then not only became head of »Carnation« but also of business in the whole of America.

You see, I have always used capable people. I've always told the people: »You're part of Nestlé now. You have the same opportunities as anyone else in the company! « But I didn't just say it. I also showed it in such examples.

Psychological questions – the management after the takeover, leadership, motivation, involving the people or showing the proper regard – are crucial to the success of an acquisition in the long run.

Farsam Farschtschian: That's interesting, for you read that when it comes to post merger integration (PMI) it has to be relatively quick and smooth. Besides, I read in something of yours that you didn't, for example, integrate directly at »Carnation« ...

Helmut Maucher: In many cases I left the people to themselves. We kept an eye on them for a while and only then did we take any action. For example, we integrated a subsidiary company in Germany into Nestlé Germany because we understood more about Germany than »Carnation« did. We carefully allowed many companies that had been taken over by Nestlé to continue running and then integrated them step by step.

Of course, we were aware of synergies right from the very start: for example, from the very beginning you need less head office, and no research of your own. Integration took place step by step both in a socially acceptable and socio-political way. These are all steps where mistakes can be made: or it's just done properly.

For a long time I had two CEOs in America, who were required to report directly to me. Naturally they worked together and certain synergies were always evident – for a long time there were two. The financial analysts asked me why I didn't combine the two posts together. I told them: »Because I'm clever, unlike you«. Thus all the companies worked well and we made profits. It was only later when they had got used to and had got to know each other that the next step was taken; when we only needed one CEO in America.

Farsam Farschtschian: One of the main reasons given for an acquisition failing is that too much was paid. It is much more important for a project to make strategic sense and for the price to be of secondary importance. Would you say, however, that a premium of 40–50 % can be a reason for failure because the project cannot be absorbed financially?

Helmut Maucher: Of course you ought to know how much you can afford to pay.

There are many people who don't want to join in because they don't pay enough attention to the long-term components.

Financial analysts or pure financiers quite often advised against an acquisition if it was going to mean a restriction of profit for three years. Then I said: »But we will still make a profit of ..... ; this is a once-in-a-century decision. If we don't do it now, we'll never position Nestlé where we want to in the long term«.

I paid over CHF 6 billion for »Rowntree«. At the time, I said that the additional interest we would have to pay would have to correspond to the additional profit margins, so that the sum would remain the same, but we wouldn't make the same progress with the profit in the next 2–3 years. However, as I said, that was a once-in-a-century decision. In the field of confectionery and bar products, there were only two companies – « Mars« and »Rowntree«. If we wanted to stay in the chocolate business, we would have to make this acquisition. It has paid off long since.

The question as to long-term or short-term is vital and has to be discussed with the Board of Directors, too, for it is all part of strategy.

Farsam Farschtschian: Does the Board of Directors base its decision entirely on the CEO's assessment of the target or does it call in external financial experts?

Helmut Maucher: No, it doesn't. If the Board of Directors requires additional information, it is the CEO who obtains it, not the Board of Directors. There would only be intrigues if it were done differently. If the Board of Directors wished to have additional information, they let me know and either I informed them that we didn't need it or I obtained the information for them. At any rate, everything went through me. Anything else is a vote of no confidence which a good CEO would never accept.

Of course the price is a vital aspect. In my experience, the most expensive acquisitions were the best ones and the cheapest were often the worst ones.

Anything that has a real value in the long run has its price. You pay for this goodwill which is often far more than the book value – but you get it back again with the profitability.

Farsam Farschtschian: it is said that deals paid in cash are more likely to lead to success …

Helmut Maucher: Financing is an entirely different matter. It depends on how you finance a company. I can run a company on little equity and a great deal of borrowed capital or vice versa. It is a question of how willing the company is to run financial risks.

We have principles that are quite clearly stipulated in our strategy. For example, we said that we would never go as far as the Americans. We Swiss are more careful. As a rule I said that the net gearing – i. e. all the credits we have less cash – should never be more than 50 % of the equity. The Americans easily go as far as 100 %. We don't do that. We don't want to get into difficulty in uncertain times. Besides, it depends on how much cash flow I have. If I have more cash flow; I can risk more than if I have little cash flow.

Financial policy and risk policy are independent of acquisition but the acquisition influences this policy. When making an acquisition I have to take into consideration whether my risk policy is financially safeguarded or whether I need to go to the capital market to get new equity. With regard to an acquisition, checks are made as to whether my financial policy is still correct or whether I need to reconsider. Whether cash is financed or not depends on my financial strategy.

Farsam Farschtschian: That's the point of view of the company you've given me, but what I'd like to know is how, in your opinion, the financial markets judge that?

Helmut Maucher: That is a topic we haven't touched on so far: the whole subject of investor relations (IR) and financial markets. Of course, as CEO, I have to take that into consideration.

However, as a rule it is taken too much into account. Of course these topics are particularly important to companies wanting to return to the capital market again because then the cost of capital rises and then the price is too low.

But in principle, we have to do what is correct in the long term. That is why I have criticized financial analysts. Their opinions are short-term and the facts are important in the long term.

Of course, in general, I have to include in my considerations how the capital market will react. But because we almost never needed capital from the capital market, I didn't see why it should bother me if the price dropped for six months. If the Management Board only thinks of their stock options, they don't act in the interest of the company. I knew the price would remain stable in the medium term. If business improved and earnings rose, the market would react accordingly.

If I were to take this short-term thinking constantly into consideration, I would be running the business incorrectly and certainly not in the long term. I've never done that.

In general I have to consider the opinion of the capital market in my deliberations – but then I have to be able to explain it. That means we have to have an IR Committee or a meeting. On the whole, I always succeeded because the share price always rose.

Farsam Farschtschian: Then that is also a task for the CEO and not the Board of Directors?

Helmut Maucher: Correct. But the Board of Directors does look at it, too.

The information the Board of Directors receives regularly includes the share price compared with the share price of our competitors and with the Swiss index. The CEO always reports on his visits to markets and his conferences with investor relations. That is all part of his obligation to report.

That way the Board of Directors can take action. However, the Board of Directors cannot go directly to the financial markets. That is not their job. They are informed in detail about what is happening and how the share capital is distributed between the Americans and the Swiss.

Moreover, I always reported on my trips and my contacts to financiers and statesmen and women. That was all part of my obligation to report. But if the Board of Directors thought they needed to do it without me, then they could have looked for a new CEO.

Farsam Farschtschian: What I would like to know in this context is: When is it the Chairman who acts and when the CEO?

Helmut Maucher: The two of them have to arrange that between them. For a time I held both positions. At first I was only CEO, then both and finally only Chairman. We always laid down exactly how the tasks were to be divided up.

When I was CEO – and I was a strong CEO –Mr. Jolles was Chairman and Secretary of State in the government. In my position of CEO, I was at that time principally responsible for 90 % of the contacts made. The people wanted to see the company head and that was me.

Mr. Jolles had general contacts, for example, in the government. But all the contacts that mattered, contacts where business was negotiated or where Nestlé had to be represented in public, fell to me.

When I was Chairman and not CEO any more, Mr. Brabeck and I decided jointly that he should take charge of all the contacts connected with his position of CEO. I didn't go to press conferences anymore and didn't conduct any more IR meetings. Those are all the things he had to do as CEO. That meant that 70–80 % of the contacts were handed over to the CEO immediately – even though I was an active Chairman.

Only when certain issues were involved, where I had old connections, did I continue for a little while longer. For example, I remained President of the European Roundtable. Or if it happened that I knew the Prime Minister of India better, it was I who went to meet him but only after consulting Mr. Brabeck.

Even though I was a strong Chairman, I had basically handed over most of the contacts to him; not because I couldn't have done the job but because I was of the opinion that these things belong to a CEO's position. He has to discharge such duties; he has to make a name for himself; has to show his authority and become known.

Today I'm proud of the fact that I took a back seat in this respect, for it was certainly in the interest of Nestlé's future.

Farsam Farschtschian: I was aware of course that Nestlé's management was very good, but what I didn't know was that there were such definite guidelines.

Helmut Maucher: Yes, that was also in our articles. Whether you like it or not: the CEO, whether he's Chairman at the same time or not, is the key figure in the place.

If he doesn't function properly, you can have the best Board of Directors, and the company will founder nevertheless. We have a saying in Germany: If a company is managed well, the Board of Directors is superfluous, and if it is managed badly, the Board is helpless. There's something in that.

I've never seen a company anywhere in the world where things went well under a bad CEO only because the Board of Directors was good. On the other hand there are numerous companies that work well where the Board of Directors is mediocre but where the CEO is good instead.

Farsam Farschtschian: Let´s talk about the success factors that you publicized at Nestlé. You say that an acquisition has to strengthen the core business or that it ought to provide access to a major market where one has a key competence; or that the acquisition is to shorten the length of time to adopt a new product line which in turn fits the strategy....

Helmut Maucher: ... You are speaking here of growth strategy. In growth strategy there is generally always the alternative: acquisition or internal growth. The latter has to be there otherwise the company has no momentum anymore.

But certain processes can be shortened by making an acquisition. In the short term you pay more because after all you pay the price for the success of the others, but that way you can achieve certain objectives more quickly. After that, you need to see whether it is profitable or not.

In my case I achieved two-thirds with acquisitions and one third with internal growth for a time because I had to lead the company into a new dimension within a short period. I had to do it before everyone realized the meaning of globalization, water or »pet food«. I was able to shorten all that. Ten years later it would all have become a lot more expensive.

You need to do both: grow internally but also enter new product fields which you think have potential in the future. That was the reason why I went into »pet food«, water and nutrition.

An acquisition can also make sense if you want to strengthen your presence in certain countries. Acquiring »Carnation« was one of the strategies for strengthening our business in America. We acquired »Rowntree« because we wanted to occupy a leading position in the confectionery sector. That is why we had to go into this segment – and not just into bars of chocolate and chocolates.

When I began to buy water, people laughed at me at first. No one laughs today. Nowadays, we sell 15–20 billion liters of water. Water is like oil: either you have it or you don't. In the meantime, water is a major line of business at Nestlé. We had to do that via acquisition.

There are other growth theories, too. I wanted to create equilibrium between the product groups. When I came to Switzerland, 50 % of the profit was generated by Nescafé. I said: »That is all very well, but it's dangerous in the long term«. And so we expanded our product range.

I also said: »We can't make more than 50 % of our profit in Europe permanently, if the world is growing in other places«. That's why I invested in America and Asia etc. There were also some gaps in some countries where we were scarcely active.

However, those are things that are specified in the total strategy with the Board. I discussed them with the Board and as a rule the Board gave me their support. In this respect, the Board was able to participate in a long-term policy because I was still in a position to increase profits every year. If you can only promise long-term earnings and no short-term profits, the public, the shareholders and the Board become nervous. However, because the share value and current profits always continued to rise and consequently productivity, too, people were satisfied with my work.

If there is something wrong with one component, the Board asks questions, and justifiably so. But I was always lucky that things always went relatively well for me.

Farsam Farschtschian: One of the fundamental principles you followed with each of the acquisitions was that there had to be a willingness to learn from each other. That's why, as a matter of principle, you didn't make any hostile takeover bids. But there were exceptions....

Helmut Maucher: In the beginning, I made no hostile takeover bids but then

I changed my mind. In the meantime hostile takeovers are made because it sometimes doesn't work any other way.

»Rowntree« was partly a hostile takeover. Nevertheless, I went into the company immediately, motivated and convinced the people and gave them a chance, whereupon they accepted the situation because what I told them made sense. I protected the people. I pursued a policy that was socially sound and I also gave the new people a chance. If things work that way, people realize at once that it's a good thing.

Farsam Farschtschian: And so there were never conglomerates and no vertical integration in that sense either.

Helmut Maucher: No, there weren't. I never did any of those things. There was a time, about 30 years ago when diversification was all the rage. I didn't buy bike factories, so that later, when consolidation was in vogue, I didn't have to sell any. It's as simple as that.

Farsam Farschtschian: Do you think that these specific factors were only successful with respect to your acquisitions at Nestlé or can they be applied in other companies, too?

Helmut Maucher: I think these principles apply generally. That means: *firstly* using in acquisitions the psychology I mentioned and *secondly* not buying things about which you have absolutely no idea. If you do that, the company needs to be completely restructured because then you are a financial holding that lets the companies run individually and only controls them on the basis of their financial data.

We have always said that we wanted to run businesses we understood. We wanted to practice genuine business management. That's why buying things that weren't right for us were out of the question.

Source: Farschtschian, Farsam: *The Reality of M&A Governance: Transforming Board Practice for Success*, Springer 2012, pages 189–209.

Marketing, Advertising and Communication

Fast moving consumer goods: current and future aspects

In the following lecture Helmut Maucher talks about traditional marketing and the importance of the corporate brand. He comments on the importance of integrative branding policy, the importance of family and single brands and trademarks, and the importance of product design in general. He also addresses topics like advertising, co-operation with advertising agencies and the future of marketing.

There are two remarks I would like to make to begin with:

At the ›German Marketing Day‹ on October 12, the question was asked under the heading of »Marketing for the Future« whether traditional marketing no longer works, and recently a lecture on breaking the rules was held at Grey's.

Today we are attending a meeting at Metro, one of the largest business groups in the world, and thus from a location point of view we are right at the center of the action.

I would like to divide my lecture into three parts in which I will address three questions:

A) What is left of traditional marketing?
B) What does the situation look like today and what is changing?
C) What do these changes mean for the future of marketing?

First of all: What's left?

1.

Despite all the critical remarks from the relevant side about the apparent loss in the importance of branding, brands still continue to rate high with the consumer. In fact, they tend to have gained in importance. There are a number of reasons for this:

In the increasing anonymity of our living conditions and rising uncertainty, and the many changes in our lives with which we are steadily confronted, human beings search for elements and fixtures which provide continuity, safety and orientation. Brands can also contribute to this.

Despite the increase in the bargain-hunting mentality and price awareness over the past few years, quality is something that is still appreciated. It constitutes a longing for product safety and stability, and a striving for prestige and the gratification of emotions etc.

Brands have the advantage of being on offer everywhere (so-called ubiquity). This circumstance affords them an additional advantage over trademarks.

Of course no two brands are identical. Although the name and the logo are important, these alone don't create a brand. What is paramount is that in a certain product category, the brand-name product covers the upper quality segment and that there are no quality fluctuations so that the brand – i.e. the quality it stands for – remains trustworthy. Moreover not only must the quality remain constant (improvements in quality are naturally permissible!), but that applies also to the image of the brand and to the marketing strategy for the brand.

Part of the marketing strategy is the steady promotion of the product because otherwise the image of the brand and the customer's preference for the brand are weakened and preferences are transferred to other rival products.

[...]

In addition, branding policy needs to be pursued holistically. Apart from the name and the logo, the overall design needs to add up; from the product to the design (label) and from the marketing strategy to all the other manifestations with which a company goes public. That also includes the type and style of the sellers, even the design of the offices and naturally the reception and telephone exchange in particular. Even business reports and other PR measures need to fit the entire image we want to create for a certain brand among our consumers and the public.

Usually in a company we have a corporate brand image and apart from that there are numerous family and single brands. It is crucial that the overall branding concept and the framework dovetail. To start with, there is of course the design of the *corporate brand*. Let me say something about this using Nestlé as an example. Even at that time, Heinrich Nestlé the founder laid down, in our case, the basics of the *corporate image* in an ingenious and ideal way. He linked his name Nestlé to a bird's nest in which a mother bird is feeding her three young. (The name Nestlé means »little nest« in the Swabian dialect). Thus he lent the Nestlé brand a huge emotional value that moreover fits our industry (food) precisely. There's only one thing that can said about that: You only need the luck to be called Nestlé!

A further question that is constantly discussed a great deal is whether each new product should be given its own brand or how much use should be made of existing brands or even the corporate image. Many companies such as Unilever and Procter & Gamble have always been very strong in developing single brands. Recently, however, they have started to make greater use of family brands and the corporate image; whether for economic reasons or because they have ascertained that an individual brand can benefit from the corporate image just as much as the corporate image can benefit from the individual brand. We always had a more balanced policy at Nestlé. However, in my day I made sure that greater use was made of the corporate image and the family brand than had been the case prior to then, and that produced the well-known advantages I've just described.

On the other hand, care needs to be taken that a particular brand or family brand isn't too segmented and that all kinds of products aren't attached to the brand – this is generally known as »brand stretching«. It can even go so far that it dilutes the basic brand value. Good branding policy requires a great deal of thought, fine tuning and feeling to find the right way.

I'd just like to say one more word about trademarks, which are a vital factor in the food and beverage and tobacco industry and in a few other sectors where the products are sold via the food trade. You need to be aware of the fact that the producer wants to create a distinctive image for single brands. However, the retail market wants to create a distinctive image for its entire trade chain and any means is justified if this promotes the unique position of its chain including among other things trademarks. Of course, trademarks are also there to offer consumers a favorable price. For various reasons, therefore, trademarks have a place in the commercial range of goods offered by the retail trade. The task of the producers of branded goods is to ensure that the importance of trademarks and private brands does not increase too much. In principle, that requires the following policy:

1. The difference in quality should be apparent to the consumer (this is known as perceived quality).
2. I need to create as much preference for my brand as possible with branding policy, and advertising etc. to curb the sales of trademarks further.
3. Strict cost management Is necessary to ensure that the gap between the price of our brand and the trademark does not become too wide and at all events remains within a limit so that a large number of consumers continue to prefer to buy brand-name products.
4. Finally, I need to develop custom-made actions, among other things, in collaboration with and in conjunction with the retail trade, actions that promote our own brands and are also interesting for the retail trade.
5. A technological lead serves to strengthen the position against other trademarks.

I have always stressed, moreover, how vital it is to take care that – apart from attention to the retail trade and the creation of good relations to the trade organizations – we maintain a competitive edge over our fellow competitors with regards to quality, brand, and price etc. If we do that, the consumer will notice. After all, the retail trade ultimately sells to consumers what is going to generate the largest turnover.

2.

What elements of traditional marketing instruments will be valid in the future, too?

I would like to comment as follows:

Product policy

Logically, all marketing deliberations and activities begin with product policy. For which products is there a direct or latent demand and can such a product be produced at a price acceptable to the consumer? It is a common saying that the development of a product must be market-oriented. Besides, researchers and technicians often have ideas which the market never even thought of and which ultimately lead to products that are accepted by the market. Establishing a need, research and very often a dazzling idea by a company have always been the trigger for new solutions and products, which have provided progress and improved living standards. Of course, there are also other, less fundamental, revolutionary products and the development of products that are very promising. For example, an existing product – even one by competitors – can be improved considerably with the result that market volume is enlarged or quite simply market share is gained. New manufacturing processes afford an opportunity to manufacture the product more cheaply and that means prices decrease etc. It is crucial ultimately that establishing a need, having ideas for products and research combine to create a promising product.

And then the new product needs to be sold!

The first steps in this direction are the *product design,* the packaging, the label, the design etc. The importance of these deliberations cannot be stressed enough. Frequently, failure can be put down to bad product design. Many designs might win a prize at an art exhibition, but the consumer doesn't like them. The design of the label, the instructions for use etc. need to be legible, understandable and attractive, but they shouldn't be overloaded. Look at packages for the consumer from this point of view and you will ascertain that they are often done badly. One modern bad habit is putting the writing or the name of the product vertically. Sometimes this is necessary because there isn't enough space; besides, it looks cool but the writing is difficult to read. Instruction manuals for technical appliances – including cars and cell phones – are often a fiasco when it comes to understanding them, as they are often written by technicians with poor communication skills. To highlight this, I would like to point out, for example, how important the design of a car is in addition to the technical data, the price and the brand.

Moreover, it is important to avoid small print and to think of senior citizens!

Product design also includes a precise description of the product, its name and the brand; but I've already talked about that.

Pricing policy and sales conditions

Another marketing instrument is pricing policy, but at the same time this presents one of the most difficult problems in marketing. First of all, everything has to be done to keep manufacturing costs as low as possible without any loss in quality (!). In order to determine the price, it is necessary to calculate the manufacturing costs that are possible if a certain sales volume is reached. (These are often considerably lower than the manufacturing costs of the first production). Then the difficult question has to be answered as to how many products can be sold at a particular price. Unfortunately, market research and tests aren't much help. Naturally, the price has to fit into the competitive frame of reference and take the value of the brand into consideration.

If the product is brand new, it is often launched at a relatively high price to serve the upper segment, which is willing to pay this price. In a second phase, »market penetration« begins at a lower price and with mostly lower manufacturing costs.

In summary, I would like to say on the subject of pricing policy that it is difficult, despite sophisticated instruments thanks to market research and calculations etc., to determine the optimal price (with the largest long-term ROI) precisely and that is why we are often obliged to undertake corrections and changes according to the market trend.

With regard to pricing policy I would like to say a word about strategies for sales conditions: These have gained tremendous importance in my industry due to the concentration of the retail trade and the strong development of purchasing power. On the one hand, the policy for sales conditions needs to ensure that large quantities, larger annual sales, large-scale orders per unit of account or special performances in sales are rewarded appropriately in the retail trade. On the other hand, there should be no yielding to blackmail and unreasonable demands because otherwise the other traders will suffer discrimination. These improprieties would not remain undetected if purchasers change frequently, and when there are mergers!

Sales methods and sales policy

With regards to new and existing products, it is advisable to think about specifying distribution channels and sales policy. Here I can merely sum up some of my thoughts in the following questions: Should you sell directly or via a middleman? Do you use your own sales force, or sales representatives and agents etc.? How much do you actually need to invest in sales to keep the costs down on the one hand and to successfully achieve optimal sales on the other?

Advertising

It is well known that advertising as a further marketing instrument is an important feature of the »marketing mix«. The more products for the mass market are involved and the more emotion and prestige are at play, the more advertising is a key success factor. What many people don't understand is that advertising is an integrated feature of the market economy. You cannot be in favor of a market economy and oppose advertising. Advertising looms large because the suppliers of goods and services depend on it to explain to consumers what they can buy and what benefits they can get from the product. *The quality of advertising is usually much more crucial for success than the size of the advertising budget.* According to Ogilvy, one of the greatest advertising gurus of the last century, the difference between good and bad advertising with regard to the success of a product is 1:17. But even if it were only 1:3, you can gauge how important it is to do everything to improve the effectiveness and quality of advertising.

Today you can often see advertising which is supposed to be creative and arouse emotions. In reality, advertisements are all too often questionable gimmicks which don't make the least contribution to selling more. In fact it quite often happens that you have no idea what the commercial is supposed to be about. It's just a pity that this also helps to lend consequence to those advertisers who meet their colleagues in the bistros in the evenings. And the worst thing is that some entrepreneurs, (and politicians, too!) tolerate this nonsense because they don't understand anything about it or they simply want to be »cool« (by the way, the same applies to the purchase of works of art or art exhibitions).

There are some nasty assertions that a third of advertising is done to please the bosses – the ones who take the decisions, a third is to impress colleagues in the advertising industry or simply to attract attention and only a third is to have a positive impact on consumers so that they ultimately buy more. *I think it is important to bear the following in mind if you are interested in good advertising: a good advertisement introduces the product and the brand, gives understandable information on the product, attracts attention (a particularly important point in view of the flood and density of advertising), arouses emotions and ends – if possible – with a good catchy slogan that needs to be repeated in every ad over a longer period. (Even a piece of music that is played continually can strengthen the brand image and encourage a liking for the product.) Moreover, identical optical elements are an absolute »must«. It is important to ask with every advertisement why the customer should actually want to buy this specific product (Reason why!).*

Something that frequently receives little attention and yet is crucial for good and successful advertising is the fact that all those participants in the agencies and companies should genuinely believe in the product, should be enthusiastic about it and be fully committed to promoting it. It reminds me of the saying: »Anyone who is convinced has no difficulty convincing others« – which was after all the secret of the Apostles' sermon at Whitsun. What advertising requires are similar preachers and fewer producers of gimmicks.

Moreover, if an advertisement is to be good, there should be a clear briefing by the client at the start. That is often missing. For example: Is the campaign to establish and strengthen the image and the brand in the long term or is the intention to generate a short-term increase in sales? Is the advertisement to expand the market in general (for example where your own market share is high) or do I want to gain market shares? What are the key messages I want to impress on the consumer? What target groups do I wish to address in particular? In any case you can't complain about an advertising agency if the necessary information and a good briefing are missing. That means that bad advertising is often the fault of the client and the resulting poor co-operation frequently leads to a lot of frustration in the agencies. The situation isn't exactly improved by the well-known fact that although several different levels in the marketing hierarchy can reject the suggestions by the agencies, it is only the upper echelon in the marketing department that can actually approve them. At any rate, it is vital for the top people in a company to keep in touch with the agencies because that provides motivation and is conducive to understanding. Besides, agencies shouldn't be changed for the slightest reason just the way it happens with football trainers. An agency needs to be given an opportunity to know what exactly is being criticized and to present suggestions for improvement.

With regard to advertising in the various media, care should be taken that the general advertising theme, the basic message is included everywhere but at the same time is adapted to each target group. A reader of the »US WEEKLY« has to be addressed differently from a reader of »TIME«.

Another key factor in advertising is insisting on the continuity of both the advertising campaign and the advertising design – the same also applies to the branding policy. Continuity is often violated in branding policy, either because due to the frequent change in marketing and advertising staff, the new ones want to make a name for themselves or because people lose patience if there is no immediate success with an advertising campaign geared to the long term.

B) The present-day situation

On the one hand there is greater consumer awareness and a bargain-hunting mentality and on the other hand there is an increasing awareness and appreciation of the importance and the quality of brands. However, striving to obtain value for money persists.

At events like »Best Brands« in Munich, increasing trivialization and commodity character can be observed. Google, fast cars and the development of cell phones to a multi-functional instrument are to the fore. Maggi and Persil are no longer of tremendous interest but they generate huge sales nevertheless! New trends are, for example, nutrition, wellness, ecology, organic foods, and to a lesser degree Fair Trade products and social motivation, exotic products from other countries and a striving for identity. A preference for products that provide a feeling of home and a trend towards global products are also becoming apparent.

The image the producer has is becoming more significant. Consumers want to know where the goods come from.

The situation in the retail trade appears as follows: the retail trade will continue to become more focused (probably the increase will be 50% soon), which is due less to an increase in private labels and trademarks but to the fact that brands are being included in the range of products. Progressive professionalization in logistics and data acquisition is leading to more and more professional management.

More frequently individual chains of retail shops (see REWE) will come up with an overall strategy and an integrated market appearance; sub-brands are likely to remain reserved for the various distribution channels.

There will be an increase in internationalization in the purchasing departments which will raise the question whether and when trademarks should be put on the markets.

C) What ought to be done?
(In the following remarks the focus is on the problems of the producer)

1. Boosting innovation and research

The innovation of a company is a decisive factor when it comes to strengthening the competitiveness and sustainability of a company, thus ensuring its existence and success in the long term. For that reason I am of the opinion that one of the major managerial functions is creating an innovative climate.

It is, therefore, crucial for the success of a company that everything is done to promote innovation, the capacity for innovation and the spirit of innovation in a company. But it isn't just a matter of dramatic phases of innovation and discoveries but it can be many small innovative steps, which I term renovation.

Innovation isn't only necessary with regard to new products but also to all areas of a company – for example technology, methods, organization, human resources policy, leadership style etc. Of course not everything that is new is automatically good and »innovative«. Anything new needs to be assessed and judged critically.

Innovation is particularly vital in creating new or improving existing products. The question is frequently asked where the ideas and stimuli for new products are to come from. All I can say is that they come from all over the place: from the market, market research, employees from every department, from customers, suppliers, science and technology, consultants and naturally from research, too. Considerable investments need to be made in the field of research and these must be long-term and suitably target-orientated. (In this case it is crucial to open one's own research to science and technology and other institutions.) Moreover, it is important to mobilize people and to listen to people who are not in the mainstream of thoughts and trends. Frequently it is they who have the most original Ideas. There is an expression for this in French: »penser à côté«. That is why it is absolutely essential to develop more tolerance towards unconventional thinkers (and perhaps even towards »oddballs«).

Therefore a key managerial function is collecting all suggestions and ideas without bias, checking them and assessing them. Often, more needs to be invested in research – if an idea for a product seems to be useful or attractive – so that it can be realized.

A significant factor for increasing the capacity for innovation is promoting creativity. More creativity can be created by deliberately selecting employees with creative, innovative talent. To that end we need to put up with the conduct of employees who are somewhat less conventional. However, it isn't always easy to distinguish between really creative employees and the oddballs whom one can well do without. Capacity for innovation and creativity can be promoted to a certain extent by specific methods, systems and measures.

And finally: if innovation and creativity are to be promoted, everything possible must be done to ensure that there are no obstacles in the way. Almost 20 years ago a book entitled »Die anonymen Kreativen« (The Anonymous Creative Ones) was published by Gabler Verlag, a German publishing house. It contained the following 10 provocative rules for obstructing creativity:

»1. Distrust any idea coming from below – simply because it is new and comes from below.

2. Insist that people who need your permission for an action also obtain permission from several higher authorities.

3. Ask departments or individuals to criticize each other's suggestions. (That saves the bother of making a decision; you need only reward the one who survives.)

4. Voice criticism immediately and never praise. (That keeps up pressure on people.)

5. Treat exposing problems as a mistake so that no one hits on the idea of informing you when something doesn't work.

6. Monitor everything carefully. Make sure that anything that can be counted is counted frequently and checked thoroughly.

7. Only make decisions on reorganization in secret and then take your employees completely by surprise. (That too keeps the pressure on people.)

8. Ensure that demands for information are always well-founded and make sure that it is not for nothing that information is made available. (Information should not fall into the wrong hands!)

9. Use your powers of delegation to make subordinate managers in particular responsible for putting cost-cutting measures and other threatening decisions into effect and get them to do so quickly.

10. And above all: never forget that as one of the ones at the top you know everything there is to know about the business«.

2. Marketing

In the field of branding policy, focusing on the image and the strength of family brands ought to be stepped up as product-specific single brands are becoming less important, particularly for economic reasons. But watch out! Segmentation among a family brand shouldn't lead to excessive stretching and weakening of the brand.

Moreover, the brand needs to be protected even more by the quality associated with it. The power of the brand name needs to be increased so that the brand functions like a friend to the consumer. Moreover, the brand should be integrated much more into life style.

3. Product policy

Instead of conducting phony activities and launching lots of products that aren't in fact new, greater emphasis should be placed on real innovation and improvement in quality. In this respect there is generally a danger that the range of products might become too wide.

Usually this has little to do with creative innovation but serves the pseudo image of people in marketing.

For example, there is a company that has a market share of 2% in the food trade, where it offers 500 articles despite a total range of approx. 5,000 to 6,000 articles in the retail trade. Therefore, these 500 articles account for 10% of the range of goods in the retail trade whereas the market share only amounts to 2%. Currently, 35,000 new articles come onto the market, the majority of which end up as flops.

Such things lessen the credibility of the producer. On the other hand there are new segments and new consumer trends that need to be addressed more consistently – as for example nutrition, health-conscious foods, the needs of singles and the older generation.

In this connection convenience continues to be important; likewise the trend towards products from other countries and apart from that the more consistent improvement in quality play a significant role (at Nestlé a 60:40 system).

4. Advertising

A much debated question today is the extent to which the new media have ousted the old. I'm referring to the Internet, teleshopping, virtual shops, and the many possibilities for direct marketing etc. I think that these trends need to be studied carefully, but I also believe that the traditional media will retain their raison d'être, especially because the favored target groups can be addressed more effectively and more directly through today's variety of newspapers and magazines, radio stations and TV channels.

Moreover, as far as improving the quality of advertising is concerned, I would like to refer to a new development that comes from brain research and is known as neuromarketing. Although the field is very new, it seems to me that, thanks to it, we have gained valuable insight into what makes the consumer really »tick«, and which emotions play a significant role.

Advertising policy confronts multinational companies with the further question as to how uniform or how different an advertisement should be for the whole world.

I know from experience that certain basic arguments and advertising campaigns can be applied world-wide, but everything else needs to be adapted to suit the locality: firstly, because mentalities and traditions vary and secondly, because we find ourselves in individual countries with varying market phases (e. g. launching new products, established consumption, or different market shares each of which requires different advertising strategies). Generally it can be said that in the case of products that are of a more technical nature and are universal the world over, the advertising message can be uniform whereas in the food, beverage and tobacco industry, for example, there are perceptible limits, as these products vary considerably in taste or in the degree of convenience in the individual countries. Moreover, it will always be difficult to sell an advertising message with Anglo-Saxon humor to a German.

It is important for multinational companies to organize world-wide collaboration with specific agencies. In general, it is better not to use too many agencies for the product and only to change if there are serious reasons for doing so.

One of the advertising media used with increasing frequency today is so-called sponsoring. Here activities or events are supported in the hope that mention of the company or the product in connection with the event will produce a liking for, goodwill towards and a brand image for this product. Doubtlessly this is a means that in many cases may be justified. The problem is that it is more difficult to prove that sponsoring has a greater impact than normal advertising; sometimes some sponsoring doesn't really suit the product, but corresponds rather to the interests and hobbies of the boss (or his wife!). If you spend the shareholders' money and you want your strategy to succeed, these means need to be analyzed very carefully and level-headedly and checked frequently as to whether the results you expected have actually been achieved.

5. Sales policy

One of the questions that are asked frequently is where, in the world, our products need to be made available to the consumer. Certain products no longer necessarily require the traditional food trade. Nowadays we have product groups 50 % of which are sold outside the normal retail trade.

As far as collaboration with the retail trade is concerned, it can generally be claimed that interests will also vary in future (profiling brands and profiling chains), but that all in all, the objective is to sell more. But the question arises as to how far brands ought to be advertised in national campaigns and how far it is right to have tailor-made promotions. The answer is that both are needed.

Something that is often ignored by producers is that it is decidedly important to maintain continuity in the visits by sellers to the retail trade. Too many changes are not beneficial to business.

With regards to sales policy, I would like, in conclusion, to remark on the fact that executives who are inclined to be particularly intellectual and theoretical underestimate sales as a marketing instrument; or they do not pay enough attention to it and are not sufficiently aware of the value of human relations and connections in the sales business. Personally speaking, that is why the Chinese proverb – despite all technocratic achievements and the computer – still applies today:

>*If you cannot smile, you should not open a shop*«.

Building up confidence in the retail trade, a confidence that is ever so important for sales, is destroyed by the short-winded corporate policy that can often be observed on account of the pressures from the financial side or from fiercer competition, too. Naturally a zigzag course, where no one knows what the company stands for or where it wants to go in the long term, is particularly bad. Changes in corporate policy are only justified if new technological developments, market conditions or new consumer trends make these essential.

6.

In today's national and international competitive situations, cost competition plays an increasingly major role. Strict cost management permits a pricing policy that is more competitive – even against trademarks.

In conclusion, I would like to comment on the changes that, from my point of view, are required in the retail trade.

On the one hand, the retail trade needs to strive for more uniformity of presence and more consistency in the pooling of its purchasing power; on the other hand, the interests of the individual locations ought to be maintained because each location is concerned with a different consumer segment and operates in a different competitive environment which leads partly to a varied product range and different sales measures. With the hurly-burly that we can frequently observe in the retail trade, too, it will be crucial to have more continuity again, which will further more commitment to the customer.

This can also be achieved by not continually changing the arrangement of products in the shops, something which is known to be a source of annoyance to consumers.

We all know that the retail trade has not yet reached the end of its scope in the field of modern organizational methods. I only need to refer to the subject of logistics and IT.

Internationalizing the retail trade is understandable on the one hand because it leads to a growth in sales; however, it is doubtful whether it produces a competitive edge in a particular country as in contrast to producers the same synergies are not generated in the retail trade by internationalizing.

Closing remarks

In order to shape the future optimally we need, therefore, to give continuous thought to what will remain, what is still valid today, and what will change. In general it can be claimed that as far as values and management issues are concerned there will be hardly any changes. In this respect we, at Nestlé, are relatively conservative, too – I'm thinking for example of what I term marketing basics: creating, advertising and selling a product that is in line with the market and at a fair market price. On the other hand, new trends in technology, in competitive market structures and in consumers need to be recognized swiftly and acted upon at once. I always say to this: »Be first, be daring, be different«. A time advantage provides a competitive edge.

I would like to say in closing:

Today we talk about »fast-moving consumer goods«. Success for the companies concerned is only possible if they are »fast-moving companies« too.

Source: Helmut Maucher, »*Fast-Moving Consumer Goods: Current and Future Aspects of Marketing*«: a lecture given before the Marketing Club, Düsseldorf in November 2006.

Product and branding policy between image and dilution

In the following lecture Helmut Maucher addresses topics such as product and branding policy, brand segmentation, brand extension and brand transfer and in conclusion makes some significant remarks on advertising.

Ladies and Gentlemen,

Today's market situation is characterized by low economic growth, in some cases stagnating markets, structural shifts in consumption, demographic changes, informed and responsible consumers, a bargain-hunting mentality, brand-name products which frequently become commodities, less loyalty to brands with increasing concentration in the retail sector, discount stores and – linked to this – a strengthening of trademarks. All of these do not make life any easier. There is only one consolation which you have to remind your employees of quite frequently: it's no different for competitors.

Furthermore, there are, of course, other factors such as globalization and the internationalization of competition with its attendant opportunities but also with its new threats and the increasing fierceness of competition.

What does all this mean with regards to our topic today?

First of all it should be said that there is no longer any such thing as easy business. In competition today and in the future, only those who produce top performances can survive. In companies in the consumer goods industry, this certainly includes products that fulfill consumers' wishes, that stand out from those of competitors and that are offered at a fair market price. This product policy needs to be supplemented with a branding, advertising and sales policy, which generates corresponding sales. That all sounds self-evident and plausible. Nevertheless, such truisms are frequently ignored and result in serious mistakes.

Today, as requested, I am merely going to deal with product and branding policy.

First of all I would like to make a few comments on product policy. In this connection, my own guiding principle is: »Be first, be daring, be different«.

Ladies and Gentlemen, the key to the greatest competitive edge is being the first to have a certain product or idea for a product and launching it onto the market as quickly as possible. Timing and speed are paramount. But what can you do to ensure you are first?

Certainly, market research and trend-scouting are not enough. After all, these are the things that operate in all professionally managed companies at the same time and in the same direction. A huge amount of information needs to be processed and combined, trends sensed and technological developments exploited etc. In this context I have been asked frequently whether I work intuitively or with ›scientific management‹. My reply is that as far as I am concerned, intuition is the creative use of information.

For example, it was quite early on that I discovered the potential of mineral water and that a good friend of mine began to sell potting compost which also proved to be a great success. That shows that it isn't merely a question of identifying but also discovering consumer requirements. If you want to be first in new countries, you often have to fulfill the second requirement: »be daring«.

I apologize for always quoting examples from my professional life, such as China and Pakistan, and Southeast Asia and Russia when they got into economic difficulty. In this context »daring« means having staying power, too – something which often tends to be forgotten today. A certain optimism is also necessary but without »wishful thinking«. I would like to tell the following little story by way of illustration: It's about two men, one of whom is a shoe salesman, who have been to Alaska. The first man, a market research specialist, comes back from Alaska and tells us that there is absolutely no market for shoes because no one wears shoes there. The second man, a salesman, comes back and says that there is a huge market waiting because no one wears shoes there.

With regard to the last requirement »be daring«, I would like to point out that that involves the collaboration of market research, technology and research and a gut feeling deep down that consumers sometimes want something quite different.

And now to branding policy!

Branding policy begins when the corporate image and the corporate brand are in tune. The corporate brand is often the basic brand (see Siemens, and Nestlé, too). Depending on the strength of the product differentiation or the heterogeneity of a product range, family brands or sub brands are meant for individual products. Sometimes single brands are successful without segmentation because sales are large enough and thus it is possible to maintain a first-class profile (see Jägermeister, Red Bull, and Miele).

Nestlé's branding policy consists of making clear use of the corporate image (Nestlé) on the one hand and using family brands for certain product groups on the other hand. However, the family brands are always linked, to a certain extent, to the corporate image Nestlé.

Historically, Unilever and P&G come from single brands; with the many trends today the corporate image or family brands are gaining a stronger presence (see the new UL sign). The reason for such developments is that a general image has become increasingly important to the consumer.

Of course, it can be generally claimed that the greater the pooling under a corporate brand or a family brand the less distinct the individual profile becomes. The more single brands are retained the more expensive marketing and advertising become. Moreover, the positive reinforcement by a corporate brand or family brand is also missing. In any case, very good individual products under the same family brand can also strengthen the image of the family brand.

In the case of the special problem of acquisitions, it is of course sensible to make use of and exploit the new brands that have been acquired, but these brands ought to be integrated gradually into the corporate brand e. g. Nestle (for those who know, refer to Alete).

And so I have come to a central aspect of our topic today: branding policy with regard to the clarity of the profile and dilution.

Both of these constitute one of the most difficult problems in marketing and in branding policy. On the one hand, there is a desire for segmentation and an extension of the brand, and on the other hand, the question arises as to how far a brand transfer can go. Usually it can be said that the more a new product differs from the basic product, the more difficult and problematic it becomes to use the core brand. It becomes particularly difficult if at the same time you are struggling against a competitor's mono brand. Maggi is a clear example of an outstanding family brand, but an expansion in the direction of sweet products is just not possible here. In the case of Kit Kat, originally an excellent single brand, an expansion in the direction of Kit Kat Chunky, Kit Kat with new flavors etc. is possible.

Attempts were made with other products without the typical Kit Kat-shape, but – thank God – they were abandoned; because that would have meant a considerable weakening of this excellent brand.

Some other examples are:

Nivea was originally a single product. Later a very clever and effective expansion took place with the result that Nivea has become a family brand, which for my taste, however, has become too diluted.

In the field of mineral water there are basically only single brands, as water in its origins lives from its source. Nestlé Aquarel is an example of another policy that has been successful.

In principle, the question arises time and again as to how much segmentation, expansion and stretching a brand can tolerate. For years the Nestlé corporate brand has been linked to the slogan »Good Food, Good Life«. The big problem was our engagement in pet food. In the end the decision was taken not to connect pet food with Nestlé.

The success of brand stretching is naturally dependent on the strength of the brand; the basic image should not suffer. A good example of this is the Porsche Cayenne.

Brand stretching can also result in upgrading the brand which is evident in the example of Maggi: originally renowned for seasoning and soups, Maggi progressed to delicatessen soups, ›Fix‹ products, simple ready-made meals (›Pastaria‹ etc.) and Ravioli. This development has also produced positive interaction: the extension of Maggi in association with its upgrade benefits every new Maggi product nowadays.

A few more remarks on the question as to whether stretching
and segmentation cause a dilution of the brand or not:

In this case it is important to check thoroughly whether the extension of the brand fits the brand core. A decisive factor is also how the brand stretching is done from an optical point of view.

With regard to the description and the optical design, it is necessary to make a differentiation in the extension to facilitate recognition; on the other hand the general brand image should not be jeopardized. Good examples of this are: Aspirin plus C, Aspirin forte (Norgesic Forte), Aspirin; and Nescafé as the basic brand with variations (the same characteristics, Nescafé logo and basic colors). A common slogan or a common jingle can have the effect of putting a general bracket round the brand stretching.

[...]

It is evident from all this that the entire problem of brand profiling and dilution are manifold and require very different solutions in different situations. The optimal design requires experience; but it is a matter of judgment, too. That is why in general – as always in marketing – the marketing mind is more important than marketing techniques.

[...]

Nevertheless it is absolutely vital that the top management and brand management addresses these questions systematically and seriously. See my book »*Marketing ist Chefsache*« (Leadership in Action – Tough-minded Strategies from the Global Giant).

Finally a word about the importance of marketing and branding policy as opposed to trademarks: Here it is crucial to pursue a consistent branding policy (and there is any number of successful examples of this). Too much compliance and too many unsatisfactory compromises should be avoided. The price gap to the trademarks has to be organized by means of cost management, quality policy and brand management so that the gap is acceptable to the consumers (at least to the majority). A closer eye needs to be kept on competitors, and that includes trademarks.

Lastly: in view of today's uncertainty and consumer mobility and the devious and short-term opportunistic marketing tactics which can still be observed, more needs to be invested in building up long-term confidence in quality and the brand. People want safety, orientation and reliability. First of all, that means not changing the quality and design of brands continually, even when careful modernization occasionally appears necessary. We frequently observe questionable promises about or advertisements for products where these do not bear any resemblance to reality or the type of advertisement does not match the product.

In the long term these damage branding policy. It wasn't for nothing that Hans Domizlaff, probably the most eminent expert for branding techniques in the last century, published one of his standard books entitled »*Die Gewinnung des öffentlichen Vertrauens als Grundlage für eine erfolgreiche Markentechnik*« (Winning public confidence as the basis for successful branding techniques).

Therefore, it's important to build up the confidence of consumers in the long term or of customers in so far as the goods are sold in the retail trade. Developing confidence begins with the consumer as the real focal point. Sometimes we need to ask ourselves matter-of-factly: Do we really focus on consumers, or is it not more a question of many marketing initiatives having little to do with their actual needs.

More frequently they are the product of the profiling neurosis of individual marketing people, the infatuation of individual employees with certain ideas for products, or they even reflect the hobbies and priorities of technologically inclined employees or of research.

The constant changing of jobs by employees or executives and in general too many changes in marketing initiatives which are unnecessary and do not constitute genuine innovations do not do anything to promote confidence.

A frequent mistake in large-scale enterprises in particular is that the managerial staff changes too often. The need for job rotation has to be weighed up more against the advantage of continuity.

In addition, there should be no excessive stretching of the range of products or extensive segmentation – irrespective of the danger of weakening that I have already mentioned. Usually that has nothing to do with creative innovation but furthers the pseudo profiling of marketing people.

[...]

Creating sustainable confidence and commitment requires a long-term advertising policy rather than a continual, frenzied change in advertising campaigns, which only confuse the consumer.

The following example will serve to illustrate how to really put the consumer at the center of our thinking. We once had a commercial for baby food where the baby was sitting in the CEO's presidential chair. The baby was surrounded by marketing people who asked: »And what precisely do you want, Mr. President; what do you want us to do, Mr. President? « I showed the commercial to my marketing people, who were rather amused. Then I told them that the commercial wasn't just amusing; it was true because this little child really was »Mr. President« telling us what we should do.

An essential feature of creating consumer and customer confidence is promoting the confidence of our own employees and executives. This is often forgotten. If the employees have no confidence, there is no motivation and no commitment to the common objectives of the company. That is the reason why credibility is one of the major leadership attributes in top management. If they are committed, employees can market better, can sell better and thus make a considerable contribution to the success of marketing. For that reason the following two statements which I found recently in a collection of quotations are very apt:

- »The sales department is not the entire company but the entire company should be a sales department«.
- «You cannot expect your employees to delight your customers unless you as an employer delight your employees«.

Moreover, it is particularly true that the head of the company needs to be the head salesperson!

Naturally good branding policy also requires good advertising, which is the major communication instrument and an extensive topic as such. At this point I would just like to say one more thing on the topic of advertising: The decisive factor is not always the size of the budget but rather the quality and impact of the advertising.

[...]

We find ourselves faced with fierce competition, and a company that does everything right will have a competitive edge over those who neglect things.

Ladies and gentlemen, after I finished writing my lecture I happened to catch sight of an article in the periodical »*werben&verkaufen*« (Advertising and Sales): it was entitled »*Wenn Innovationen zum Milliarden-Flop werden*« (When Innovations turn into Billion-Dollar Flops). The article included the results of a study by the GfK market research agency and I would like to quote some excerpts from it:

»The sobering findings of the study are that 70 % of all new articles are no longer on the market at the end of a year and therefore they are flops. Just about 17 % of all new products are a success from the very beginning; a genuine hit achieving an initial buying rate of 5 % in the first twelve months and then a repurchasing rate of 30 %«.

Mistakes made in development and in stocking brands are sheer destruction of value; the authors of the study put the investments in launches which flopped at € 10 billion annually. According to GfK, »innovation weakness is the major mistake. The sustainability of family brands is often overestimated«, says GfK.

Thus, Ladies and Gentlemen, I come to my closing remarks.

1) A product policy is optimal if it is really geared towards the needs of the consumer or it focuses on what the consumer considers to be attractive and fascinating and what meets his prestige requirements.

   Furthermore, the quality and design of the product and the marketing must stand out from that of the competition.

2) The product needs to support the branding policy with a strong and appropriate profile; it needs to show the consumer the advantages of the product and it ought to distinguish it clearly and visually from that of the other competitors. This should be coupled with an attractive and eye-catching advertisement that is sales effective and is appropriate to the product. Moreover, advertising needs a great deal of continuity and not continual, frenzied changes.

3) To start with, segmentation and brand stretching have economic advantages and are often sensible because they generate additional sales. But

segmentation and brand extension should in no way lead to a weakening or diluting of the core brand.

4) Branding policy needs to be regarded in its entirety. Nothing should be done to undermine the consumer's confidence in the brand.

5) The significance of all these issues needs to be addressed by the top management. Marketing is after all a matter for the boss!

Source: Helmut Maucher, » Product and branding policy between image and dilution«, a lecture given at the 3rd International Brands-Colloquium in May 2006.

Credibility and communication as elements of modern corporate and branding policy

The following lecture by Helmut Maucher addresses three elements of good branding policy: credibility, good communication strategy and advertising.

Introductory Remarks

The presentation of an award is a festive occasion, when no lecture is given but some general thoughts are expressed that are pertinent to the subject matter and the content of the prize.

However, it is of course appropriate to talk about the great future of brands and to present the key factors of successful branding policy in detail.

These are things which are familiar, to a large extent, to the many experts present here this evening.

For that reason, I'm going to take the liberty of singling out two elements of successful branding policy that in my opinion have been given little attention in discussion or whose deeper and wider significance do not receive nearly enough recognition. I would, therefore, like to say a few words today on credibility and communication as elements of modern corporate and branding policy.

Winning consumers and motivating employees is difficult if no attempt is made to create trust. Professional communication is in a significant position to promote successful marketing and branding policy, and a positive image.

Today this applies more than ever when we look at the well-informed, critical employees, the consumers and investors and the public in general. If that is the case, everything needs to be done to promote trust and to organize communication optimally. These things need to be a major feature of modern corporate policy.

1. Credibility

1) What can be done to guarantee trust and credibility? The key condition is the qualification of the top management and managerial staff. It is crucial when selecting management staff to take into account not just the professional credentials and experience but more specifically the personality and character – and especially the credibility of a person. Credibility means that people can rely the next day on what was said the day before.

In addition more continuity is needed in management.

Credibility is not created by paying out huge salaries to the members of the Management Board when earnings are good and at the same time appearing before the workforce and telling them that cost-cutting is necessary and that sacrifices have to be made or even that 10,000 people will have to be made redundant.

[...]

Credibility also needs to be established among shareholders and investors. That requires giving neat, transparent reports and avoiding an excessively optimistic show – when the results don't turn out so well later on.

2) More credibility is needed in marketing, too. Quite often there are questionable promises about or ads for products where the advertisements do not bear any resemblance to reality or the type of advertisement does not match the product. In the long term these damage branding policy. It wasn't for nothing that Hans Domizlaff, probably the most eminent expert for branding techniques in the last century, published one of his standard books entitled » Die Gewinnung des öffentlichen Vertrauens als Grundlage für eine erfolgreiche Markentechnik « (Winning Public Confidence – the Basis for Successful Branding Techniques).

Therefore, it's a question of building up the confidence of consumers in the long term or of customers in so far as the goods are sold in the retail trade. Developing confidence begins with the consumer as the real focal point of interest. Sometimes we need to ask ourselves matter-of-factly if we really focus on each of them.

[...]

3) An essential feature of creating consumer and customer confidence is promoting the confidence of our own employees and executives.

This is often forgotten. If the employees have no confidence, there is no motivation and no commitment to the common objectives of the company. That is the reason why credibility is one of the key leadership attributes in top management. If employees are committed, they can do better marketing, can sell better and thus make a considerable contribution to the success of marketing. When someone has been given the benefit of the doubt, it is my experience that this has a positive effect. Even if there are some disappointments, it produces more motivation and performance on balance. That is why I am more in favor of decentralization and more delegation of responsibility, which leads to a greater identification with the task, greater market proximity and more flexibility. However, this requires more care in selecting staff – my maxim is: Look more in the eyes than in the files. And at the same time, this requires fundamental policies and a consistent removal from the job if trust is not justified or is disappointed. Ladies and Gentlemen, all confidence-building measures rebound positively on the company because employees, clients, consumers, investors and the public have more confidence in the company.

4) Confidence in the retail trade, a confidence that is ever so important for sales, is destroyed by the short-winded corporate policy which can often be observed on account of the pressures from the financial side or from fiercer competition, too. Naturally a zigzag course, where no one knows what the company stands for or where it wants to go in the long term, is particularly bad. Changes in corporate policy are only justified if new technological developments, market conditions or new consumer trends make these essential.

5) On the subject of trust and control, I would like to pass on two quotations. The first one is by Lenin: »Trust is good but control is better«; the second one is by Goethe: »If you treat an individual as he is, he will remain as he is; if you treat him as if he were what he ought to be and could be, he will become what he ought to be and could be«.

Both statements have an element of truth. It is assuredly correct not to trust blindly but to look and discover who you trust and can trust – according to the German proverb: »Trust – but look first to see who you can trust«.

6) Finally I would like to make few general remarks on the subject of trust. Currently, it is possible to observe an increasing distrust of and a dwindling confidence in all institutions and structures of responsibility, especially with regard to politics and companies. This tendency is dangerous and ought not to be underestimated. It is also a danger to the acceptance of our market-based, liberal systems and thus to the acceptance of everything we do or launch on the market. Compared with earlier, we are not given the benefit of the doubt, which is what I just demanded for employees. And meat scandals etc. don't help either. For that reason we need to do everything to win back our customers and the public. Certainly we need to be more consistent in penalizing abuse. Apart from that, Ladies and Gentlemen, it is here that there is a great opportunity, especially for companies producing brands, companies that are generally in a better position because of their policy, to win back trust and to put across the safety of products to the consumer.

2. Communication

Good communication strategies and measures were and are a key factor of success especially in today's world. Among the top leadership attributes I include the ability to communicate – internally and externally. In the end, however, if corporate policy is not up to standard and lacks responsibility, the best communication can have no positive impact.

It doesn't work like the cock that crows at 5.00 in the morning and thinks that it is he that causes the sun to rise.

For our communication purposes I have modified Kant's Categorical Imperative as follows: »*Don't do anything that can't appear in the press tomorrow*«. That does not mean that in a specific case we always want to have everything published, but it does mean that if something is published, we can justify it and stand by it.

Of course we all know the usual means of communication from the business report via the company newsletter, via internal documents to press releases and interviews etc. Obviously, they all have their place. But what is decisive is that communication needs to come from the manager of a company to a greater degree. It is and remains »a matter for the boss«. People want to see and hear the »first man«. For that reason a manager needs one major characteristic – being credible and able to communicate in a way that is convincing and easy to understand. This makes a considerable contribution to success. However, one problem that can arise is that executives cultivate their own image instead of promoting the corporate image.

Another important aspect which is really self-evident but is not always observed: communication needs to be geared to the recipient (see the various target groups – the consumer, customer, company newsletter, executives, investors and shareholders). But take care! What is communicated to the investors is read by everyone else, (the personnel, the public and the trade unions). That is why I advise against communication from finance departments that as a rule tend to speak the language of the investors.

[...]

Concluding remarks

Ladies and Gentlemen, in the present day there is, on the one hand, a lot of hypocrisy, fraud and glossing over the facts, and the addiction of some managers to self-glorification has increased. On the other hand, we are currently experiencing an enormous concentration of the media. We are dealing with more and more critical people, consumers and citizens etc., who have the most diverse wishes, inclinations and life styles, and with an increasing globalization of markets and communication. In such a world, winning trust and good, neat, and professional communication gain even greater significance.

I would like to congratulate today's award winners. It is an incentive for you to continue to work successfully. However, it is also an incentive for all those who did not receive an award. I am convinced that such an event promotes competition for the best ideas and thus can make a significant contribution to successful marketing in Germany and thereby to improving our location.

Source: Helmut Maucher, »Credibility and communication as elements of modern corporate and branding policy«; a keynote speech at the presentation of the reward for »Best Brands« in February 2006.

Cultivating simplicity

»Take care! « – so that genuine understanding becomes possible again ... In the columns below Helmut Maucher speaks on the importance of the ability to communicate at a personal level.

When fancy concepts such as »sustainable« are used excessively, it should not come as a surprise if you are not understood.

As is well known, we are taking gigantic steps into the age of global communication. Television, Internet and other modern communication tools have given rise to a situation today in which every news item can be spread all over the world simultaneously and we can all communicate with each other at any time – and, if desired, face to face across thousands of miles.

However, at the same time, I have noticed that the ability to communicate on a personal level is declining; whether due to a deterioration in the command of language and the mode of expression or because language has either become more primitive and vulgar or so frightfully artificial, pompous and complicated that it tends to make understanding more difficult.

A van belonging to a family-owned company comes regularly to fetch washing from a hotel, where I stay quite often. It can, therefore, be assumed that the company is a laundry. Far from it! Of late you can read on the van: »Hygienic dynamics, powered by Leo«.

A freight forwarding company that I have known since my youth has started to call itself »Intelligent Logistics«.

In general it has become common to pep up simple titles with bombastic and portentous words. Consequently the Market Research Department is now called »Market Intelligence«. Frequently there are no memoranda in a company that do not contain words like »sustainability«, »strategic«, »competence« or »win-win situation«.

Naturally a need to internationalize or use English comes across in these examples and this is understandable and even necessary in a global corporation. Nevertheless, we ought to communicate in our own language when we talk to our own employees in the factory, for example.

In the case of the many releases and the information produced by the PR departments, I have the feeling that a lack of practical experience is replaced by highfalutin brochures. There has never been so much talk of sustainability and value orientation, for example; at the same time these two principles have never been violated to such an extent (see the financial and economic crisis).

In conclusion, a word on today's tendency by some media to dramatize news, to exaggerate and to distort by giving the wrong emphasis or using misleading headlines:

The result is that with the concentration of the media today, people receive considerably more information but at the same time they receive disinformation more and more often, too.

What can be done? We can all help by bringing clarity, truth and simplicity back to our language.

Perhaps we should take Schopenhauer's recommendation more to heart when he said: »One should use common words to say uncommon things.« – With this in mind: »Take care!«

Source: Helmut Maucher, »Cultivating simplicity«, in *Bilanz* no. 13/2010.

The Economy, Politics and Society

Is Rhineland capitalism sustainable?

Is the social market economy or »Rhineland Capitalism« still sustainable? In this contribution Helmut Maucher describes developments over the last few centuries and deviations from the original concept.

A.

First of all we need to consider what exactly Rhineland capitalism is. The concept has become a catchword and thus shares the fate of all buzzwords: everyone has an idea of what it means but no one knows exactly what it is. In my opinion, Rhineland capitalism is nothing other than the social market economy as it was conceived originally. Pure capitalism was fortified by social principles from the social doctrines of the Catholic Church and from the social ethics of the Protestant Church. As far as the market economy itself or even freedom on the market are concerned, the social market economy follows the constituent principles of the organization of competition as set down by the economist Walter Eucken of the Freiburg School: legal, firmly anchored and enforced private property, freedom of contract and freedom of trade, open markets, a clear public liability law, the safeguarding of functional competition, stable currency, and over and above that a reasonably steady government. It is thus freedom on the basis of specified rules and is also known as *ordoliberalism*.

As far as the social aspect is concerned, the concept is based first of all on the positive effects of an open market with dynamic growth and competitive structures which all in all not only afford the largest possible »cake« but equality of opportunity, too; apart from that, it also provides for state intervention. At the same time it was in the form of a collective mutual insurance that was to make the system altogether more effective and social but with the objective of affluence for all as the focus of attention. To this end, there was to be an adjustment to the distribution of income by means of a progressive tax system and the social safety net of collective basic public services.

As to the influence of Christian social doctrine, three concepts in particular were defined: 1. Personality, (human dignity is inviolable or the human being is the center and objective of social order); 2. Subsidiarity: personal responsibility for oneself and the individuals such as family and employees entrusted to one; that means in particular that the state and society should not deprive individuals of what they can achieve themselves; 3. Solidarity: the obligation to be responsible overall for each other as far as it is within one's power to do so.

These three principles express an ethic of Christian actions; that means that on the basis of knowledge anchored in faith, action should contribute to realizing a humane society.

The social market economy thus focuses on human beings, their individual freedom and their social commitments. In this respect, it is of particular significance because the social market economy stands and falls with non-economic and moral commitments.

In total, Rhineland capitalism or the social market economy is concerned with the principle of combining freedom on the market with that of social balance.

That therefore is my interpretation of Rhineland capitalism – the development of »pure« capitalism to »Rhineland« capitalism!

It is interesting to note that historically the concept was secretly developed during the Second World War, particularly among the resistance in Freiburg; it was developed by economists, lawyers and theologists, too, and was to serve as the central theme for a liberal Germany after the hoped-for collapse of the tyranny of the National Socialists. Apart from Walter Eucken, it involved lawyer Franz Böhm and the economists and social scientists Alexander Rüstow and Wilhelm Röpke, too.

The actual concept *social market economy* was fashioned by Alfred Müller-Armack (a member of Ludwig Erhard's staff) in 1947. He wanted the social aspects of society and the market to interfuse. The social market economy was to be an open, »progressive« concept needing concrete form; its unshakeable cornerstones are self-responsibility, the principle of commensurability, competition, subsidiarity and social security.

Ludwig Erhard regarded the concept per se as a pleonasm because as far as he was concerned the market was in principle social and did not need to be made social first. Erhard put this thought into concrete terms by stressing »the more liberal the economy the more social it is«. Nevertheless, he recognized the integrating impact that could be achieved with the Müller-Armack label.

B.

After these introductory remarks by way of explanation, the question arises as to the sustainability of Rhineland Capitalism. This question consists of two parts:

1) How far removed are we from the original concept?

I do not claim that what I am going to say is comprehensive but I would like to address some significant developments and deviations:

a) The perceptible influence exerted by Anglo-Saxon capitalism on the financial markets and on corporate policy in particular: In the context of the globalization process, developments arose which all in all led to the recent financial and economic crisis. Meanwhile there is a growing realization that with increasing globalization and free trade world-wide there is a need for institutions and regulations to support these developments and to channel them correctly. Therefore it is a question of world-wide ordoliberalism which we have always associated with the introduction of the market economy in Germany. Progress in this direction has been achieved meanwhile but further improvements are necessary.

b) Corporate policy and entrepreneurial responsibility: Although from a social point of view German companies have, on the whole, always shouldered their responsibility, there has been negative spin-off, which has damaged both the corporate image and the acceptance of our market economy. These include rationalization and restructuring which have not always been socially acceptable; short-term action associated with short-term greed for money and profits, and some, even if only a few, inacceptable remunerations at Board level. Public discussion, corporate governance regulations and the steadily growing endorsement of a sustainable, social and value-oriented corporate policy imply positive adjustments.

c) Social issues and industrial law: What we have in Germany is not really a social market economy, but rather a social state economy that in international comparison has an immensely dense network of regulations and has produced an almost uniquely high level of incidental wage costs and a high tax and contribution ratio. Some of this is sensible and is part of a social market economy. I am very much in favor of a social network, but I am not in favor of a social hammock. Many establishments which promote social dialogue as, for example, trade unions, Works Council Constitution Act etc., make sense on the whole and have had a positive impact on social consensus in Germany. Some things, however, can only be seen in the light of power politics, and in a very negative way these have restricted the competitiveness and the speed and flexibility which are often necessary in business life.

d) It is well known that our energy policy is strongly influenced by ideology and in total is leading to higher costs in Germany and to restrictions in competitiveness. Some relief has been achieved due to the fact that the life of some nuclear power stations has been extended. It also makes sense to carry out research into alternative energy systems. Our problem is that there is no support for alternative energy sources and the very high attendant subsidies either by our neighbors or by other parts of the world. It means that, all in all, we make a ridiculously low contribution to global climate protection, but on the other hand we are the only country to increase its costs due to the resulting restrictions on our competitiveness. Every expert has pointed out that we will need all the energy sources for a long time, from coal to oil and from gas to nuclear energy and alternative energy sources to cover the total requirements and to avoid being too dependent on other countries. The recent newly conceived energy policy of the German government with an even faster phasing out of nuclear energy only exacerbates the situation.

e) The influence of the state: The open break with the concept of the social market economy begins with the comprehensive jurisdiction of the state recorded in the Stability Law of 1967, according to which the state has the task of providing full employment, price stability, equilibrium in foreign trade and steady economic growth. This is reflected in a series of welfare laws and linked to this exponentially increasing state expenditure. The rate of government expenditures to gross national product is almost 50 %; public debt has meanwhile reached astronomic proportions. Linked to this is, of course, a steadily increasing degree of regulation, which is magnified even more by the influence from Brussels. A strong state is needed in many respects (also in areas where it is sometimes weak) but at the same time we need a streamlined state. What we have has nothing to do with streamlining anymore. Instead of normal regulatory policy we have growing interventionism and a policy of subsidies, and instead of performance-oriented policy we have a distribution policy.

f) On the other hand, we are also dealing with an expansion of individual interests, an increase in opportunities to make objections, in contradictions and in opportunities to protest, which together with a rigid planning bureaucracy lead to delays in implementation or even to a stop to democratically decided joint tasks, which make our neighbors and especially the Chinese shake their head in wonderment. These also restrict our competitiveness. In this context I would remind you of sections of motorway which have needed 30 years to materialize. Only think of the extension of the airport in Frankfurt or Berlin or the discussion of project ›Stuttgart 21‹ (the proposed building of the central railway station underground).

g) Demographic changes. Only some of the measures to counteract the increasing rise in the ageing population have been implemented. Our immigration and integration policy has only now been modified – which is much too late. Let us hope that it will be tackled in a way that is shaped more by the interested parties and less by a »multi-cultural philosophy«. Many more changes can only be mentioned here in keywords: the decrease in motivation and commitment, the increase in egoism and the lack of consideration for others. Furthermore: a hostility towards technology, an exaggerated need for security, abuse of freedom and the like that do not necessarily make life easier and that certainly do not increase the competitiveness and the importance of our country internationally.

2) Is Rhineland capitalism still sustainable despite this negative development?

As far as this is concerned, we need to answer two further questions: 1. Are we still in a position that is strong enough (i. e. will we have a majority in elections) to again realize the original concept of Rhineland capitalism more intensively? 2. How many rejections, deviations and deteriorations can we cope with without the whole system going to pieces?

As a born optimist I hope that we will get the majorities we need for some improvements. It seems to me that there are already some beginnings and even some recognition of what is required. In democracies things sometimes take a long time and as a rule are only altered when the catastrophe is already in sight.

In particular, I hope that we will see some progress in energy policy and in some points of industrial law and social policy and that politically we will be able to push through decisions that are the result of a democratic vote and that these are not brought down by minorities and cumbersome planning bureaucracy.

Finally I hope that Europe develops in such a way that on the one hand, it becomes more capable of taking decisions without losing importance, and that nevertheless the hands of individual countries are not tied too much by the consistent application of the principle of subsidiarity and restricted in their opportunities for development.

The pressure of globalization and the increase in international competition that this has brought will not make life easier, but on the other hand it will mean that some things such as greater productivity, efficiency and competition will be improved inevitably.

Source: Helmut Maucher, »Is Rhineland Capitalism Sustainable?« in *Rhineland Capitalism and its Origins in Catholic Social Doctrine*, published by Michael Spangenberger, Aschendorff, 2011.

Visions and innovations as a major factor of success in the progressive globalization of the food industry

In the following lecture Helmut Maucher addresses the future of the food industry under the conditions created by globalization. He elaborates on the importance of research, innovation and the time factor and comments on current marketing methods.

Ladies and Gentlemen,

It is with the greatest of pleasure that I have come to Munich this morning so that together we can take a look at the future of the food industry, particularly in the light of the continuing internationalization and globalization of the markets. I would like to address the subject under the following four aspects:

1. General trends and developments which are relevant to the food industry worldwide
2. Visions and concepts for shaping the future successfully
3. The importance of innovation for successful corporate management
4. The importance of the time factor.

In general I will address worldwide developments, but naturally this will include some remarks on Europe and the Federal Republic of Germany in particular.

General trends and developments which are relevant to the food industry worldwide

The world population today totals more than 6 billion people. According to estimates by the United Nations there will be 6.8 billion in 2010 which means an annual growth rate of ca. 1 % or an increase of 74 million people.

The development of the population and the development of the income and affluence of this population are of course the key data for the future of the food industry.

Without doubt, distribution looms large, too. Currently, the wealthiest fifth of the world population possesses 86 % of the gross world product while the poorest fifth has just about 1 %.

According to the »World Watch Institute«, the number of overweight people, which is put at 1.1 billion, exceeds the number of hungry people, which is put at 800 million at present. Currently Nestlé generates 70% of its sales to 30% of the world population.

Thus the increase in population and income in developing countries provides the food industry with immense opportunities.

Depending on the economic climate, the gross world product is growing by 1% to 3% annually, whereby in general the growth is greatest in the developing countries. Apart from that the growth in gross national product is higher than the growth in the population so that an increase in income per capita can be expected. It is only too understandable that developing countries are striving for a standard of living such as we enjoy in the industrialized world.

Increasing globalization, the increase in free world trade, the creation of common markets in major regions, the constant transfer of technology, information technology, and general technological progress are sure to accelerate these trends and lead to a steady increase in affluence in the developing countries. 500 to 600 million people have left the poverty threshold behind in the past few years – due to globalization alone.

There is a steady increase in the number of people in developing countries with increasing potential purchasing power. We know for a fact that the increase in sales in the food industry is highest among people with a pro capita income between US$ 1,000 and US$ 15,000. Thus the increase in population and income in developing countries furnish the food industry with immense opportunities.

The development of the industry

Unquestionably, there will be further concentration and structural improvements, and a considerable increase in the business generated by multinational companies. In addition, new multi-national companies will emerge; some of these also from within the developing countries. The process of mergers, acquisitions and co-operation (joint ventures) will be continued with a view to long-term oriented, strategic decisions. Unilever/Bestfood and Nestlé/Ralston Purina are some of the latest examples. But in our industry there will always be very many small and medium-sized businesses that are important regionally and cater for certain niches. Our industry in the Federal Republic of Germany still numbers 5,000 companies, but it is highly likely that there will be adjustments and the number will decline in the next 5 to 10 years. Nevertheless only 18% of the total sales are generated by the 10 largest food producers in Germany. As the largest company, Nestlé's share of sales in the food industry in Germany is approximately 3%.

There are two clear trends evident here: on the one hand, the continuation and expansion of global segments whose products are placed unchanged and often successfully on the market. Coca Cola, Nescafé, Kit Kat, McDonald's and Nike are typical of such companies. On the other hand, there is the trend towards regionalization and to an identity of one's own and to the retention of regional tastes and consumption habits. Traditions, cultural and religious factors and climatic influences will continue to loom large for the majority of people.

In this context I would like to mention a further trend which is of importance to the food industry: the worldwide distribution of attractive products originating in a particular country or region. We need only think of pasta, for example, Asian dishes or even ethnic food.

In the industrialized world convenience, quality and health play a considerable and ever more important role. Due to the increase in the number of households consisting of one or two persons there is a more frequent demand for small packaging and for increasing convenience. Eating-out is on the rise. Establishments such as canteens, restaurants and schools are but a few examples. There is also a certain trend towards vegetarian food; meat consumption is falling – and that is not just due to the recent BSE scare.

A significant indicator of affluence is beverage consumption, which amounts to approximately 600 liters per capita. We have observed considerable movement within this consumption: the consumption of spirits and beer has fallen perceptibly in the last 10 years, the consumption of wine has remained constant – i. e. it has risen slightly – and the consumption of coffee has remained more or less the same whereas the consumption of mineral water and soft drinks has risen considerably.

Of course, in developing countries the quantitative provision of the population remains important but with the changing life style which imitates our habits more and more and with the simultaneous growth of the middle classes, convenience is gaining increasingly in importance.

The current consumption intake of ca. 50–60 kilos of meat per capita is inconceivable in developing economies due to the high costs and prices, due to energy and water consumption and for ecological reasons. There needs to be a greater trend towards food which doesn't use animals in the process. In this way, apart from anything else, the seven-fold rise in prices and costs can be avoided.

Development of trade and retail channels for consumers in general

We can still observe a further increase in concentration and purchasing power here, a slight increase in the trend towards trademarks, but at the same time a rise in alternative retail channels (kiosks, public swimming pools, sports grounds, filling stations, direct delivery to households etc.). With some of its products Nestlé today generates more than 50 % of its sales beyond the traditional food trade channels. Moreover, it is of course important to continue to follow up new virtual developments like the Internet and e-commerce. An overall picture of their growth potential and their growth limits will assuredly become more evident in the next few years.

Besides, similar trends, especially in the concentration of the retail trade, can also be observed increasingly in developing countries, too.

Research and development

One element which will always be crucial is the steady improvement in the quality of the products produced by the food industry. But innovations in manufacturing processes and in the products themselves will continue to be crucial to success – only think of dehydration technology that today offers very inexpensive products and both first-class quality and convenience or think of the ever more gentle methods of preserving food with less loss in taste and flavor. Even instantizing technology has made enormous progress. Furthermore, ever more products are coming onto the market that have a medium-term durability of up to 35 days and are sold via a cold chain of 8°C. Or take the development of cereal products that has practically only taken place recently.

Further trends that can be observed are the enormous development of the pet food business and a considerable change in the structure of the chocolate industry with fewer bars of chocolate and chocolates and in their place an increasing number of chocolate bars and snacks; and we must not forget the growing segment of calorie-reduced or low-fat products (ice-cream, yoghurt, cooked meats and sausage that have little or no loss in taste or flavor).

These are changes which in the end were only possible due to the innovation and development activity of the food industry.

I would like to mention one very important and forward-looking trend, namely the manufacture of value-added foods – in short »nutrition«. Research shows us an increasing correlation between food and health. As a result, the positive effect of food on health and well-being is going to become a main issue in the food industry.

2) Visions

In many respects I am cautious about using the word visions. At any rate, we are not talking about pipedreams. On the other hand, pure extrapolations are not sufficient to grasp the future. We need to do everything we can to obtain a clear picture of the future and at the same time to develop the ability to react to changes quickly and flexibly. Apart from that, the statement by Max Weber, the famous sociologist, is particularly apt:

>*»What we need is trained ruthlessness in looking at the realities of life«.*

We need to inquire into the extent to which intuition plays a role in estimating future developments. In my opinion, intuition is the creative utilization of information. In summary, creative, courageous but realistic deliberations are crucial as a basis for successful corporate policy.

Specific implications for the future of the food industry

General implications

In industrialized countries, the food industry needs to continue to follow the trends of convenience, quality, variety and health and support these consumer trends with innovations. That means specifically that the needs of individual consumer segments have to be satisfied, as for example: small households, various life styles and different age groups. In connection with the latter, demographic changes in particular need to be borne in mind. This also seems to indicate a further growth potential in the industrialized world.

To maintain competitiveness and the successful development of the individual companies, measures to reduce costs and rationalization measures will still be unavoidable; but this should not be at the expense of quality – which unfortunately is often the case nowadays. Finally, competitiveness also requires first-class marketing; however, this often needs improving. There is less need of intellectual vocabulary and »huzzah marketing« and more need of »back to basics« or the right advertising and the right selling of the right products. Despite short-term pressures, brand management needs to be practiced long-term. In general, advertising needs to improve – i. e. it needs to provide more information; it has to rouse attention, to highlight the »reason why« and strengthen the brand. New media and direct marketing need to be employed to this end.

As already mentioned, there needs to be greater collaboration with the alternative retail channels than has been the case so far; the expansion of bulk consumer business in particular is crucial in this case.

Just a few words on consumer focus; this is mentioned frequently and receives special emphasis nowadays. This is something I do not quite understand. In a market economy determined by the sale of products to consumers and customers it has always been important and correct to think in terms of the customer.

Specific aspects of developing countries

As I said at the very beginning, there are immense opportunities due to the increasing potential within the consumer group which has an income pro capita of between ca. US$ 1,000 and US$ 15,000. But it should be pointed out that value creation in these countries needs to be increased not by exports alone but rather by building factories in these sales areas and, where it makes sense, taking local tastes into consideration. In the food industry, only some consumer habits are valid globally. The theory that world-wide taste has become standardized due to globalization and global activity by companies has not proved true. The deployment of the so-called double strategy in developing a product (i. e. a strategy worked out at Nestlé for the developing countries in addition to the traditional product strategies, whereby products are developed on the basis of local raw materials which are suited to local tastes) opens up the opportunity to expand sales and at the same time to create more inexpensive products.

It is important to strengthen our brands further in order to ensure stable business in these countries in the future! The degree of familiarity, the success and the continued existence of a brand can be explained by a combination of international synergy assessment and emotional traditions that are dear to the consumer. But it should not be forgotten that in every marketing approach to individual markets the different competitive situations, trade structures, consumer habits and legislation of each country need to be taken into account, too. A reassessment of the measures to be taken at global level and those to be taken at local level is needed time and again.

3) Innovations

Being innovative and creative affords a decisive competitive edge in a world of increasing competition. Creating differences in quality and in innovation affords more success with the consumer and the trade as far as competition is concerned.

I would like to develop this topic as follows:

a) In general, it is vital to create an innovative climate (providing time and space, encouraging employees to come up with innovations, tolerating and accepting mistakes). In selecting executives it is particularly important to pay attention to a capacity for innovation.

b) How do you promote creativity? Here are some steps to be taken at three different levels:
   1. Stimulating with the correct structures (with the right signals and incentives, the right people and the right atmosphere).
   2. Listening to the market but having ideas yourself which the consumer may not have hit on. In this connection research and development have a significant role to play. Nestlé takes this key aspect into account with its Basic Research Center in Switzerland and approx. 17 research centers on four continents and an international workforce of about 3,500 employees.
   3. Reducing obstacles to communication with regards to innovation (in short: unblocking). In this context it is necessary to emphasize how vital it is for information within the company to flow freely and directly. Creating trust and security, and pursuing an open information policy with employees are ultimately a basic prerequisite for a creative and innovative climate.

We can also achieve more creativity by a purposeful selection of employees, whom we employ because of their creative and innovative talent and not on the basis of a rational check list and credentials (Goethe once said: »If you don't feel it, you'll never get it«).

In general the following applies: The selection of executives is at least as important as training (if the right employee is chosen, then perceptibly less training will be necessary, whereas if ability is lacking, training will only bring about a marginal improvement).

- We need to promote more free and horizontal communication flow; that includes flat organizational structures, permeability and encouragement.

Moreover, apart from general measures, conditions adapted to the individual employees and departments need to be created as prerequisites for providing scope for creativity. This also raises the question as to which »types« of employees we can accept. Can »crackpots« and »screwballs« have a role to play? On the whole I would answer in the affirmative; subject to certain limits, however!

Nor should we forget that there is greater creativity if there is the right »fighting spirit« – and last but not least if there is competitive pressure.

Over and above that there are naturally systematic methods for promoting creativity:

- Promoting creativity through »cross-fertilization« (battling against the »not-invented-here« syndrome)
- Using brainstorming
- Using analogies (i. e. transferring certain findings to another area or product)

And sometimes it is also simply a matter of shaking people up a little. Provocative statements trigger off thoughts, reactions and processes more often and more quickly than would otherwise be the case. In this context I sometimes talk of »management by provocation«. I also consider occasional graphic sayings like »I want more pepper, less paper« to be very effective.

But it is not just products that require companies to be innovative. Innovation is just as vital in marketing, advertising, systems, organization, management style and measures to reduce costs. One of the major managerial functions is creating an innovative climate to facilitate research and development and new ideas. To achieve this, it is necessary to have the co-operation of all the departments and the people who are involved in innovation or in the development of new products within the company. However it is important to see that it is not just the large innovations that are crucial but that renovations and the small steady steps to improvement are just as crucial.

4) The right timing

Globalization accelerates every development. In the event of a successful outcome, timing and the swift and immediate implementation of the necessary decisions and measures are crucial to further success. »Be first, be daring, be different«.

5) Concluding remarks

1. Although it is a platitude, it is frequently forgotten: ultimately everything is done by people (by executives and their employees in equal measure), which is why the selection, the training and the motivation of the management and the employees is of ultimate importance.
2. More than in the past, globalization and open competition will mean that in the end good performance and achievement will be rewarded more substantially and poor achievement will be penalized more severely.
3. Increasing competition and globalization require an even more agile fighting spirit – true to Bertold Brecht's motto: »Who fights can lose; who doesn't fight has already lost«.

Source: Helmut Maucher, »Visions and Innovations as a vital factor of success in the advancing globalization of the food industry«: a lecture given at the 3rd International Whey Conference (WHEY) in September 2001

The social responsibility of companies in the age of globalization

Helmut Maucher believes that long-term management and ethical and moral conduct form the basis of corporate success – even and above all in times of growing globalization. Maucher illustrates what implications globalization has for responsible corporate management.

Globalization and social responsibility

Despite all opponents and criticism the following still holds true: globalization is ultimately in everyone's interest. 500 to 600 million people have been able to leave the poverty threshold behind in the past ten years – thanks to globalization and liberalization. Nevertheless, a great deal still has to be done to solve the problems:

1) Our markets need to be opened considerably wider to the Third World. It is here that the WTO has a key task to perform. Only if the industrial world behaves more favorably and openly in this respect can the developing countries benefit fully from globalization.

   Difficulties ensue from the demand on the part of the industrial countries that developing countries need to observe stricter standards of quality (especially social and ecological standards). This can lead to new protectionism by industrial countries, which is why we ought not to go beyond minimum standards and should leave the rest to other organizations. »Social standards« should be left to institutions like the ILO; agreements on minimum regulations to protect the global environment should be kept separate (as happened with the agreements in Kyoto).

2) As with every transition, increasing globalization creates problems (keener competition, restructuring and a greater need to rationalize). Consequently, globalization needs to be accompanied by the necessary social measures – both by the countries and by the companies.

   Companies should not only export; they should also enhance the value added in the developing countries by setting up production locations there. That also has many other positive effects on these countries because as a rule multi-national companies pay higher wages, provide more social benefits and training for employees and have a favorable impact on the environment of a production plant (this includes suppliers for example). In this respect Nestlé provided, so to speak, development aid with ca.

300 plants in developing countries, before the word had ever been coined. Apart from that, multi-national companies make a vital contribution to mutual understanding on account of employing people of many different nationalities and cultures.

3) If the world becomes a market, there need to be more global institutions and world order, similar to what was done per country under ordoliberalism and the social market economies.

For example: organizing competition, creating reliable legislation, and no case-by-case decisions which, as is generally known, encourage corruption.

Concluding remarks

All in all I believe that a social market economy, combined with long-term orientation and responsible conduct by companies, and supplemented by an expansion of ordoliberalism can well serve as a model for successful globalization that also benefits all sections of the population.

Source: Helmut Maucher, »The social responsibility of companies in the age of globalization«: the opening statement to a panel discussion at the Conference held by the BKU (Association of Catholic Entrepreneurs) in October 2001.

The proper degree of moderation

In this article Helmut Maucher comments on the problems of democracy, managers' excessive salaries and the advantages of long-term corporate policy.

Gentlemen,

currently the Federal Republic of Germany has total debts amounting to 1.5 trillion euro and annual interest payments that are not only heading in the direction of 100 billion euro annually but which will entail a burden for generations to come. The reasons are manifold; we are all familiar with them. They are most certainly an expression of our society with its generally higher expectations and the tendency in democratic constitutions to spend more than it has on account of the competition between the individual parties to win over voters; at the same time they blatantly go beyond the bound of what is acceptable and appropriate – which of course brings me to today's topic.

A second issue that is the subject of much discussion concerns the salary of some managers. Frequently, however, not enough recognition is given to the fact that the managers of flourishing companies need to be properly rewarded. Moreover, not sufficient attention is paid to the fact that thousands of companies pay their managers sensibly and moderately. On the other hand, what provokes criticism, Gentlemen, is the conduct of some, a very few entrepreneurs, all of who hit the headlines unfortunately. These top managers appear before their workforce with tears in their eyes and say: »We have to make sacrifices«, but at the same time they pocket tens of millions of Euros. That is something no one can understand. Of course it does not matter one iota what individual top managers earn in companies making a net profit of 5 or 6 billion. However, no one can understand it if at the same time employees are expected to make sacrifices and short-term redundancies are made. Moreover, it jeopardizes the acceptance of our social and market-oriented system. It is for this reason that I myself have occasionally expressed criticism. But care should be taken to avoid such excesses, not just because the bounds of what is acceptable and appropriate are exceeded but mainly because it is more prudent to do so. Apparently a lack of restraint and greed win at the expense of common sense.

A third situation currently: greed and short-term thinking (and probably stupidity, too) are part of the present international financial crisis which is assuming ever larger proportions – a testimony to an intemperance which is almost unsurpassable.

These introductory remarks have brought us right to the heart of this far from simple subject. I am fully aware that views on the subject vary considerably and I can only express my own opinions. Moreover, it is impossible to define the proper degree of moderation in mathematical or objectively precise terms.

The dictionary that one painstakingly consults in such cases says: »The proper degree of moderation is midway between too much and too little«. That is certainly true but the question remains as to what is too much and what is too little. In the following remarks I would like to deliberate on the proper degree of moderation in different fields and in the economy and corporate policy in particular. I am going to explain the connection that exists between long-term policy and the proper degree of moderation; I repeat: between long-term policy and the proper degree of moderation. If a long-term policy is pursued, it is indeed more than possible to maintain the proper degree of moderation.

And now a few remarks on corporate management first of all. A company cannot survive without long-term policy. Therefore, long-term investment in the market, including long-term development of image and brands as well as long-term human resources policy, are absolutely essential despite all short-term constraints on account of competition and the financial market. We all know that today many of these are not complied with. Of course, we ought not to neglect generating on-going profits. As a rule, the financial market or the owners want to achieve a return in the current year; in other words, if you make a loss and you are up to your neck in it, it is difficult to pursue long-term policies. Finding the right balance, the right degree of moderation between long-term strategy and the short-term realization of profits is one of the most difficult but at the same time one of the most crucial tasks. Apart from that, there are many areas in corporate policy where it is essential to find this balance, the right degree of moderation. For example:

1. Long-term versus short-term aspects
2. Centralization versus decentralization
3. Marketing priority versus controlling or spending versus saving
4. Variety and diversification versus focusing
5. Essential regulations and rules versus individual scope for development
6. Performance and competitive acumen (especially in HR and wages policy) versus social responsibility and social protection

7. National and cultural identity of the company versus international claims and worldwide activities.

In this context I would like to say a few words about corporate culture. I said at Nestlé: Our corporate culture has to be such that it differs from that of other companies. If we merely state »Man should be noble, helpful and good«, it is no different from what is stated at Unilever, Shell or anyone else. Moreover, if our conduct is too specific or too Swiss, we do not encompass the different cultures of the world where we do business. As a result it is essential to find something that is specific for the company but that does not offend the cultures and traditions of the other countries where we operate. That is what constitutes proper corporate culture. However, there are any number of things that fit everywhere (more industriousness instead of laziness, integrity, more pragmatism than dogmatics to name but a few), and which can therefore be found in our corporate guidelines.

The proper degree of moderation for corporate management and for the executives of the company also includes personal life style and a careful check of one's own conduct and one's own vanity [...]. At Nestlé I developed a principle that can be found in our management principles and that states: *We are modest but we have style.*

Another point is the manager's handling of power and its inherent responsibility. The subject of »power« has been partly exaggerated by imbuing the word with mystical overtones (»Just look at how powerful we guys are« etc.). Of course it is absolute nonsense. Firstly, competition is the best distribution of power and we are all subject to this and secondly, we have public controls because we have administrative bodies, works councils etc. who automatically control this power. And nevertheless, I believe there is something else, something that causes managers to combine the power they have with its inherent responsibility so that negative spin-off can be avoided. Power and responsibility, therefore, need to be congruent.

As far as the organization of leadership is concerned, it seems to me that a balanced relationship between the authority of leadership and a co-operative leadership style towards colleagues is the most sensible. However, as we all know, opinions on this diverge considerably. My views are as follows: I am in favor of a team with a leader and not a team of leaders because I firmly believe that at every place a »point de crystallization« as the French say, is essential so that no one can say afterwards: »Well, I wanted to, but he didn't«. This is my experience: have dialogue and a team, but with one man in the team who cannot simply shift responsibility onto his colleagues. Sometimes the top management consists of two personalities – in Germany at least it used to be held in high esteem– a Chairman with technical know-how and a Chairman with business acumen. That may well work as long as things go well and the two of them get on well together. But in this case I would quote the well-known Turkish proverb: »*A ship with two captains sinks*«. That means that the proper degree of moderation between leadership skills, loyalty to colleagues and co-operation is essential if a company is to function well, which put in a nutshell means: Authority yes, authoritarian no.

With regard to moderation, the correct conduct and the right motivation of employees, I propagated three things in my company:

1) The so-called Value-Added Leadership Principle, which means leading less with formal authority but rather considering every day whether one has contributed to increasing the value of the company. That is a different question to asking »What authority do I have?«

2) The Employee-Involvement Concept means discussing changes and improvements with employees in good time and in detail in order to learn their opinions. Due to the fact that they have a better understanding of the practical aspects, it is often possible to take better decisions than the ones »higher up« would take on their own. Moreover, that way, decisions are reached which are supported by the employees, too. It is as simple as that, but quite often it is not done that way.

3) I mentioned this earlier and I have deliberately come back to it again: the principle of a long-term human resources policy. A long-term human resources policy that gives employees long-term security is a powerful incentive. It corresponds to goodwill towards the company and is an asset that is second to none! Yet today it is ignored non-stop. And then people are surprised at the kind of team they end up with. Of course we have to do everything within our power to rationalize and to lower costs. If we don't do that, we will stop being competitive some day. But the question I ask myself is, how it can be done – and it is in this process that many lapses occur. If a company earns – let's say – 5 or 6 billion and the very same company goes and says next day: »By the way, we have to make 6,000 people redundant in the next three weeks« then employees' security and motivation are gone.

This will harm a company – both internally and externally – for a long time to come. For that reason I am in favor of the following approach: If a company makes such profits and needs 6,000 people fewer, the cutbacks should be carried out over a period of 3–4 years without compulsory redundancies by making use of normal fluctuation, retirements and possible retraining. In the first year that might mean costs of 400 million, in the second year 300 million, in the third year 200 million etc. The ensuing reduction in profits is perceptibly less harmful to the company than the drastic approach described above. Such an investment in the personnel will maintain motivation, guarantee security, ensure loyalty and outwardly the image of the company does not suffer any harm. That is certainly one of the best investments that can be made in the interest of the company! And nevertheless, it is done incorrectly all the time. My opinion is that there has to rationalization, but the question is: how?

A leadership attribute which I think is part of moderate but efficient management is credibility. I consider it to be essential because today so many promises are made, so many lies are told and there is so much blether and populist talk. If on Monday people cannot rely on what the boss proclaimed on Sunday still applying, he has lost their trust in the long term. That is why I think that credibility is one of the key leadership attributes today.

Another important aspect of moderate and balanced corporate policy is how values, in other words value-oriented management, are handled. We all know that value orientation is currently very much in fashion. I have never experienced a time in which there has been so much talk of values and at the same time so many values have been trampled on or disregarded. At Nestlé I have always said that we are absolutely progressive and dynamic in our pursuit of new consumer trends, in technological developments and in research and innovation policy, but that we are conservative in retaining fundamental human values. Here too it is a matter of the proper degree of moderation and the correct values; in other words, it is a question of how we behave.

An interesting field to be considered with respect to the proper degree of moderation is also corporate governance – an issue which is widely discussed today. The optimum distribution of tasks and competences ought to be regulated among the annual general meeting, the Supervisory Board and the Management Board; moreover, a decision ought to be taken on what should be laid down by law and what should remain within the jurisdiction of the company. Lord Cadbury, the former Chairman of Cadbury, was one of the first to address this issue which he defined as follows: »Corporate governance is a system by which companies are directed and controlled«. The various, current deliberations and discussions tend to strengthen the rights of the annual general meeting and the Supervisory Board over the Management Board in order to thus guarantee that the owners have greater influence. That appears to me to be justified to a certain extent. However,

I consider an expansion of the rights of the annual general meeting to be wrong in the case of a publicly held company. After all, a company cannot be managed by a broad shareholder democracy. At present there are even discussions on whether for example the salaries of the Management Board ought to be determined by the general meeting. I think it is much more vital for shareholders to elect a Board of Directors that acts in their interest and really takes its responsibility seriously and monitors the Management Board. In the shareholder structure today there are, however, developments towards larger shares of institutional investors and hedge funds that, in view of their substantial interest in the company, want to strengthen their influence as owners; in such a case this also makes sense, but we don't need laws for that. On the other hand, we observe in large, publicly-owned companies that individual shareholders – often with only one vote – abuse their rights and speak out on all sorts of topics at the general meeting. That prolongs the general meeting unnecessarily; regulations to remove this abuse ought to be created by strengthening the position of the Chairman of the general meeting for example. That is more important than what is being discussed at present.

On the other hand, as far as the Supervisory Board is concerned I think that this body should be granted more rights with respect to current German legislation. The current tasks of the Supervisory Board basically concern dealing with everything the general meeting has to decide, all matters concerning the Board of Directors and their obligation to report. Beyond that, the Board is almost autonomous according to current legislation: it can determine new strategies, undertake acquisitions, it can do anything it wants. These all-embracing competences are often limited however by the statutes and procedural rules, by business being specified that requires the consent of the Supervisory Board. That is one way of solving the problem. But in Germany there is the additional problem of co-determination: everything that falls within the responsibility of the Supervisory Board is also determined by the trade unions and workers' representatives. That is why in Germany we face a certain dilemma in this respect. I think that independent of this specific German problem the Supervisory Board should be strengthened in any case and more strongly integrated in all strategic decisions. That includes major acquisitions or engaging in new business or investment plans. There is one point that in my opinion does not receive enough attention and which is not to be found in these new regulations: it concerns the Supervisory Board's task – to discuss specifically the long-term aspects and impact of business decisions on the company and incorporate the results of their deliberations in the decision-making process. Why do I say this? I say this because a long-term policy is absolutely essential for the company – I have said this on various occasions – and due to the pressure from the financial world and the growing fierceness of competition as a result of globalization, the Management Board and executives tend more and more to think in the short term. In that case, the Supervisory Board can be a corrective factor.

In general, I think that today's discussion on the subject of corporate governance ought not to result in too many regulations. Excessive regulation is always a problem and can never take the different circumstances of each company into consideration. That applies to Siemens or Bertelsmann or Shell – they are all different in kind and in size. Besides, a great deal of regulation cannot ultimately prevent inappropriate conduct. That is why it is much more important to appoint the right people onto the Supervisory Boards; at the same time these people don't have to be experts – these need to be in the company – but personalities with character and experience of life and business, who on the one hand will stand by the company and the CEO in difficult situations and on the other hand are prepared to act and vote members of the Management Board out of office should this appear to be indicated.

Therefore, finding the proper degree of moderation in the distribution of tasks and competences among the general meeting, the Supervisory Board and the Management Board is a vital topic and has a considerable impact on the proper functioning of the company.

I would also like to say a few words on financial policy. It is well-known that on this subject there are two opinions that differ widely: on the one hand, there is the opinion that holds that it is better to work only with equity, to avoid long-term debt thus creating a high degree of safety for the company, but at the expense of profitability. The opposing policy favors a very strong leverage, which has recently been the practice of hedge funds in particular: that means maximum debt and thus higher profitability of equity but with a corresponding reduction in safety. In view of the diversity of companies it is difficult to find the proper degree of moderation. There is just no formula; it depends more on the size, the structure, the earnings position, the cash flow, and the mentality and the risk disposition of the owners. I once had a professor who said: »There are two ways of doing business: you can eat well or you can sleep well«.

I would like to address a few remarks on the proper degree of moderation in other fields. However, I am only going to outline a few topics, which I cannot possibly deal with in detail here.

There is for example the proper degree of moderation in food and drink, which is known to be good for the health and influences the aesthetics of human beings.

Obviously love and sexuality are a topic to be considered in the light of the proper degree of moderation. However, to be on the safe side, I think it would be better not to express my views on that subject.

Furthermore: we have a democratic constitution on the one hand and the requirements of leadership on the other hand; bureaucracy, regulations and harassment as opposed to more freedom for citizens and subsidiarity. This also includes the topic of »safety for the citizen«, whereby more protection should be granted to the victim compared with the culprit, but at present this tends to be treated the other way round.

The question of »central state or federalism « needs to be looked at in a worldwide context, in view of increasing globalization and with regard to the European Union. It is well-known that in this context the Federal Republic of Germany, like any other country, hands over competences and functions to superordinate committees. Thus, the competences of the nation-state are restricted. On the other hand, bearing in mind a preference for subsidiarity it certainly makes more sense to transfer as many decisions and measures as possible to the individual federal states or local authorities. What is the proper degree of moderation therefore in dividing up competences and tasks among the UN, G8, and Europe, the state, the federal states and local authorities? I believe that these are issues that at present have not been thought through properly. I only need to think of the European Parliament! On the one hand, we are endeavoring to grant rights to this parliament. However, at the same time, the nation-states have no desire to hand over any of these rights but wish to exercise their competences via their own national representatives in the Council of Ministers and take major decisions there. But you can't work both ways. As far as I am concerned the problem has not been thought through properly.

It is not surprising, therefore, that for some time the French have said that the European Parliament is only a »talking shop«, as long as we, the democratically elected, go to Brussels from our own countries in order to arrive at decisions with the others. Giscard D'Estaing went to a great deal of trouble to regulate some of the problems in the new constitution but there is still a need for further action.

In another area, necessary joint tasks at national level on the one hand and the individual interests of owners and civil rights movements on the other need to be brought into line. In this context I would like to refer to the expansion of the airport in Frankfurt or in Berlin. I think we are the only country in the world that has difficulty building a decent airport in a capital city within a specified period of time. Any small state can manage it. Various objections that have been raised have, for almost twenty years, prevented the building of stretches of the motorway between Lindau and Munich. I am very familiar with this because I come from the Allgäu. Where, therefore, is the proper degree of moderation between individual and community interests?

We just need to compare it with other countries like France or America. The Chinese nearly split their sides laughing at our practices.

Another area raises the question as to whether we should have a free market economy à la Hayek and Friedman or ordoliberalism à la Freiburg School or a greater emphasis on the socio-political components by the social state that makes so-called provision for the population and that the SPD (Labor Party) aspire to, or even a planned economy without private property?

There is certainly a general consensus on some kind of social market economy in Germany but there are fierce arguments on what it should look like in detail. Personally, I think that currently we are going too far with the social aspects and the bureaucracy this entails and that we give too much room to potential abuse and the principle of indiscriminate, all-round distribution. In this context I would like to mention Röpke, an economist from last century, for whom I have a very high regard and who once said: »There is a tendency for any system to come to grief on its own excesses«. There has never been a truer word spoken. That seems to be in the nature of mankind. However, there are, I believe, many genuine social problems that we have left out of the reckoning. Where is the proper degree of moderation in economic and social policy?

I would also like to say a few brief words on the subject of sports where we also tend to exaggerate at times. Even the slogan we chose for the Olympics »Faster, Higher, Further«, smacks of excess. The excesses seen recently in doping, payment of top stars, and the like has nothing whatsoever to do with a fair sporting spirit. Society needs to consider where it should apply the proper degree of moderation.

Apart from that, we tend towards exaggeration and overreactions in many other fields. Certain reactions to some developments in high technology are certainly comprehensible. It is easy to understand that people are no longer able to understand them; that they do not understand the world any more. But here in Germany, the reactions to such things have assumed extreme forms. We need only think of *waldsterben*, bizarre activities in what are after all sensible ecological endeavors, disputes about nuclear energy, bio-technology, and green genetic engineering and similar issues culminating in the youth movement of 1968.

In Germany we have taken things to extremes and have certainly not been moderate. But then I always say that in Germany we were always better at mysticism and romanticism than we were at classicism.

Finally, I would like to ask whether the proper degree of moderation always makes sense. I would like to say first of all that the proper degree of moderation does not mean preventing initiative and obstructing a courageous forging ahead; nor does it mean giving up in resignation; that is not the way it is to be understood. Sometimes the normal or proper degree of moderation has to be exceeded. In a company it is often necessary to make courageous and far-reaching decisions, which, at that point in time, appear to many people as *excessive or at least which not everyone can conceive in their entirety*. This can be perceived in many examples from history: Would Alexander the Great have achieved what he did if he had been satisfied with our ideas, with my ideas today of what is the proper degree of moderation? Or what would have become of Churchill, who, in difficult times, was called to lead England. In »normal« times, he would never have become Prime Minister of England. Incidentally, this same Churchill held a moderate speech in Zürich just after the war in which he attempted to end the friend-foe relationship and propagated the idea of a United States of Europe. Then again, Columbus would never have gone to sea if he had acted according to our principles of what is the proper degree of moderation.

But let us return to moderation and my concluding remarks. As you can see, the discussion on what is the proper degree of moderation is an inexhaustible subject that encompasses all fields of society and the economy.

It goes without saying that I do not mean mediocrity when I speak of the proper degree of moderation. It seems to me to be quite useful to refer to Plato's four cardinal virtues in this context. It is well-known that one of these four virtues is moderation: modesty, which is supplemented by the other three virtues of courage, wisdom and justice. These four virtues have accompanied me all my life and I think they are a good basis for observing the proper degree of moderation.

Moreover, Chinese sages do not appear to think it very realistic to expect a proper degree of moderation before a certain age has been reached. Confucius, the famous Chinese sage, is supposed to have said in his dialogues (Lun Yu) on life: » At sixty I could follow all my heart's desires without transgressing the norm!«

There is also a poem by Goethe – you can always quote Goethe; there is a quotation for every occasion – that has always occupied my thoughts. It is one of my favorite poems entitled »Nature and Art«. The second part of the poem is as follows: »*Such is the case with all forms of refinement: In vain will spirits lacking due constraint seek the perfection of pure elevation. He who'd do great things must display great restraint; the master shows himself first in confinement, and law alone can grant us liberation*«

What wisdom is contained in these sentences! If we had paid more attention to the advice given in this poem and followed it more exactly, we would have been spared a great deal of trouble throughout history.

Finally I would like to quote a poem by Mörike, the famous Swabian poet and Church minister. I am going to become very personal here for this poem has accompanied me all my life even though I do not entirely share his philosophy in the poem because I – and doubtlessly you, too, – would like to approach my future and my life with a more positive attitude and willpower. Nevertheless, I would like to close with this poem:

»Lord, send what you will,
love or sorrow.
I am content that both
come from your hands.
Do as you wish with joy
and do as you wish with sorrow
but do not lavish it on me.
Somewhere in the middle
is sweet modesty! «

I hope that with these remarks I have only lightly exceeded the proper degree of moderation in the time allotted to my speech. Thank you for your attention.

Source: Helmut Maucher, »*The proper degree of moderation*«, a lecture given on the occasion of the Carl Friedrich von Weizsäcker Talks in January 2008.

Economic opportunities for Upper Swabia in the world of today

Regarding current problems and trends, Helmut Maucher draws a picture, in the following speech, of the direction in which the business world could develop and what this could mean for companies.

Ladies and Gentlemen,
My topic today is: Upper Swabia in the world of today.

That is why I would like to call to mind the world of the present and the future in brief:

- Globalization and internationalization will continue to increase as will free trade and the international intertwining of the financial world.
- We can observe a rapid progress in digitalization and application of technology – i. e. the entire world has been taken over by computers, Internet etc.
- Moreover, we can observe a demographic development with regard to increasing population ageing, the shift of a proportion of the world's population to other regions (to Asia in particular) and to the progressive increase in the world's population and the rise in affluence.
- Geo-political shifts can also be observed as regions beyond America, – i. e. China, Russia, India, Brazil etc. – assume more and more significance.

The question therefore arises as to how important Europe will be in the future and which role it will play. I hope that Europe will also have a decisive role to play in a geo-political context in future. Among other things, that will depend on how far Europe develops politically and economically; on how far it will succeed in speaking with one voice and if it succeeds in becoming more capable of making decisions within its internal structures.

It is vital for the future that the EU concentrates more on its core tasks: foreign, security and immigration policy, safeguarding peace and the affluence of its citizens, and giving more consideration to the principles of subsidiarity and decentralization.

Greece is a good example of the weakness of current regulations.

Apart from that the euro, too, only makes sense if there is greater discipline and co-ordination in economic policy and tougher sanctions in the case of inadequate performance.

Moreover, some reduction in bureaucracy and in some of the excesses in social policy is needed.

Which heads of government there will be in Europe in the future will be of importance. It is to be hoped that in the future we will have fewer »Prime Ministers« and more statesmen and women (see Adenauer, Kohl, and Mitterand) – something that cannot be said about most of the present heads of government.

Linked to these geo-political shifts we are marching from a G7 towards a G20 whereby it is to be hoped that this will be accompanied by an improvement in global co-operation.

- For some considerable time we have experienced – and this can also be expected in the future, too – global peace especially between the Great Powers such as has never been experienced before, although local wars and terrorism continue to abound.
- We observe certain trends in society mainly in the direction of more democracy – even outside the United States, Japan and Europe.
- Despite local and isolated setbacks, we are moving more in the direction of market economy systems. These are linked to an ordoliberalism, as it is defined in our latitudes.
- Despite the current crisis we are moving towards more social and ecological responsibility and this includes the issue of climate protection.
- This whole area also includes the increasing water shortage as well as the growing discrepancy between the supply and demand of agricultural products and the reduction of farmland due to urbanization.

    Water is a resource that is in short supply. Agriculture uses 70 % of all the fresh water that there is. China is experiencing the worst drought for more than five decades (there has been only a slight alleviation due to recent rainfall); in India they are drilling to a depth of seven meters in search of ground water. A price needs to be put on water. The share of Nestlé's mineral water business is merely 0.0067 percent of the total water consumption.

    [...]
- At present the trend all over the world is towards more regional co-operation, even beyond the EU. It is to be hoped that we will achieve a strengthening of institutions and regulations which will be valid worldwide so that globalization can be allowed to take effect without negative spin-offs.

What does all this mean for companies?

1) First of all it must be stated concisely that more globalization
means more competition.

That also means that performing well on the market meets with substantial rewards and that failure is penalized severely.

I have always held that leadership consisting of a team of colleagues doesn't work in difficult times and this applies even more in view of this fiercer competition. That's why I am in favor of *a team with a leader and not a team of leaders.*

Apart from that: the world is revolving faster and faster especially in the field of technological changes and scientific knowledge (findings double about every three years). In such a situation the time factor, speed, plays an increasingly major role. That is why I say: *»Be first, be daring, be different«.*

Anyone who is first – and therefore ahead of the others – to recognize trends and developments, who decides on necessary changes in good time and implements them quickly and consistently will simply be more successful.

2) Before addressing opportunities for Upper Swabia in detail
I would like to comment in general on opportunities
for the Federal Republic of Germany and Europe.

Geographically we are not sufficiently aware of the fact that Europe is the geographic centre of the globalized world, which means between America and the Far East. In addition, Europe has other advantages which need to be called to mind occasionally:

- We have a temperate climate that provides Europe with sufficient rainfall and there is consequently no water shortage
- Europe has relative safety, high quality standards and the population has a good standard of education.
- Technology has made immense strides and the political situation is quite stable.
- In general, economic structures boast a good balance between industry, the service sector, small and medium-sized businesses etc. (this applies to the Federal Republic of Germany in particular).

3) Opportunities for Upper Swabia

Many people may not be aware of the fact that Upper Swabia lies right in the centre of the North/South axis of Europe: between Sicily and Narwick. This applies to Switzerland, too.

Apart from that, Southern Europe is going to become significantly more important despite current problems in the financial sector and a downward trend in employment figures.

It is about time that we stopped thinking of Upper Swabia as being in the outermost regions.

Apart from that, online technology enables contact to the entire world at any time with the result that anyone with a small or medium-sized business can operate internationally and be a multi-national company.

4) Development and opportunities in individual fields

Agriculture (see also my introductory remarks)

Agricultural products worldwide are becoming increasingly scarce and this applies particularly to countries in Asia where generally the population is on the increase and prosperity is growing. That is a genuine opportunity for agriculture in Upper Swabia.

We should not allow ourselves to be affected too much by the current crisis with regard to the price of milk.

The increasing water shortage mentioned earlier affords Upper Swabia a further advantage because literally the water flows from the mountains and prices will therefore be lower than in many warmer countries.

In talking about agricultural products we must not forget the different types of fruit, wine, and hops to be found here (the weather conditions are particularly favorable in Upper Swabia).

However, structural improvements will have to continue. The average size of a farm in Upper Swabia is 25 hectares whereas in Mecklenburg it is 250 hectares. Hybrid forms, too, (plying a trade and running a farm on the side) have chances of survival.

Besides more imagination and initiative should be brought to bear on alternative sources of income (see such examples as bio-energy, holidays on the farm, consumer trends etc.).

Upper Swabia is better than its reputation. There are many good firms here (e. g. Liebherr, VAUDE, Ravensburger, Böhringer, ZF Friedrichshafen, Vetter, MTU, Hümer and of course Weishaupt).

Moreover, there are a large number of small and medium sized businesses which have a reputation of being relatively stable. Therefore, I would particucularly like to add a few words about small and medium-sized businesses.

- Such companies are often managed by families and that leads to more sustainable policy. However it is vital that the question of a successor is addressed in good time and solved optimally.
- Such firms are often more flexible and closer to the market. (It is not the large-scale enterprises that swallow up the small ones but the faster ones that swallow up the slower ones.)
- The development of the service sector provides the small and medium-sized businesses with perceptible opportunities.
- With the steadily growing differentiation of consumer behavior it is and will be immensely important for companies of this size to exploit niches that are not or are only insufficiently served by enterprises.
- The opportunities provided by Internet connections for operating worldwide have already been mentioned.

All in all, Upper Swabia is therefore well positioned in the industrial sector.

Tourism

This area is a growth industry!

I can foresee excellent opportunities for Upper Swabia: Lake Constance, the Allgäu, wine-growing areas, an enormous wealth of art and culture, the Barockstraße (a route with famous Baroque sights), the climate and countryside in general and many family-friendly programs.

The topic of health must not be forgotten in this context. In Upper Swabia, many facilities have been established meanwhile in the field of rehabilitation, health centers, spas, and lakes (see for example Neutrauchburg) and there are further facilities at Lake Constance.

Taken as a whole, there is a huge need for Upper Swabia to address and highlight this industry to a greater extent and especially with regard to prevailing market requirements. Perhaps individual towns and areas need to join forces and make an even more concerted effort.

5) Problems

Not everything can be seen in a rosy light, however. There are many aspects which make a positive development more difficult. Some of these problems are not peculiar to Upper Swabia, but also affect the Federal Republic of Germany and sometimes the whole of Europe; e.g. excessive bureaucracy and the sheer number of rules and regulations. These also include the excesses in the entire social network, in industrial law, in the Works Constitution and co-determination. To avoid any misunderstandings, I would add that all of these make sense to a certain degree and that I am merely decrying bureaucratic excesses and the danger of abuse to which they are subject. Moreover, we are much too slow in planning sensible joint tasks. I would call to mind the two sections of the motorway between Lindau and Munich, the extension of the airport in Frankfurt or Berlin or the central station in Stuttgart. In general, Upper Swabia needs better transport connections. Some progress has been reached with the extension of the airports at Friedrichshafen and Memmingen. Stuttgart, the capital of our federal state, occasionally needs to be reminded that Upper Swabia is not in Siberia!

With regard to the sheer number of rules and regulations and excessive bureaucracy, I would like to mention two further areas: the overburdening of doctors and chemists with bureaucratic tasks (a chemist who is a friend of mine told me recently that he needs a full-time employee to cope with all the red tape in the office).

A further example is the anti-discrimination law. Although it comes from Europe, it was partly initiated by lower-level German bureaucrats. The latest bizarre proposal in this area is the demand for anonymity in job applications to avoid potential favoritism!

All in all, these things naturally increase our costs and reduce our speed of action: two things that are crucial in increasing global competition.

Another problem is our general hostility to technology (see nuclear energy and genetic engineering). In this context, Upper Swabia is developing particular trends such as the Alliance of Conservative-Christian Forces with the Greens, or the great difficulties in or the obstacles to developing new and sensible industrial estates. The slogan »Protect Creation« is frequently abused; it appears to have been forgotten that the world has always changed and will continue to do so! Here in Upper Swabia there are so-called GMO-free regions; moreover, it is difficult to obtain permission to erect pylons because people are afraid of radiation and imagine they can be contaminated. (In general the Teutons and particularly the Upper Swabians were always better at mysticism and romanticism than they were at classicism.) And as far as I know, the Upper Swabians were the last to give up their belief in witchcraft.

Therefore, I would advise you to keep a critical eye on things, to remain vigilant and not just leave discussions of such matters to our objectors.

Evidently we need a sensible balance between the economy, and ecology etc., but without overloading with excessive ideology.

> 6) Now I would like to return to the positive developments, regardless of the positive facts mentioned objectively at the beginning of my talk.

I would like to stress once again that the distinctive structure of small and medium-sized businesses will have a favorable and sustainable impact on the development of Upper Swabia. Beyond that, I would like to mention in a few key phrases that we have relative political stability (to which I would add the word: common sense), a good mixture in the population between tradition and being open-minded about changes, and on the whole a healthy mentality. Secondary virtues and attributes such as diligence, realism, loyalty and consideration are still appreciated. In general, the Upper Swabians have little time for political or other utopias.

7) Summary

I would like to state succinctly and with conviction: in the future, Upper Swabia has excellent opportunities due to its geographic, structural and economic conditions, and to the quality and mentality of its population. This also applies to a certain extent when compared to the rest of the Federal Republic of Germany.

Various developments and trends worldwide, as I mentioned at the beginning, provide Upper Swabia with new opportunities.

However, three things are essential to bring Upper Swabia to the fore and to help it to really cope with the future:

1. We have to be prepared to take an active part in shaping the future and in no way ought we to rest on our laurels.
2. The negative trends mentioned need to be tackled with greater courage and persistence.
3. We also need to learn to communicate better and highlight all the things we can do and all the things we want to do; in short, we need to improve

our marketing of Upper Swabia so that in future the term Upper Swabia does not just denote a higher lying region but also the fact that we are »on top« in every respect.

Thank you for your attention.

Source: Helmut Maucher, »Economic opportunities for Upper Swabia in the world of today«; a speech given at »Talks in Upper Swabia« in May 2010.

Remain true to yourselves!

As a German, Helmut Maucher became one of the major economic leaders in Switzerland. In the following interview he talks about the various experiences he has had with respect to both countries.

[...]
Mr. Maucher, do you know what Henri Nestlé and you have in common?

Let me think a minute. Heinrich Nestlé went to Switzerland and there he founded an excellent company. I was brought to Switzerland to advance an excellent company. He invented the logo of the mother bird feeding her young. I prevented the nest being replaced by a new logo. Both of us understood what unique positioning and marketing mean.

Both families come from the state of Baden-Württemberg and both ended up at Lake Geneva via Nestlé's German headquarters in Frankfurt.

That's correct. And we both felt very much at home in Romandy.

Nestlé even embellished the name of the family and the company with a French accent ...

... not really. He was called Heinrich Nestlé to the very end and only became Henri Nestlé after his death – a pragmatic adaptation to the French-speaking part of Switzerland. *Why not?* Nestlé, however, never became a Swiss citizen.

But he did remain in Switzerland and he died in Montreux. You, on the other hand, returned to Frankfurt after you retired from professional life. Why?

I love Switzerland, but I felt a need to be close to my children. And in particular, I wanted my successor to be able to go his own way – without my presence in the background. When you hand over power, then it has been handed over once and for all.

When someone like you leaves Switzerland of his own free will, the Swiss are put out – despite complaints about the large number of Germans working at the universities and hospital in Switzerland.

226

The Swiss often offered me Swiss citizenship. However, I have simple principles in my life: you never change your religion, your wife or your fatherland
without good cause. When the Swiss heard that they said: *You're right, of
course.*

Apropos dialect: when the Swiss try to speak ›Hochdeutsch‹ (the equivalent
of Received Pronunciation in Britain), it still sounds to Germans like a dialect – i. e. somehow cute! On the other hand every German, no matter how he
speaks, sounds like Goethe to the German-speaking Swiss.

People like Franz Blankart have always said: We need to uphold ›Hochdeutsch‹ as a common language, but in addition we need to continue to cultivate our dialect, which is more colorful and more original. Switzerland could
do with working at maintaining the balance between international communication in German and the local dialect.

It was also Blankart who specially pointed out the Swiss penchant for mediocrity.

He said that in Switzerland the happy medium is passed off as proximity to
its citizens.

You're joking. Mediocrity is the manager's enemy.

I perceive the trend of giving anyone a bash on the head if he towers above
mediocrity as a perversion of social justice.

Economically, Switzerland has found its place as a location for the production
of quality products; there can be no more talk of mediocrity. And if nothing
else, thanks to the expertise enlisted from Germany. Nevertheless, they had to
get used to Germans occasionally running the major Swiss companies.

The economic areas have moved closer together; management is an international commodity. That's a sensible development which benefits all concerned. But you are right, of course: a German running the largest company
in Switzerland was a bit revolutionary in the early 1980s. Nevertheless, I was
made to feel very welcome. It was partly my own doing and partly the Swiss'
doing. If you come to Switzerland and complain about a hostile environment,
it's your own fault. I didn't run around like Lord Muck; didn't lead an elitist

life and that was noticed. When I came to Vevey, I visited all the wine-growing villages among which Nestlé lay like a Moloch, drank a *verre d'amitié* with the people and said: If you have any problems, come straight to me. That was very much appreciated.

As someone from the Allgäu, you probably found that easy.

Well, I think I can safely say that I have a flair for the Swiss mentality.

That all sounds very harmonious. But Berlin and Bern argue about taxes; Baden-Württemberg and Zürich have been debating landings at their airports for years. That is a problem of communication and therefore of mentality.

I wouldn't place too much emphasis on it. If the world had no other problems than the ones between Germany and Switzerland, we would be living in a wonderful world. Neighbors always have different interests. No doubt, there were a lot of accounts in Switzerland that were associated with undeclared assets. I am against tax evasion and have always declared my accounts, but when taxes are high, it is only natural for someone who has worked for 30 years and put a considerable amount of money aside to ask him/herself whether he has to pay tax on it all over again. On the other hand, the Swiss had to realize that the world has changed and tax fraud, sorry: tax evasion is just not possible in Europe any more.

Switzerland has defended banking confidentiality like a fortress for such a long time and has suddenly changed to an over-eagerness to comply. What does the strategically trained manager say to that?

Switzerland had its back to the wall. It was difficult to come off unscathed. That's why they tried to rectify matters. But Switzerland ought to adopt a clear position in this case: preventing tax evasion is one thing, protecting financial privacy is another. Protecting privacy happens to be part of Switzerland. And I say: People of Switzerland, do not forget that!

Anyone protecting privacy consistently has to accept the fact that he is protecting a black sheep sometimes.

Transparency is good, total transparency is dangerous. Switzerland can say: Of course we are opposed to tax fraud, but it is not our task to act as a police force for the whole world. Recently, I experienced something myself where I have to say: Damn it all, that's going too far – in the other direction.

What happened?

There was this business about the sale of the Kärntner ›Hypo Alpe Adria‹ Bank to the Bayerische Landesbank (Regional Bank of Bavaria). A few years ago, asset manager Tilo Berlin, whom I have known for some time, was looking for investors to acquire a considerable interest in the Alpe Adria. I invested and got a good deal when the bank was sold to the Bayerische Landesbank. However, the Free State of Bavaria and the Bayerische Landesbank lost quite a lot of money in the transaction, which sparked off a public dispute. At first, the Bavarian public prosecutors wanted to charge the former head of the Landesbank and the sellers from Kärnten. Then they began to investigate Tilo Berlin for possible criminal offences. They found nothing. So they went one step further and investigated the investors. With what appeared to be a very arbitrary reason that investors might have paid a kickback or an illegal commission, the public prosecutors in Zürich were asked if access could be gained to my account with a large Swiss bank. The request was granted and my data was released on the grounds of a very flimsy suspicion – without my consent; I was only informed after the event. The laugh of it is that the Austrians said that there was not enough suspicion to warrant disclosure of details about the accounts. I wondered what the point of having an account in Switzerland was if anyone with a flimsy request for information could obtain access to details about my account. Of course I hadn't paid a *kickback* and that has been confirmed by the public prosecutors meanwhile.

Switzerland has been made insecure. The economy and the government say that they uphold banking confidentiality but de facto they are abolishing it.

You said that!

Many people in Germany think that Switzerland is removing Germany's guaranteed taxes. It is a matter of principle: Can the recipient country be blamed for that?

No, it can't. I can understand companies transferring their headquarters to Switzerland for tax reasons. That's their decision. We can't approve of competition and globalization and then prevent people from acting accordingly.

The Germans might need to start thinking about what they can do to keep companies in Germany. But I can tell you what I do object to.

Offshore companies?

My objections apply to men like Schumacher and Vettel, who sign a contract with a community whereby they spend 80 days a year in their Swiss abode. They have no objections to being acclaimed as German icons all over the world and then they move to Switzerland to save taxes. I think it is cynical and wrong of such icons that have hundreds of millions and live off their image as Germans.

What would you advise Germany to do to increase its relative attraction for companies and private individuals?

Germany should ask what Switzerland does better. It doesn't matter whether we elect a socialist or a middle-class government; excessive taxes are always a reason for people moving away. It's about time the Germans understood that they are not alone on this earth.

»Competition« has become a word with very strong connotations for the German public. When Guido Westerwelle spoke recently of late Roman decadence, it created a similar stir to the word »consumer waste«, which you used at the end of 1996. Where does this hysteria come from?

We have many advantages in Germany. We have good infrastructure, and good people. Industry has done its homework in the last 10 to 15 years. That is the reason why German companies are successful worldwide. I always say: The Germans were always better at romanticism than at classicism. Mysticism arose in Germany, the youth movement was the strongest, and we had the Pietists in Swabia. But for all our efficiency we have a slight eccentricity. As far as this mindset of too much regulation and planning periods is concerned, these are still grounds for criticism. The technological lead that we have in many areas is becoming progressively smaller. Every day the Chinese learn a little more about how to build machinery with precision.

But people in Germany and Switzerland are still well off. A certain psychological pressure is missing.

The affluent society is a recent phenomenon! For 100,000 years human beings had to struggle daily to ensure that they didn't starve, freeze and were not eaten by lions. We have got rid of these uncertainties bit by bit. Fritz Gerber, the former head of Roche, once told me about his great-grandparents, who came from the Emmental region and who only had enough to be able to support one son. The other children were given 20 Francs to take them to America.

That's a long time ago!

Germany and Switzerland, too, have made enormous progress. Thank God! But if we all turn into softies and someone refuses to be transferred from Frankfurt to Munich because he's a member of a tennis club in Frankfurt, then I can only say: Those aren't people with whom you can win global acclaim.

A similar materialism can also be observed in Switzerland. Is Switzerland simply a belated Germany?

In many respects Switzerland is different but many trends are similar. We had an *association du personnel*, but not anchored in the Swiss Works Constitution Act and I think that is a good thing. Switzerland should look at Germany occasionally and thus avoid the mistakes that Germany has made.

Is Germany ahead of Switzerland – for better or for worse?

For historical reasons Germany will always be one of the best democratic pupils but this sometimes causes somewhat over-hasty political decisions. Civil rights have been pushed so far that specific interests can block nearly everything today. There are phenomena like »Stuttgart 21« in almost every German city when anything new is to be built. Berlin has been trying to get plans for a proper airport off the ground for 15 years; when it came to an extension of the airport in Frankfurt, all the marmots in the area were examined and calculations were made whether all the butterflies would have to shift their touchdown by five meters. The mixture of specific interests and irrational ecology are an obstacle to many projects. Wilhelm Röpke, one of the economists I admire most, said aptly: » There is a tendency for any system to come to grief on its own excesses«.

The Chinese government does the exact opposite: If they want to build a dam, thousands of people are forcibly relocated. That can't be the answer either.

Of course that goes too far. Even in France, Great Britain and the USA things happen faster than in Germany – that applies not only to government infrastructure projects but also to the building of privately owned factories. Meanwhile, in the Middle and Far East it is not only the population that is growing; affluence is growing, too.

You were one of the first to go to these countries and you established Vevey as a globalization platform.

I have always tried to understand the world. I made it clear at Nestlé that we are a multi-national company; we sell our products to the whole world and have employees and shareholders from all over the world. It is not the passport that counts but whether someone fits into our corporate culture or not. But if we operate in Brazil, we adapt to Brazil and have no intention of forcing a different way of life on to anyone. At the same time I, as a German, have always emphasized that Nestlé is a Swiss company with Swiss origins. Our culture is Swiss and we cultivate Swiss virtues. That is not only the right thing to do; it is also an advantage that we have over our competitors with regards to our image.

Switzerland needs to make a huge effort to translate economic strength into power on the international stage; Germany needs to conceal its true power within the EU. What's better?

In my experience, it is better to stick to the truth. However, it depends on how you tell it. I always used a slightly modified form of Kant's Categorical Imperative for our communication policy: *»Don't do anything that can't appear in the press tomorrow«*. That doesn't mean that I always want everything to be in the press tomorrow. But if it is in the press, you have to be able to justify it. If I have power and deny it, no one will believe me. The Germans should exercise sensitivity when dealing with their power; but they also have to say: We are also prepared to assume responsibility. And my advice to the Swiss is: Remain what you are and defend your position. You have been successful with it and it suits your country, its size and its structure. Don't give it all up for the sake of opportunism.

Source: Florian Rittmeyer, »Remain true to yourselves! «, in *Schweizer Monat* (Special Edition no. 4), issued in October 2011.

Education for the future – Thoughts of an entrepreneur

In this lecture, Helmut Maucher expresses his general views on education. He speaks about future trends, which knowledge and skills are needed to be able to survive in the future and which contradictions exist in this respect.

An anniversary is not only a reason for celebrating but is also the right moment to think about the future. For that reason, the headmaster and senior staff invited me to speak to you today on the topic of »Education for the Future«. Today it is not an educationalist, an expert or a teacher who is speaking to you but someone who has very different experience and responsibility. But education is a topic that should be of interest to us all because it has a considerable impact on how the future will develop. I have broken down the topic into twelve sections.

1) As a person who thinks in terms of a company and the economy, I naturally ask first of all what education can actually achieve. We know increasingly from science how profoundly we have been shaped by the past and our genetic make-up; we know that some of the philosophers of earlier centuries were incorrect when they started out from a *tabula rasa* and thought that only education and society shaped a person. Consequently, education has its limits but that does not restrict the value or the importance of education in any way. We also need to be aware of the fact that there are other influences which bombard young people: their environment, the media, the *zeitgeist*, the community in which they live, the sports clubs with their facilities and activities, sports and cultural influences etc. Of course it is important that parents accept their responsibility with regard to education. A young person can fulfill his potential best if parents, school and many other institutes co-operate and make an effort to act in concert.

2) When we talk about education for the future, we need to have an idea of what this future will look like. I would like to make a few comments on this:

   - The importance of modern communication and information technology will take another gigantic leap forward and change our lives. These technologies are steadily transforming the world into a global village with all the resulting impact on our social and political institutions and our life together. Other technological developments, such as bio-genetics, new energy sources or brain research all play a part, too.

- These developments are accelerating: our knowledge doubles at least every ten years and 90% of all the scientists who ever lived are still alive today.
- In addition, there are enormous demographic developments (a sharp rise in the population in today's developing countries with a high proportion of young people, a relatively substantial stagnation of the population in industrial countries with a steadily rising proportion of elderly people). We also know that, in coming years, for example, 50% of the increase in the gross world product will come from Asia, regardless of the current crisis. All this involves huge structural shifts of relative proportions of the population and of economic strength in the different parts of the world as well as greater self-confidence.
- At the same time, there is a new desire for regional and personal identity to compensate these developments.

3) A major factor in education – that must be stated here – is naturally the quality of teachers and their commitment to everything concerning education and young people. That requires dedication from teachers, a continual updating of their knowledge, an observance of current trends and the integration of these in lessons in a correct and sensible measure. Certainly those teachers have it easier if they are personalities and not just experts in their subjects, and certainly society has many reasons for recognizing and honoring the accomplishments of schools and teachers. Touching on this I would like to mention that schools need to increase their efficiency and cost effectiveness by making use of the resources provided by today's communication and information technology (PC).

4) We also need to ask ourselves what we ought to be learning, what priorities we should be setting, and what skills and knowledge are necessary for the future. I cannot elaborate on this at length today and would prefer to leave that to the experts; besides it depends on the different types of school which prepare young people for various professions etc. However, I think the following is important:

- General knowledge about our world and not just specialist knowledge needs to be taught.
- Furthermore, it is crucial that in the syllabus greater emphasis is placed on the basics e. g. on arithmetic and writing, and on good general knowledge (11% of Germans believe that sun moves round the earth and 9% aren't sure).
- A command of language is important; and today that doesn't only apply to one language but to a number of languages because otherwise we will not be able to communicate internationally.

- Every citizen ought to have a basic knowledge of and an interest in politics and know the major principles of our constitution. After all, that is one of the duties of a responsible citizen, who is frequently called upon to vote or take other decisions. Apart from that, it would also be nice if it was again obligatory for pupils in German schools to learn the text and melody of the national anthem as happens all over the world.
- Schools in secondary education should make young people familiar with the latest major scientific and cultural developments. That includes knowledge of the economy and the essential characteristics of a social market economy (it is sometimes astonishing how little even relatively educated people know).
- Every aspect of modern information technology is becoming more and more important.
- Worldwide co-operation requires young people to develop an understanding of other cultures. They need to develop an interest in their own cultural development and a general interest in cultural matters.
- Increasing globalization requires us to know the whole world and not just Upper Swabia, Baden-Württemberg, Germany or Europe. But perhaps it might not be a bad idea to get to know Upper Swabia again before becoming familiar with every village and town in Mallorca.

5) I also believe that we need to openly acknowledge that conduct, attitudes, standards and the like are important. We need to think about how we want to shape our community and our society, how we want to live together and how we want to treat each other.

The President of the German Teachers' Association said recently:

»School policy is in the Bermuda-Square between Rousseau, Skinner, Markuse and Greenpeace: that means between a utopia of equality, the delusion of feasibility, the pleasure principle and an alarmism of doom! In this square, personality development, a sense of reality, a willingness to make an effort and a zest for life are gradually lost«.

6) This topic also includes finding the correct balance between individuality or egoism and a sense of community, between a proper understanding of equality (in terms of equal opportunities, freedom and free development) and the limits to freedom (in terms of commitment and responsibility etc.). Here are two quotations in this connection which are worth thinking about

The first one is taken from the famous English philosopher Hobbes, who lived 300 years ago and is as follows: »*Freedom requires an understanding of necessity*«.

The other is by Goethe, from his famous poem *Nature and Art*; the last part is as follows: »Such is the case with all forms of refinement: In vain will spirits lacking due constraint seek the perfection of pure elevation. He who'd do great things must display great restraint; the master shows himself first in confinement, and law alone can grant us liberation.«

7) Today there is much talk about education in so-called social competence. In principle, that is okay if it means real social behavior and not abstract, collective and socialist demeanor. As you know, social behavior begins at home and in the immediate environment and cannot be replaced by demonstrative declarations about problems occurring somewhere thousands of miles away.

8) In view of today's wide-spread mentality of thinking only of one's own wishes and demands, we need to encourage young people to develop more courage towards initiative and self-help. We are certainly all in favor of a social network for the needy, the weak and the old, but I am strictly against a social hammock. The state should not become a self-service store, which is frequently demanded by the very same people who repeatedly argue in favor of the responsible citizen.

9) We need to be aware of some contradictions in schools. I mean the following, for example:
   • We are moving in the direction of a service society whereby the service mentality is decreasing at the same time.
   • We find ourselves in the middle of a communication society and at the same time the ability to hold a real conversation is on the wane.
   • We need to make it clear to people that safeguarding one's rights also means fulfilling one's obligations.

10) Within the framework of the afore-mentioned acceleration of technological developments and the numerous changes in the whole world young people need to be educated to have an inner willingness to live with these continual changes and to address them consciously. This also entails the will and the willingness not to stop learning when you finish school but to know that today you have to continue learning and to adapt to new situations. This also needs to be a feature of future flexibility because that is the way to contribute to the current serious problem of unemployment.

11) We need to be absolutely willing to understand and shape this future but at the same time we need to understand our history and consciously accept it. A famous philosopher of our times, Bodo Marquardt, once said:

»Future needs an origin«. That is why we also need more open discussion and it is to be hoped a greater consensus on fundamental values, moral issues in the broadest sense and a sense of the rule of law. If we continue to move in the direction of a »permissive society« or according to the slogan »anything goes«, this society or Europe will stop playing a role in the global context and run the risk of destroying itself.

12) Today, having an understanding of modern technologies and environmental issues is very important. We need to reduce irrational attitudes, hostility towards technology and fears that are partly unfounded scientifically, and at the same time promote a responsible handling of technology and the environment. *Angst* is a typical German word and often this *angst* has to do with the fact that compared with earlier times things have become more complex, more abstract, and less easy to understand.

Ladies and Gentlemen, let me say in summary:

1. Education can't do everything but it can contribute considerably to raising the standard of citizens in respect of quality and personality including their conduct, their attitudes and their responsibility.

2. Acquiring skills and knowledge needs to be geared towards future requirements. Apart from purely factual knowledge of subjects, it is important to understand general developments and interrelations from politics and economics to culture, science and globalization.

3. A good education presupposes capable teachers, good schools and intact parental homes. In this case, we need to remember that the youth of today are the parents of tomorrow; that we do not get good schools if we do not spend money on equipping them properly; if we do not acknowledge their achievements and if we demand not only sound knowledge of their subjects but commitment to everything concerning education.

4. Education must also contribute to our reaching a greater consensus on fundamental values, behavior and attitudes including moral issues in the broadest sense.

5. Ultimately it must be the aim of education, to put young people in a position to understand the future better and thus enable them to shape it in the best possible way. This includes knowledge of our history and the acknowledgement of and respect for values and experiences which have proved to be useful, sensible and advantageous in the history of mankind.

In this context I would like quote from an article by Mr. Gerhardt the current leader of the FDP (Liberal Party):

»Anyone who does not get a minimum knowledge of history at school will have problems assessing developments and have difficulty getting his/her bearings in Germany and the world. Anyone who does not acquire a minimum knowledge of foreign languages will experience considerable disadvantages in communicating in an increasingly international society. Anyone who is not offered a minimum of science and mathematics in school will understand increasingly less of our society with its technical developments and ecological challenges. Anyone who has not acquired a minimum knowledge for dealing with technology will quickly become a loser in our information society and on the labor market. Anyone who does not have a minimum education in tolerance, in democracy and social action will face our society and its values and the discharging of responsibility with indifference or rejection«.

I would like to add something more to this: Anyone who does not have a minimum knowledge of the economy and market economy will be frequently led astray by superficial slogans.

Apart from this I would like to add another quotation by Goethe which briefly says almost all that needs to be said about education. I quote: »*There are only two things we can give our children that last: the first is roots and the second is wings*«.

If we seize, understand and take this completely to heart, we will do many things in society better as teachers, parents and persons of responsibility.

I would like to congratulate the Commercial High School in Wangen on its 30th anniversary and wish it every success in its efforts to make a significant contribution to the education of our young people and thus to the shaping of our future.

Source: Helmut Maucher, »Education for the future – Thoughts of an entrepreneur «; a lecture at the Commercial High School, Wangen in October 1998.

Part 3

Discussion between Helmut Maucher and Fredmund Malik

Thoughts on Management and the Economy

Below is a discussion, which took place especially for this work on management, between Helmut Maucher and Fredmund Malik in 2012. It was chaired by Farsam Farschtschian, who is very well acquainted with the approaches to management and the schools of thought of both Maucher and Malik and who has accordingly elaborated on and accentuated these approaches in his own books.

Introduction to the discussion

Farschtschian: The following debate, a special summit meeting between Fredmund Malik and Helmut Maucher, is intended to act as a »lighthouse for sailors in times of storm« by providing reliable navigation for today's generation of managers. This appears to be of particular importance in the current economic context and in view of the present-day turbulences.

The significant content of this work is supplemented and rounded off by the exchange of thoughts of two eminent authorities on major issues of management and the economy.

It is particularly interesting that, for the first time, some issues are raised that are of great importance but about which hardly anything has been written until today. One reason for this might be that there are some things which are so obvious to Helmut Maucher that he never regarded them as anything special and therefore, there was never any need to address them in the past. It is just like someone having a particular strong point of which he is unaware because he finds everything so easy, as if it were the most natural thing in the world. Professor Malik aptly expresses this as »*The obvious is not so obvious*«.

Over the last few years numerous conversations have afforded me an opportunity to follow the views and the development of both personalities closely. Looked at clearly, Maucher's and Malik's opinions on most major issues are very similar or even identical. However the following transcript of our discussion makes it very evident that, prima facie, the opinions of two such personalities on some issues differ considerably. But in thrashing out such issues it can be ascertained that both of them come to similar conclusions in the end but by different paths.

Those taking part in the discussion are:

- Helmut Maucher, one of the most successful and exemplary business managers, who headed Nestlé, the market leader in the sector, for almost two decades. Mr. Maucher always thought and acted for the company in terms of sustainability. He never succumbed to the errors of the *zeitgeist* and developed Nestlé into one of the major multi-national corporations.
- Professor Fredmund Malik, the leading management pioneer, who has influenced a whole generation of managers with his school of thought. He is one of the most distinguished consultants, academics, entrepreneurs and bestselling authors, and has been described by Peter Drucker as »the leading authority on management in Europe« and »the major voice – in management both in theory and practice«. He always clearly foresaw the challenges which have eventually faced companies.

The key issues for discussion are as follows:

1. *Corporate Governance, Business Organization and Strategy*
2. *Effective Management and Daily Management Routine*
3. *Politics, the Economy and Society*

Corporate Governance, Business Organization and Strategy

Shareholder value and corporate management

Farschtschian: Let's start with Anglo-Saxon corporate governance. Both of you, Dr. Maucher and Professor Malik, were among the first to criticize the principle of shareholder value. Why do you believe that this principle is a misdirection of corporate management?

Maucher: I think we could say that our opinions vary a little. In principle I do not oppose shareholder value but there are three things that went absolutely wrong. That is the reason why I was just as critical of shareholder value as Professor Malik.

Firstly, shareholder value is an end product. Therefore, to better understand the matter you have to start talking about the company. And, funnily enough, only when it is being managed well – and that means successfully in the long run – does the share value rise. That is putting the cart before the horse. That is the first point.

Secondly, what I was particularly critical of was the fact that shareholder value boosted short-term thinking more than ever. I called these people shareholder value fetishists. In many instances, short-term thinking and acting is wrong in the long term.

And in your recently published book, Mr. Malik, you said on the subject of strategy what no one has ever really said: Even if people currently record a huge profit, that doesn't reveal anything about how good the company is – perhaps the strategic approaches for the future are heading in a completely different direction or they are just happy with the profit generated today and tomorrow. The moment thinking begins to focus on shares, success, profit or returns on investment for the shareholders, the entrepreneur becomes responsible for looking at the matter from a long-term perspective. I have always

said that we don't only want to win a battle; we want to win a war. We have to think in the long term and if you think in the long term, a lot of the nonsense that happens today because of short-term thinking is automatically ruled out. If I pursue marketing short-term, lower prices and stop spending money on advertising in order to generate profit for the next two years, this has a catastrophic impact on the company. The point of my criticism of the whole matter is that, due to thinking in terms of shareholder value, perspectives are becoming narrower and thinking is becoming more short-term oriented.

And the third point is the main one: that with short-term thinking in respect of shareholder value there is not only no thinking in the long term but all the other aspects that are vital in life and in the company and which ultimately – from a long-term point of view – benefit shareholder value are completely neglected.

That is the reason why I opposed this approach, which has resulted in a lot of annoyance and in catastrophe and has ultimately led to the financial crisis, too. These are essentially my three objections although in principle I say: it is only fair that if someone has invested in a company, he should have an increase in value in the *long term*; but the aspect of long-term focus has been totally pushed aside.

Farschtschian: That means that the share price should actually be the consequence and not the origin of the whole thing....

Maucher: Yes, you shouldn't put the cart before the horse but think in the longer term.

Farschtschian: Seen that way, you entirely agree with each other. Mr. Malik, in what way does your point of view differ?

Malik: Essentially we are indeed of the same opinion; perhaps there are a few nuances where we differ. I would like to mention a few more things. I'll start with something which I think is really a matter of the greatest urgency at the moment, namely that it is important to recognize that one of the major causes of the crisis in which we find ourselves is actually this shareholder value – due to its one-sidedness....

Maucher: ... due to this short-sightedness.

Malik: Precisely. That is one of the major causes.

Maucher: Absolutely.

Malik: To be sure it wasn't something anyone wanted – but that is de facto the way it turned out. I took an early stand on this and said that anyone who focused on shareholder value – and *only* on this – maximized the probability that his decisions were more likely to be wrong than right because he was focused on the wrong star.

Then the question arises as to what the alternatives are and that way you come to a very good basis for corporate management. Of course there is also the fact that a company thinking in terms of shareholder value is exposed to the random movements on the stock markets. Everything may well look wonderful if the stock markets are booming. But shareholder value leads, for example, to very dubious systems of performance bonus awards. Although I have always been (and still am) in favor of executives earning very well and even better, I have never had any problems with the issue, but what I would wish for is that executives are awarded a bonus for the right things. I am not in favor of this short-term orientation, but prefer a long-term focus ...

Maucher: ... yes, I'm all for long-term development.

Malik: I call it *enduring*: I have to take a decision so that the company can be successful in the long term; that the likelihood of this happening is maximized. Apart from that, the cause of the crisis, even though we are now entering the fourth year since the crisis began in 2008, is still not known, even today. I don't see this aspect addressed in the media and before that happens I don't think that the purely economic measures taken will really be successful. There weren't even any demands made on the banks to change their mode of operation; the one could have been linked to the other. Instead of that, people in finance basically continue in the same way as they did before the crisis. Yes, basically, it all boils down to the fact that politics wants to save the old system or is de facto saving it. However, we both seem to agree that ...

Maucher: Yes, indeed.

Malik: ... that it won't work that way. In addition, there is the fact that today's shareholder has an excellent return on his investment. However, I must point out that I am naturally in favor of shareholders being able to make good profits ...

Maucher: ... yes, but long-term – if I may just interrupt a minute – which is why I have always said that I am very much in favor of shareholders but not share traders.

Malik: That is precisely the point I want to make. Today's shareholder is not like the former owner, the former shareholder who thought long-term; who basically did not want to sell his shares but preferred to bequeath them; who consequently bought Nestlé or General Electric shares or blue chips that were in turn properly positioned in pension funds and so on. But today we are faced with something entirely different – that is reflected in the average holding period of shares which even in Germany has fallen below 12 months; we're faced with traders and share flippers ...

Maucher: Yes ...

Malik: ... or share turners – or whatever you like to call them – and thus the company is exposed to the random movements on the stock markets and to financial managers.

Maucher: Yes, that is almost the most important of all the points you've mentioned. It's clear that the stock market value depends on all kinds of factors: on these short-term traders, on pronouncements by financiers, on the press ...

Malik: True.

Maucher: ... in fact on all kinds of things. If I allow myself to be influenced by the entirely uncertain, queer shareholder value of the company, I'll make even more mistakes. Apart from the problem of short-term/long-term thinking, it is this modern mindset of shareholders, the stock markets, the financiers and so on that can distort the shareholder value completely – i. e. hike it up or force it down. But all of that has nothing to do with the progress of a company. That is a very important amendment. You know what I mean?

Farschtschian: Mr. Maucher, with regard to this you once said to analysts: »Hopefully we share more values than the share-value«.

Maucher: Yes, I did. Such comments always occur to me at the appropriate moment.

Maucher: And remember that that is at least as important as this share value.

Malik: Exactly! And that is why I have come to the conclusion that shareholder value as understood in this short-term and fashionably distorted way is hostile to real investments; because the stock market doesn't appreciate every investment – not even the right or long-term one. Besides, the stock market is also hostile to innovations because some innovations simply take longer than the exchange clientele's patience. Consequently, it is bad for the economy in many ways.

Maucher: In this context it is also important to understand that the moment a company makes a long-term investment or acquisition that will only be profitable after three years the price falls even though it is the best thing the company could do.

Malik: Precisely.

Maucher: It can be seen from that how opinions can distort the share value – contrary to the interests of the company. If I am guided by that, I will do everything wrong.

Malik: That's precisely how it is. In many instances, the stock market penalizes the right action and rewards the wrong one, which can prove to be a disaster – especially for large corporations. That's why I have come to believe that – to the best of my knowledge – we are dealing with the greatest misallocation of economic and social resources in history.

Maucher: Absolutely!

Malik: This is particularly evident in the example of the USA, which in a thoroughly tragic way has mismanaged the real economy and yet the financial economy is flourishing – and yet they are dealing in turn with a cancerous growth of credits that cannot be covered – in other words with debt problems. In the financial economy, this is aggravated by two further problems: on the one hand, where these resources are invested at present, they don't manage to create real values; they only create pseudo values because the whole thing rests on a mound of debt. As a result there is basically no value added – apart from commission payments and fees to lawyers and consultants. On the other hand, the most talented are not being utilized – when I think of all the university graduates ...

Maucher: That's another important point!

Malik: ... who then want to go to consulting companies or into investment banking, but not into real economic companies, as these are not necessarily to the fore.

Maucher: That is exactly the way I see it, too.

Malik: I think this trend really needs to be set right. What is absolutely crucial is an entirely realistic understanding of what the actual objective of a company is or what it is supposed to be. Naturally you are free to decide what the wrong, the right or the best star is for the company or the management to steer by; you have the freedom to decide what constitutes a healthy company. You ought to ask yourself what exactly a healthy, powerful company is; one that is viable in the long run, and that as a rule provides the shareholder with much higher – and at the same time healthy – profits, which are also invested sustainably.

Maucher: Precisely. That is my opinion, too.

Malik: And so I come to the conclusion that I have to give top priority to what makes the company healthy and not to some group of stakeholders. Otherwise, the company will become an object of prey for the changing balance of power among the shareholders. First of all there are the trade unions, the shareholders, perhaps the media or other groups that make leadership difficult. The executives need almost superhuman strength to tackle all these – and that is something that interests us especially Mr. Maucher –these trends of *zeitgeist*. For that reason I'll finish by saying that the best thing to do is to focus on the customer. Then of course everyone says: »Yes, but that is banal anyway! « – It may well be that from a logical point of view. It is trite but it hasn't been put into practice in the last 20 years. A company that has satisfied customers will always be able to provide shareholders with a decent share of the profits.

Maucher: Yes, that is clear enough because ultimately we are in a market economy and if we no longer have anyone who would like to have our things, then we will have lost from the outset.

Malik: Yes, of course. And that is an entirely different aspect.

Maucher: And secondly, we need to achieve unique selling points because we are competing with many others. What can we offer the customer that the others don't offer? If you don't know the score with regard to these two points, you won't be successful. In this context I have always said: You can do all kinds of things in the right way but keep three things in mind that in my opinion are vital: »Be close to your people«, »Be close to your product« and »Be close to your customers«. If you have understood that, it is impossible to do everything wrong.

Malik: Exactly! Even if you take that to heart, there are still some risks, but you won't actually make fundamental mistakes any more. That's the point and that also leads to a robust corporate management which isn't dominated by fashionable trends.

Farschtschian: What are the other consequences of shareholder value in your opinion?

Malik: It has led to – put the other way round, it has highlighted again – performance bonus awards systems that for their part are harmful to the company. The media was particularly quick to take this up and this has led to a renewed hostility towards the business world; people have always found it difficult to understand the business world but now we have these effects of envy etc. on top of that.

Maucher: Associated with the mentality of many managers, who gear their behavior to the annual bonus.

Malik: That's it exactly. Naturally this is linked to an almost open invitation to practice extraordinary bookkeeping in order to change the figures. This has been recognized meanwhile and has been contained somewhat; but cases like *Enron* and the like are still remembered or at least they ought to be remembered. As I have also ascertained time and again, shareholder value in this context also results in a certain type of person taking over the management of a company who would hardly have stood a chance 20 years ago. Good old Peter Drucker – of whom we both think very highly, Mr. Maucher – said that he always sold his shares in a company if the Chief Financial Officer became CEO. That is not intended as a criticism of CFOs because naturally we have need of them. Moreover, I would like to point out something where, in my opinion, shareholder value definitely has a positive effect. CFOs need to act the way they do but if they have unlimited power as CEOs, things do not work well as a rule. Shareholder Value has definitely led to the fact that one has to submit to financial discipline – and that is something very positive.

Maucher: And when stakeholder theories gained the upper hand, I said: »Do me a favor. Please, don't forget the shareholder! «

Malik: ... and then something really new was discovered in finance: key indicators and so on. That is an advantage but as a management principle, the shareholder value principle is dangerously misleading.

Maucher: Yes, I have often said that when a controller comes, he will certainly rescue the company and it will survive for another 3 months. After that, however, it is all the more certain that he will cause a disaster simply because he gives no thought whatsoever to the long term and cuts off all the investments that go towards the future.

Malik: Precisely.

Farschtschian: Mr. Maucher, how did you deal with the subject of bonuses at Nestlé?

Maucher: In my day, I introduced a bonus system at Nestlé that was geared to the annual profit, provided this was not corrected by measures that were long term. If anyone only made the annual profit by cutting advertising by a million or by altering things with extraordinary bookkeeping, than I said that both had to be corrected. That way I prevented them from adopting measures to achieve their annual profit for that would have been damaging in the long term.

Farschtschian: Many companies do not take this into consideration.

Maucher: Precisely. The whole business is exacerbated by the fact that there is a frequent change in leadership nowadays. If people are only there for two or three years, they do all these things in the short term so that they can still leave as heroes. They don't keep an eye on the long term to the same extent as someone who says: »I'm in the company and I'll be here for the next 20 years« or »I'm one of the family that has owned the company for three generations; let's see to it that it will be in our possession for the next five generations.« That means that these things you have mentioned are only aggravated by the attitude of the personnel or by executives changing jobs after a very short time.

Malik: That's it exactly, and that way one of the most crucial regulatory measures is restricted, namely that I as an executive have to weigh up the impact of my own decisions ...

Maucher: ... then I'm up and away ...

Malik: ... then I'm up and away, as you say. I can harm the company profoundly; after that I disappear and have even been given a golden handshake. Such a practice doesn't only corrupt these persons; it corrupts their employees, too.

Maucher: That's absolutely clear.

Malik: And it has an enormously harmful impact on the workforce; on all those who are excluded from these bonuses. In this respect I experience considerable agony, loss of trust, doubts, despondency, and even aggression towards executives. And then, when these people are needed because we have to be more productive, it is very difficult to achieve a good corporate culture again.

Maucher: Yes, these are all extremely important points that we are discussing. Moreover, I haven't addressed the subject with this precision or in this context, not even in my book.

Malik: This whole shareholder value principle and its impact give the media and people with their ideologies a lever with which they can moralize over executives.

Maucher: That, too, is an important point ...

Malik: ... and proceed with a moralistic cudgel.

The importance of long-term corporate governance

Farschtschian: The implications of shareholder value bring us to my second question. We have seen from your remarks that shareholder value – due also to pressure from the stock market and so on – frequently leads to short-term action. Moreover, your publications, Mr. Maucher, show that it is really the task of the Supervisory Board to introduce long-term aspects of trust and confidence. It would be interesting if both of you, as a lighthouse for sailors in the storm raging in the current economic environment, would express your views on the situation.

Maucher: I always say on the subject of corporate governance: One of the key factors in the functional specifications of the Supervisory Board is placing greater emphasis on long-term focus. As Supervisory Boards are somewhat further away from operative business and therefore cannot be totally corrupted, it is their task to say to the management now and again: »Wait a minute, does that work in the long term?« Although there are all sorts of things in the functional specifications of the Supervisory Board, this is not one of them – or at least I've never read it anywhere. In the current climate I consider it to be one of the major tasks. The thing is, it requires members of the Supervisory Board who are capable of doing it.

Farschtschian: You yourself thought long-term to such an extent that your results often didn't become visible until long after you had stopped being in charge. What needs to happen so that the Supervisory Board succeeds in thinking long-term and that the management accepts how important such long-term aspects are and acts accordingly?

Maucher: When the Supervisory Board is being selected, greater attention must be paid to personality. Frequently, there are a number of people who think that a Supervisory Board requires experts. First of all, I would like to have people who have a general understanding of what an institution is, who have an understanding of the economy, of society, and of general things without having necessarily studied business administration. Secondly, I would like to have people who are independent, who cannot be corrupted, and who are not »paid«. And thirdly, I would like to have people who have the necessary strength of character to intervene when things are no longer functioning in the management; people who stand out because of their independence, their strength of character and their general personality; and who have a general picture of what mankind is like. That is important! It goes without saying that the experts have to be within the company.

Malik: That's very important.

Maucher: I mean, there has always been a problem for example between industry and the banks. We always had close contacts to Credit Suisse and I said that that was generally a problem: on the one hand, I was one of their clients and therefore they were dependent on me; on the other hand, they kept tabs on me as head of the company. That is why they needed to deal with such matters very carefully indeed. I said that we definitely needed personalities who could cope with this problem because banking know-how is vital for the Supervisory Board, but a banking mentality is harmful. Do you know what I mean? Now, I was lucky I had Rainer Gut. There was no way anyone could corrupt him for he was his own man.

In my Board I had personalities who had the courage to say no when I threatened to get out of hand or began to talk rubbish or whatever; who had the guts and strength to act. Otherwise there is an even greater danger if you have such a powerful man at the top like I was.

Farschtschian: You showed greatness – although that is not in the books but I know it from our conversations – by restricting your power of your own accord so that when following a strategy which went beyond that which had been arranged with the Supervisory Board, you had to obtain approval from the Board. Even when you were making acquisitions exceeding a certain sum, you set yourself certain limits.

Maucher: We had our statute book, which stipulated what we could do. My Supervisory Board, however, knew two things: firstly, that nothing was kept hidden from them, simply because I would have found it embarrassing having to inform them of it – that was the first principle. The second was that anything that was relevant and of importance – whether it was in the statutes of our rules of procedure or not – had to be discussed with the Board. Thirdly it was clear that this Board had to consist of strong, independent people. That way the potential danger that ensues automatically with a strong man at the top was minimized. That was everything as far as the Supervisory Board was concerned.

There was another thing I made clear: If it comes down to one person such as me, when someone is both CEO and Chairman at the same time – which is what I was for seven years – then arrangements needed to be made so that there was someone capable of stepping in immediately if necessary.

Farschtschian: You're talking about planning for a successor ...

Maucher: It is crucial to have someone there who can – should one die in an accident – take over immediately. Every year, I gave the Board of Directors an envelope which contained the name of my potential successor should anything unforeseen happen to me. You can't endanger a company; you can't leave things to whether you have a heart attack or not. I always considered the subject of »the powerful man at the top and a safe structure« as being very important.

Farschtschian: Professor Malik, do you share this opinion?

Malik: Yes, I agree with the criteria for the Supervisory Board you have just stated. In the final analysis, I believe that I had the courage to limit it to three major things and you have already mentioned these: firstly, general experience of life including experience of the business world, combined with a broad minded view of the world hopefully underpinned by knowledge of history; and secondly, independence which you also stressed. I regard these as fundamental criteria which are absolutely indispensible. If these are met, there are still further skills that are highly desirable.

If, as you did at Nestlé, you know how to win personalities like Mr. Gut, who was able to withstand and master the potential conflict of interest supremely well, kept quiet at the right moment when it was necessary and did not abuse his position to do business and so on, then that's marvelous. Unfortunately, you can't always rely on people being like that.

Maucher: That's true. That's why I mentioned this – the relation to the »banking industry « – as the most problematic point.

Malik: Yes, but of course it was clear that his huge experience and his outstanding knowledge of finance were important to Nestlé.

Maucher: He knew what he was talking about. Moreover he is a practicing Catholic; I mean that he has a philosophy in which many things just weren't possible. That it worked well is due to the fact that we both had a kind of – let's say – philosophy or strength of character. We took many crucial decisions without discussing them with numerous people. The point was: we were still able to look at ourselves in the mirror in the evening without blanching.

Do you know what I mean? We never kept anything secret. My Chairmanship of the Supervisory Board was paramount; I mean, the other members took part, but I kept them informed about everything. I told myself that even if it were embarrassing, I had to tell them otherwise I wouldn't be behaving correctly.

Malik: Precisely. I'd like to come back to that when we get on to the subject of the CEO, the »strong man« and so on, because as Mr. Farschtschian has already said, you did a lot of things, of course, that were not in the statutes but which resulted in the Board of Directors functioning properly; of its own accord...

Maucher: Yes, that's true.

Malik: There is one point I would like to add primarily to what you said about members of the Board of Directors and that is the aspect of »knowledge«. It is crucial to have the right knowledge about the fundamentals of corporate management; this is in line with my observation that the less someone understands about what prerequisite has to be fulfilled to generate a profit the more he clings to the profit itself because in that case he can at least write down a figure...

Maucher: That's evident, of course.

Malik: ... that is quantified, that is something he can understand. I have experienced this in many such committees. In this respect, there is an enormous lack of knowledge with the result that there is also an enormous lack of consensus: What are we actually talking about when we talk about strategy? If everyone – and I mean everyone – knows what is meant exactly, working together is of course wonderful. But frequently we have, for example, ten people with ten different opinions on strategy. »What are the really important factors?« is one question. I suppose you can't expect anything else with that kind of people?

Maucher: Yes, I mean that doesn't apply to every member but the majority needs to have the necessary knowledge. There are always some aspects that for political reasons are included in a Supervisory Board: I would like to have a woman, I would like to have someone from Latin America and so on. But I need at least half of them with the necessary knowledge so that they understand what they are talking about, don't I?

Malik: Quite. Six persons of quality are needed for Supervisory Boards, even if they are not experts in the industry – and I fully agree with you that it is not specialists that are required because these are already in the company. These six are very valuable and among themselves also have an impact on the performance bonus awards: you need to know something about the market position, about quality, about the product – what you said; you need to have a minimum knowledge of pricing policy, the competitive climate and the sales situation of a company. I would simply summarize it as »market position«. A second thing which all too often does not receive enough attention in a company is innovation. This can't be completely quantified; that requires considerable powers of judgment – something which I think is vital. Moreover, I would like to add one more skill: the ability to form an opinion where it is not possible to quantify anymore and yet where action is needed; but this aspect results from the points you have already mentioned.

Maucher: You mean, where you know that despite good profits there is danger for the company?

Malik: Precisely. And of course productivity is also vital. As a rule, every company can improve – and needs to do so every day. Furthermore, it is important that the company attracts the right people – i. e. the issues relating to human resources. Then, of course, you have cash flow and liquidity also, and profitability. Currently, people have to learn again that under some circumstances liquidity can be much more important than profitability because you are forced out of the market if this is no longer guaranteed. For that reason, I think that these first four points are crucial if there is to be a common basis for language and understanding.

Maucher: Well, yes. One point I would like to add is the assessment of the risks with which a company operates. High-risk policy consists in seeing how much equity you can operate with, how much leverage etc.

Farschtschian: ... The Americans frequently differ there ...

Maucher: I always said at Nestlé: We'll never do what the Americans do. In the long term we want to be on the safe side. I made the principle clear that in the first place, leverage should only amount to half of the equity and secondly, only if we were generating a good cash flow.

Malik: That's that way it should be.

Maucher: And as far as high-risk policy is concerned I always said, too, that I would not endanger the company because of an acquisition. However, I could also afford to run a risk because I knew that Nestlé would not go bust because of it. However, if I am a small and medium-size company and am entirely dependent on that, I have to think differently. That is one of the advantages of a large corporation. The danger in a large corporation is that losses can be continually covered by other profits and no one notices.

Malik: Yes. And this financial discipline is regarded as being terribly conservative by the so-called modern business education school of thought, the business schools....

Maucher: Yes, »leverage« was the word you used, wasn't it?

Malik: ... then they tell you how much return on investment you've turned your back on. But you can see that all the companies that have been really successful in the long term never took risks which could have finished them off.

Maucher: Quite.

Malik: If necessary, you have to be able to write off an investment without the company going under. Those are principles that young people are hardly taught nowadays.

A strong CEO in power – and alternatives

Farschtschian: I think that this is a good place to move on to my next question. You are of the opinion that a »strong man« is needed. Now, in your case, of course, it always worked well because you thought in terms of the company – in other words: long-term. Unfortunately the number of Mauchers in the world is very limited, and it could be argued that the position of CEO is too important to be filled by only one person – if you don't have the right man, someone with the attributes of a Mr. Maucher –, and that it would be a correspondingly good alternative to place the power of the CEO in several hands. Your opinions on that would be an interesting subject for the readers.

Maucher: Yes, by all means; it is very interesting. Well, I can understand such an opinion quite easily because a company can be better safeguarded that way; there are fewer risks taken, and the imponderables with some crackpots etc. are reduced. Would you agree that seen that way it is a good strategy to gain more safety and to be able to integrate other thoughts and ideas which an absolute ruler won't be able to do? After all, no one can do everything. And the risk is whether you get the man who from his character, his personality, his knowledge and his openness to dialogue has the strength to do everything. Anyway, I think – and I am proof – that my system is better for the following reason: today we large corporations are faced with fierce competition. Let's assume I had introduced such a leadership structure at Nestlé – and that would have been second-best –, they would not have done anything stupid, they would have optimized and operated properly. If there had been someone like Maucher at Unilever for 20 years, then you would have seen that this man would have overtaken me after 20 years because he would have added that extra that I with my moderate structure would not have been able to achieve. And we did actually have this situation; I mean, when I took over Nestlé, our sales only amounted to 70 percent of what Unilever was generating; and when I stepped down, we had 30 percent more even though we had the same products; our profits were higher even though Unilever was always decently managed. That means that the extra from Maucher, an extra that could only be achieved via this structure, produced this result.

But I don't really have a solution because as you rightly say: »Yes, I have to have a person like this Maucher, for goodness sake! Surely among around 500 million Europeans there must be 500 who have the same talents, this combination of talents, to be able to run such companies«. I mean, Ford could never have arisen without Ford, General Electric couldn't have done it without Welch and Nestlé wouldn't have made it without Maucher. All of it might not have been possible to such extent if the structure had been different.

On the other hand, like you, Professor Malik, I would recommend most corporations not to run such a high risk with such a guy. Probably I would come to the conclusion and say: »Choose a strong man, give him a lot of power and plenty of opportunities to really exercise his talents but surround him with strict controls from an independent committee«. Action is needed the moment he shows any weakness. That's the way I always did it in my case. They didn't need to act in the end because I remained sensible.

Malik: Apparently we agree. However, I would like to express my respect for performances like yours; there are many examples where powerful characters in a company have indeed built it up into international companies by dint of their own strength because they also had staying power and powers of persuasion. We only need to think of Daimler, or Benz and many other founders. Whether in America, Japan or here in Germany, it was only with such personalities that these great companies could develop. On the other hand, it has to be said that they were controlled not by a Board but by their own success. That means....

Maucher: ... the market is always a good control.

Malik: ... right! Some failed and many went under: those who succeeded did an excellent job. When we see what is happening in our modern joint stock corporations, I agree with you absolutely and am convinced that if a company has a strong man of your caliber, he will initiate a glorious phase in the company and the company will flourish. And we are also almost in agreement when it comes to the opposite situation – I mean those executives, who are autocratic etc.; who don't have the necessary character; who lose all sense of proportion and within a short time can drag the company into a threatening situation. But it is possible to imagine some accompanying measures – some of them were de facto fulfilled by you Mr. Maucher. For example, you preferred executives who came from within the company.

Farschtschian: And who were tried and tested accordingly over many years; whose character and conduct– even under difficult circumstances – are known.

Maucher: Precisely.

Malik: Shareholder value and all these other things, the predominantly Anglo-Saxon kind of leadership, have meant that CEOs have come as lateral hires from somewhere outside. Germany also has some examples of its own – when someone comes from the car industry and is suddenly to take charge of a retail enterprise that works entirely differently. You know that can be very dangerous. These people are only there for a short time and within a period of three years you can naturally make enough wrong decisions to bring a company to the brink of ruin.

Maucher: I think that is a very valid point. If I have been able to observe someone in my company for 30 years, I know that he presents no danger when it comes to certain things.

Malik: Well, your human resources policy at the top didn't consist of getting executive search to find staff for you who ...

Maucher: Certainly not!

Malik: ... were outstanding and frequently also tried bluffing it. You tried and tested people for 30 years; that's what I have gathered from your human resources policy. In such cases there isn't much that will escape you. Nevertheless, there's always someone ...

Maucher: There can always be someone suffering from midlife crisis who gets up to some nonsense or other ...

Malik: ... goes mad, you mean? Yes, there is.

Maucher: ... but the danger is not so great.

Malik: That's it exactly. And I believe that's very important. The second thing I gathered from your publications is that you – as Mr. Farschtschian has already said – of your own accord and on your own initiative – subjected yourself to being monitored.

Maucher: Yes, that's correct.

Malik: Because on the one hand, you told yourself that alone you wouldn't always reach the best decisions and therefore it was more sensible to take decisions after discussing matters with others.

Maucher: Precisely!

Malik: Competent and independent people, who couldn't be influenced with payment, but who were really independent and strong enough to express their own opinions. You provided for your own successor in case anything unforeseen happened to you. You displayed – and I have to say this with the greatest of respect – almost superhuman candor and honesty. The temptation to hide something when things aren't going so well ...

Maucher: ... is great.

Malik: Yes, naturally it's enormous. In such a case, you also put yourself into the hands of those colleagues from the Board of Directors who can make use of it ...

Maucher: ... I lose trust. If they find out, I lose trust.

Malik: That's just it.

Farschtschian: Mr. Malik, it would be interesting in view of what has been discussed if you could tell us how you see the CEO principle.

Malik: When all these things merge, then the CEO principle in the form of one personality at the head of the company, a »strong man« – or a woman, too – is naturally the best of all. History has shown that quite unequivocally. And I believe that if you have these accompanying measures and stick to these principles, your wish might be fulfilled that among 500 million people enough executives can be found who correspond to the requirements. But if we rely on headhunting, lateral hires and this whole CEO carrousel that then arises, the danger for a large corporation is very, very large indeed.

Only if the entrepreneur has to assume liability with his assets, is he sufficiently under control because he has to accept liability for his own mistakes, too. And in that case one man in charge can also work well but obviously that won't work in big companies any more.

Maucher: That's it exactly.

Malik: It's interesting to see that in private banks only one person can be in charge and this person again operates as a personally liable shareholder (general partner). Or at Henkel, the German company, I think, it was like that for a while, too – but I'm not sure how it works today. On the other hand, that might restrict innovation in a company because the liability can be huge.

I'm very much in favor of the CEO principle that you also stated: that the company must be able to act speedily; it must be able to take forceful action and it must be able to act in the right way. If something is discussed in a democratic way but discussed to death and takes ages, competition is naturally faster. You are absolutely right.

Maucher: That's the way it is and then someone is going to be faster, of course.

Malik: Only the question arises as to whether and under what circumstances this principle can be incorporated in one and the same person or not? That is the decisive question. If the conditions we discussed just now are met, that is most certainly the best way. If for a number of reasons (considerations pertaining to the family or some such) these cannot be met, then I think that those CEOs coming from outside are particularly dangerous. Of course, things can work out well, too; that can't be ruled out. It becomes particularly difficult if the company is just entering an entirely new phase of development; when for example the technology needs to be changed. Anyone who has grown up in the photography business with analogue technology is unlikely to have a thorough command of digital technology. Then you have to start from inside the company or you need to establish a second company quasi alongside.

Maucher: Yes, I can't continue to run things with him; that's perfectly clear.

Malik: You also possessed the wisdom and the strength to gear the company, from the point of view of the business divisions, towards a corporate mission, branding policy and all those other things – you were very close to the business. You once told me that you spent 60 percent plus out in the market place. I would like to come back to that; not running a company via staff organizations means that you were basically – if you like – Mr. Nestlé, weren't you?

Maucher: Yes, I was.

Malik: And those are preconditions that cannot be fulfilled in today's top management without any further ado, I take it.

Maucher: That's correct.

Malik: Especially as executives move in other spheres, far from reality!

Maucher: But as I remarked, everything is exactly as we have said. They say that as an old man you ought not to always use the following expression, but I am going to use it nevertheless – the older I get the more I become convinced that even though professional knowledge is important, the decisive attributes of a leader are strength of character and personality. Everything else can be obtained on the market, but that is what is wrong. The headhunters only look at their checklists.

Malik: That's true.

Maucher: And that's exactly what it is: he mustn't lose all sense of proportion; he needs to keep both feet firmly on the ground, remain decent and display character in difficult situations. The latter is the rarest but the key attribute that he needs at the top.

Malik: Correct. And as that is so important, the question arises which methods will help us to recognize these attributes early enough, soundly enough and long enough. That is when the principle that you had at Nestlé comes into effect – I don't know whether it had existed beforehand or not or whether you introduced it. I'm referring to the long, long period of service in one company, which was frequently regarded as old-fashioned. Moving up the career ladder within one company was regarded in a negative light. But I think it is extremely important to test people, to be able to entrust them with more and more significant task. As far as I am aware, that is what you did and – basically we have already discussed it – you had a way of dealing with colleagues on the Board of Directors that prevented any intrigues arising.

Maucher: Yes, that's right.

Farschtschian: Perhaps I might add here, that on the occasion of our previous talks I met and talked with most of the Board members – e.g. Mr. de Weck, Mr. Kalbermatten or Fritz Gerber – and all of them said: »Maucher always kept us informed. We always knew what he was doing and everything he did made sense and was right«.

Maucher: Yes ... and there's something else. I made it easy for the Board of Directors to dismiss me. I said: »We'll set up the Board every year and I was always elected for one year only«.

Farschtschian: You didn't have a contract either...

Maucher: They approached me and asked: »What kind of contract do you want? « I replied: »I don't want any. We'll set up the Board every year. I'll be elected for a year and after a year you are entirely free to get rid of me without any legal problems or to change the entire system; but take careful note: in the year for which you have elected me it is I who is in charge«.

Malik: That is interesting. Did all the directors only hold their positions for one year?

Maucher: Yes, they did.

Malik: Right from the very beginning?

Maucher: It applied to everybody: the Chairman, the committees etc. We were set up every year.

Malik: But the election itself was only for ...?

Maucher: No, at that time the election was valid for five years.

Malik: Exactly.

Maucher: And my successor very rightly shortened it to three years ...

Malik: Precisely!

Maucher: ... so that he could be free somewhat earlier. But it used to be for five years.

Malik: I came to similar conclusions without knowing that: five years are too long.

Maucher: Yes, they are.

Malik: It isn't possible to part with someone on the Board of Directors if they don't prove their worth. Three years are okay. It is easy to solve the problem by not re-electing someone. But three years are needed for someone to familiarize himself with a company as complex as this. I think that what is disastrous -and this has become very popular – is that someone is only elected at the shareholders' meeting or the annual general meeting for one year only.

Maucher: That's true.

Malik: How can I learn the ropes at a company like Nestlé?

Maucher: The annual general meetings are given rights and responsibility which they cannot assume.

Malik: That's true! Being an elected representative for five years is too long, three years is okay but one year is not long enough. But I think being set up every year is of course a brilliant twin-solution, so to speak.

Maucher: It was I who introduced that idea. That way people were free and so was I.

Malik: Precisely. That was good. Only we cannot find such a solution in the Swiss Stock Corporation Act, for example. The legislators could incorporate it ...

Maucher: Of course, they could.

Malik: Of course, I would have expected Mr. Böckli and other Crown Jurists in matters of German and Swiss corporate law to propose such solutions. If it had been obligatory under law, much of what happened, especially at the beginning of the 2000s, wouldn't have been possible.

Maucher: I think so, too. That's the way it is. By the way, Swiss law as opposed to German law where everything is signed and sealed has one disadvantage: things can be treated very slovenly. However, it does have one advantage: things can be treated flexibly according to the person and the situation. I prefer Swiss legislation as long as the people who do it do so transparently.

Malik: Right.

Maucher: If I leave things open so that they can lead to intrigues or jockeying for power because they have not been regulated clearly by the law, I'll have problems. But where exactly is the competence of the Board of Directors if I move transparently within my own rules of procedure? Where is the competence of the CEO, the Chairman and so on? If I regulate that transparently, then I can regulate it according to the people involved.

Malik: Quite. It depends exactly on such accompanying rules that were valid for you. It was for that reason that I emphasized German legislation more strongly than you did because it is two-tiered.

Maucher: And because it is automatically provided for.

Malik: Correct. That means that no one can become an executive who at the same time controls himself. He has to submit to a control – and you mentioned previously, a brutal control – and yet the members of Supervisory Boards in Germany are good people. I agree with you entirely that there is one disadvantage in this strict, inflexible line where it is impossible to enlarge upon the strengths of personalities any more. And that is why it is in principle best to have a combination of the two systems. At Nestlé, you had de facto a two-tiered system, by dint of the fact that you subjected yourself to these rules. That way they could enlarge on your strengths – that is, you could enlarge superbly on the strengths of the others. That is the advantage of Swiss law.

Maucher: Yes, it is.

Effective management by Board meetings

Farschtschian: How long did a typical meeting of the Board of Directors last? Apparently they started the evening before and then...?

Maucher: Three and a half hours.

Malik: But if you include the journey to the meeting the evening before?

Maucher: With the journey there. Well, they had already read the documents. It wasn't unusual for those already there to sit together in the evening. The meeting didn't start until ten o'clock and lasted until one o'clock or half past one. Next morning they read again for a couple of hours and were able to talk to colleagues. They were able to walk around if they wanted to see a particular person. They appreciated that.

Malik: Well, that's one way of looking at it. I would see it differently: basically it lasted one and a half days ...

Maucher: Exactly.

Malik: ... for they had plenty of opportunity on the evening before to meet and swap ideas.

Maucher: But we only met three times, plus the annual general meeting. And of course the committee met once a month. We swapped ideas quite often.

Malik: And how long did a committee meeting last?

Maucher: In principle about one and a half days, too. But in that case they were all there. Someone wanted to have a word with the Head of Finance again (»I didn't understand page 17 « and so on), wanted to know more about product management, about the new products or such things. I said: »Just go and ask! We have nothing to hide«.

Malik: So the actual meeting from the reading of the minutes to the end of the meeting lasted three and a half to four hours perhaps?

Maucher: That's right; because I said that things had to be wound up speedily and the meeting shouldn't turn into a talking shop.

Malik: Precisely. But actually dealing with the subject matter and the opportunity to swap opinions...

Maucher: ... they had the opportunity during the day. At least!

Malik: ... which was of course much longer than is usually the case. And if you take a closer look at Supervisory Board meetings, they are so stilted that a real discussion is hardly possible.

Maucher: That's true.

Malik: No one really knows what the documents are about ... and I've just thought of something else: It would interest me to know whether any of the executives were present at your meetings?

Maucher: Well all the General Directors were present at the meetings of the Board of Directors.

Malik: Do you see? Of course that's another point, too.

Malik: Yes, that way you, as the strong man, created a strong basis you could rely on.

Maucher: But you know, strong people are not fearful types.

Malik: That's true.

Maucher: They don't have all these worries.

Malik: That's it precisely. Therefore I can conclude from what you have said that you never had the situation that a meeting of the Board of Directors turned into ostracizing the executives, who ended up in the dock, so to speak.

Maucher: No, that never happened.

Malik: I have experienced it again and again that members of the Management Board start to cover themselves, because they know exactly that one of them will be nagged »about this or that« and someone else will want to know why costs have risen by 0.5 percent and so on.

Maucher: But we had the opportunity to discuss some things without the General Directors being present. That meant that, when there was talk of the General Directors or nominations, for example, the General Directors were not present.

Malik: Of course. How large was your Board of Directors?

Maucher: Twelve or thirteen people.

Malik: That was good. Then that meant that de facto you had this two-tier system with the continuous CEO solution.

Maucher: At Nestlé it was the Board Committee that was de facto the supreme body.

Malik: And how many were in it?

Maucher: There were five including me – four or five.

Malik: And they met every month?

Maucher: We met every month. In addition, we talked to each other on the phone. They worked very closely with the company.

Farschtschian: When I talked with members of the Board, it was mentioned that you never had a hidden agenda, and that as the Board of Directors they could depend on Maucher telling them about it if anything did go wrong; they could rely on him informing them in good time.

Maucher: And that was something they understood really quickly. After all, I did it for 20 years. They knew: » Maucher doesn't cheat on us«. It didn't take them long to catch on to that fact and that was why they trusted me a lot.

Malik: On how many Boards of Directors or similar bodies did you have a seat during your active service?

Maucher: Two at the most. I was mainly on the Board of Credit Suisse but I was on the Board of ABB for a long time, because Wallenberg and De Pury invited me to join them. They wanted to have a sensible man on the Swiss side together with the Swedes. Apart from that, I was only on internal Boards. It was only when I turned 65 that I was open to doing other things. In Germany I was on the Board at Bayer and a few other similar companies. And the moment I had organized everything for a successor and I could wind down a little, I became Chairman of ICC in Paris and Chairman of the European Round Table of Entrepreneurs. Naturally these were major political positions, where I had contact to the whole world and to a great many people.

I wanted to make such activities dependent on how much I could delegate internally. Consequently, I didn't do so until the last phase of my career.

Malik: Precisely. And in the really most active phase you adhered to the principle, which was later widely debated and highly controversial, of having few external mandates – in your usual disciplined manner.

Maucher: I had very few. I always told our own people and that included the general delegates that I wanted them to have two or three mandates, but not more than that. I wanted them to concentrate on business but to hear something else now and again.

Malik: Absolutely right!

Maucher: Actually that was always my principle; that my people were involved in a few other things so that they heard something else, but otherwise they concentrated on their own business.

Malik: Fine. Under the circumstances, it can be said that it all boils down to the fact that the solution that this presents can be derived to a certain extent from what you practiced and from your principles. Naturally it isn't easy to persevere with this solution in a company to the very end but practicing corporate management at that level is not quite so self-evident either.

Maucher: That's true. I always point out there is a German word that – even though the English language is normally very practical for expressing everything – is much more precise and apt: it's the word »*Führungskunst* (the fine art of leadership) «.

Malik: You're quite right.

Maucher: Well, basically it's all very simple. But you only have to think and you have to have the strength to persevere. (Laughing)

Malik: Yes, if you have thought it through properly and can underpin it with the necessary experience, too, it is ultimately easy; that's true.

CEO and Chairman – One and the same person

Farschtschian: There is just one more question on this topic to actually conclude the discussion on this subject. Mr. Maucher, you combined the offices of CEO and Chairman for a long time and then you acted only as Chairman. And both of you, Mr. Maucher and Mr. Malik, are of the opinion that every company has to decide for itself which form they need at the present time. Mr. Maucher, when you became Chairman, you stopped making active contacts and left these to the CEO. Were there areas nevertheless where you still made contacts because these were personal contacts, whether it was to a Minister in Asia or …? It would be interesting to know…

Maucher: There were some principles which I adhered to and told myself: »I won't take part in that any more«. I didn't attend any more management conferences, nor did I attend the markets in terms of corporate management. That was in Nestlé's interest, and of course my successor knew all about that.

We arranged that all very transparently. It was vital that the people internally didn't think: »I'll go to his office now«; that they understood who was in charge of what. Before stepping down completely, I was Active Chairman for two or three years or a mixture of normal Chairman and a closer companion of the CEO. Then Gut became my successor and he was a normal Chairman of the Board of Directors – i. e. in our sense, a normal Chairman of the Board of Directors. We arranged things very transparently so that there were absolutely no difficulties.

My successors did exactly the same. Internally there were and are absolutely no problems. That is very important in such cases. On balance, I tend to think it is better to keep the two offices separate but admittedly a different solution should not be ruled out. But in principle it is right to appoint two people to the office of Chairman of the Board of Directors and to the position of CEO. That provides a bit more security and thus comes closer to the German system because the CEO is the Chairman so to speak who has been entrusted with many things by the Board of Directors.

Farschtschian: I think that concludes our discussion of the first subject area and now we can deal with the topic of »Effective Management and Daily Management Routine«.

Maucher: Very well. But there is still something I would like to add. What really gives me pleasure, I must say, is that I still know so many people who worked with me. When it's their birthday, I write them a letter which pleases them immensely. And what pleases me most is what many of them write; they write: »Do you know, apart from all the things you did, you told me that and that at

the time, and I'm truly grateful to you for that today«. Or: »You were one of the few people who listened to us«.

Farschtschian: At the time when I was doing my research on Nestlé, the employees said: »From the very first week when Maucher took over the reins, the culture changed to the very core«. The people noticed that there was now someone new and that he did things differently.

Maucher: Yes, there was a lot to be done with regards to the Nestlé culture. Someone had to come and mobilize the people again; had to articulate what was important and to set an example as to what the culture was all about. That was important to the people. But I always say: »I did the obvious«. I didn't do anything out of the ordinary.

Malik: Well, the obvious is not that obvious. That's the point. I've always wondered why something isn't actually obvious and have come to the conclusion that it is the fault of the way some of our universities and most of our business schools function; and also that our teaching staff has so little contact to the realities in the business world: it prefers to send questionnaires around the world to find out how companies function instead of experiencing it first-hand.

Maucher: True, but another question is also how far we were formed and influenced by our youth. I grew up in a village with one thousand inhabitants. Everyone knew each other; we knew who had died and who had been born; we knew who was a scoundrel and who wasn't. We actually lived in a small microcosm of the world, with all its strengths and weaknesses. It wasn't possible to behave very badly without the whole village seeing it. So you learnt not to do certain things. I believe, therefore, that all this formed my character – independent of my genes and my parents who brought me up decently, but who allowed me freedom too and saw to it that – like them – I was a good pupil.

Malik: Yes, I believe that, too, and would apply that to myself as well. Moreover, a touch of the Alemannic mightn't be such a bad thing either.

Maucher: Precisely. That's it exactly.

Effective Management and Daily Management Routine

The importance of training and education and the selection of employees

Farschtschian: Let us begin with training and education, the topic which we had just started to discuss. How vital is a university education for good managers, Mr. Maucher?

Maucher: I would say that anyone who is suitable anyway will benefit a lot from it. At the same time we need to be careful; after all, there are people who pick up things elsewhere and who shouldn't be ruled out only because for some reason or other they didn't have the opportunity to attend university. There are always people – even if only a few – who stand out from the rest precisely because they acquired things in a different way and who can be used to very great effect. I personally benefited considerably from studying at university. Before that I served an apprenticeship. While I was studying I expanded my theoretical knowledge and knowledge in many other fields – that helped me a lot. But I had a lot of colleagues who did the same thing, but who didn't benefit from it.

Farschtschian: Mr. Malik has a very decided opinion about this, especially as far as the content of education programs (MBAs and so on) is concerned. Professor Malik, might I ask you to express your opinions on this and to sketch briefly what direction you think future generations of managers will take.

Malik: I think that at many universities and most business schools the theory that young people are taught is very one-sided, and besides it is taught very uncritically. Fundamentally, it is the Anglo-Saxon doctrine which has become dominant all over the world. Many conclude that because it has spread globally that it must be the best – because otherwise it wouldn't have spread so widely. But that is a fallacy. It only spread so quickly, because it was the only one that was immediately available in English when globalization set in and management, therefore, became more and more important in China, in India and all round the world.

Consequently, thinking is dominated by the doctrine of shareholder value which is very one-sided to say the least and is ultimately the wrong doctrine for managing a company. The company is misconceived as a machine for maximizing profits. That in turn leads to short-term orientation and shortsightedness. It also leads to a systematic misallocation of capital and other resources.

Moreover talk is one-sided and almost exclusively about large corporations – which is of course also important. On the other hand, there is very little talk about what is required for managing a family-owned company. From an operative point of view, these are two different worlds.

And then I miss, for example, the fact that other subjects like philosophy are no longer part of the syllabus. This lack is particularly evident in the fact that an ethic has to be artificially grafted on to the company even though this ought to be integrated.

Malik: Moreover, what is missing to a very large extent is knowledge of history – whether it is about the economy or the general history of the state or society – and culture misses out, too. Mr. Maucher, you talked of your musical bent. I consider such things to be particularly important especially in (high) executive positions.

In addition, most of the staff teaching our subject has very little practical experience and this is declining steadily due to university structures. Subjects have been turned into a science and have thus been deprived of common sense.

There is far too much mathematizing, where precisely the honing of the powers of judgment, knowledge of human nature and such things are of key importance in top positions. To the present day, it has never been possible to dress these in mathematical formulae and I doubt whether it ever will be possible.

In that respect or at least that is what I think, university education needs to be reappraised – especially because with the debt crisis, all the turbulences and ever-changing globalization, we are being faced with large and new challenges all the time. Many of the students at university each year are badly prepared to cope with these. On the other hand, I naturally hold out great hopes – and there are definite indications – that most of the younger executives can change their ideas and attitudes very quickly. That is more or less my opinion.

I think that a special danger lurks in the fads that keep cropping up and that seem to be more rampant in management than in most other subjects. If engineers and scientists decide to study for an MBA after their own sound education at university, they do in fact also learn useful things – like reading balance sheets, preparing controller reports etc. But in the same way, they uncritically latch on to all kinds of fads because they think that everything in an MBA program is of the same high standard as their own subjects and that these have been scrutinized critically, just like the knowledge that they learnt in their own university studies. But that is a dangerous misapprehension, which is rarely called into question due to their confidence in the alleged quality of the MBA. I think it is vital to stress the differences to earlier times without becoming nostalgic. Mr. Maucher, as you were educated in *Betriebswirtschaftslehre, the version of business economics in the German speaking countries*, would you agree with me that some of that education had better theories to offer than today?

Maucher: I agree, *Betriebswirtschaft* was more specific.

Important literature and authors

Farschtschian: You have just forestalled my next question which is: Which authors have influenced your character most and what would you recommend managers to read? Perhaps you would begin, Mr. Maucher: Who had the most formative influence on you? You read world literature consistently at an early age ...

Maucher: Do you mean specialist literature or business administration or generally?

Farschtschian: Generally; what exerted the greatest influence on you ...

Maucher: I was formed by many things. In my youth I read practically everything written in the period from the Middle Ages to Hesse. People who study business management should acquire some general knowledge of culture. The higher their position, the more they need to understand what makes the world go round because otherwise they could founder in their own sector. And the second thing that I think is vital is – and you mentioned it yourself – that we don't want bookkeepers as professors but people who somehow were compelled in the course of their lives to come into contact with business management. Some competition wouldn't come amiss either as there are professors who do not progress beyond their original level of knowledge and lag behind modern practice and development. They offer nothing new because they are not compelled to. Some extend their knowledge of their own accord because they are good people; others remain at a level of knowledge which has been overtaken by practice long since. Moreover, many German and Swiss universities have not adopted all this nonsense in its entirety; they have continued to teach the right things. Therefore: I would favor a university education – even though it is not a universal remedy but ultimately it is useful.

Malik: I would recommend executives to have a look at what Peter Drucker has written.

Maucher: Yes.

Malik: Drucker is a man, who says very many things in a very thorough way. After all he is the man who – as one of the very first – realized the significance of management for a modern society; that includes the significance of organizations, particularly large-scale enterprises, which became evident in his study of General Motors at the time. Therefore I can recommend anyone striving for a high office in business and in politics, too, to read selected works by Peter Drucker.

Maucher: That is right. I can only agree with that.

Malik: By the way, I found reading the biographies of great entrepreneurial characters very beneficial. Admittedly, you have to make a bit of a distinction: there are the glamorizing and idealizing publications, but there are also good ones like Churchill's for example. Then some history is important; you need to understand something of economic history.

Maucher: I think so, too.

Malik: About the rise and fall of empires and about nations. About corporations; there are a few very interesting things about the German entrepreneurial merchant dynasty of the Fuggers in the 15th and 16th century for example. Those are topics a knowledge of which can help, in a well-understood way, someone who wants to climb the career ladder. You could even go further and say that perhaps it is necessary to study Machiavelli to avoid doing many of the things he described. The history of the Italian city states, too – only that would be never-ending, and normally no one has that much time. But I would recommend reading a selection.

Discussion on working methods and effectiveness

Farschtschian: Well, thank you very much. Perhaps the next question can go to Mr. Maucher first: What made you effective as a person and as a leader during your years in power? To be more precise: I'm thinking of your working methods – the exact way you worked together with your secretaries' office, your leadership style, your work with personal staff and so on and so forth.

Maucher: Well, I have always worked a lot and I don't think you can achieve much without working hard. That is a simple matter of fact. The most important thing is what you do at the beginning; which priorities you set. There are three things that are vital when it comes to the things you deal with yourself. Firstly: You should never deal with anything that someone else can do just as well. Secondly: You should never only deal with things that are of great importance to the company. And thirdly: You can't determine priorities once and for all. There are some things you can determine for years because they are always important; and in other cases you need to be guided by the circumstances. Take my visits to other countries for example: I certainly visited major countries at least once a year. I visited the more minor countries once every three years and the other countries according to the problem that presented itself. When we went to a new country, when we had a new or special problem, I went myself no matter whether it was a major or minor country. Some principles are needed that are flexible enough to be adjusted to what is required. As far as my own staff was concerned, you know that I never had an assistant, but always delegated where possible. And if a problem applied to various areas, I put someone in charge of co-coordinating the problem with his colleagues.

Moreover, you need to be in good health and have good nerves. When I was on a business trip, I went to bed at eleven o'clock because anything that is discussed after eleven is a lot of nonsense anyway. Then I slept until seven the next morning and was totally fit again. Many people go out, amuse themselves – I never felt the need of that. I lived sensibly and moderately. And those are all things that, in the end, are relatively important. It was natural for me – or perhaps it was due to my genes – to be able to sleep on a plane; I had good nerves and I never felt under stress. These attributes are very important if you have a job like mine. What is particularly crucial is being interested not only in the problems you have to solve but being interested in people, too. Anyone who is not interested in people, who doesn't work with them, who doesn't listen to them, who doesn't lead them or convince them or who doesn't tell them anything – I believe that at some stage he will come to grief. Being aware of that is probably the most important of all.

Farschtschian: How did you stay physically fit?

Maucher: I didn't do anything. I mean, I lived sensibly; as a rule I did some exercises for five minutes every morning, to loosen up. I played golf. If I was at home, I had a swim (we have a swimming pool) and in winter I went skiing.

Malik: That was indeed living sensibly.

Maucher: Besides, I had nerves of steel so that I never felt stress or exhaustion. I think that was just the way it was.

Malik: It just came naturally?

Maucher: Naturally? Yes, that was it.

Malik: But perhaps a little of it was due to your working methods – the fact that you never really worked with personal staff in the closer sense.

Maucher: No, I didn't.

Malik: You worked directly with the line managers, if I understood correctly.

Maucher: Well, I didn't have a personal assistant; I only had a secretary and that was enough for me. And secondly, I only had personal staff to deal with specific tasks such as logistics, for example. But otherwise I had relatively few of those back-slapping fancy talkers. In cases of doubt, I always gave the line managers more opportunities and gave them preference. I did have a staff department consisting of real experts, who really did what the factories and countries needed.

Malik: But then it was they who also reported to you?

Maucher: I also delegated as much as possible to the divisions – if specific staff was involved as for example in finance. I had few higher-level staff. I even disbanded the planning departments because I said that the line managers had to do the planning and they only needed a qualified bookkeeper who laid down the entire system for everyone – what had to be included in the plan and so on. Otherwise I always compelled these people and not my staff to do the planning, because they were the ones in charge and therefore they needed to know what was going on. Moreover, there was staff that discovered mistakes in Germany or elsewhere and said: »There's something wrong: we'll have to intervene«. Whereupon I replied: »No, we have to give everyone a chance to improve and rectify things himself«. That is the easier way. You don't central-ize something because a few people have made mistakes. If necessary, you have to put someone who will make fewer mistakes into the job. And we have to accept a few mistakes as anyone involved in business can make a mistake anytime.

Farschtschian: And how did you deal with making use of consultants?

Maucher: Well, I was always of the opinion that the consultancy profession does have many sensible tasks because a consultant has to have certain skills and experience. Firstly, he usually has some training in analyzing methodolog-ical problems. Secondly, he has time which one's own people don't have – we pay for time after all. And thirdly, he is under pressure from the market; he has to produce success. This staff of consultants function all the better the clearer the tasks are that they are given; the more firmly you keep contact to them under your control so that they don't run riot; and the more you pay attention to not using them where a head of department wants to use the work of the staff to get one over on someone else. Such consultants are a sensible addi-tion to one's own firm if they are deployed sensibly and to the right extent so that they don't start to take over running the company. That is the way I always looked at it and practiced it.

Malik: Mr. Maucher, I would like to enlarge on a few apparently unimportant details about working methods and co-operation with the secretaries' office. What role did the computer have for you personally, in order to be effective?

Maucher: None at all.

Malik: None? Well what about letters? Did you dictate them?

Maucher: I dictated my letters or I told my secretary what I wanted in the letter so that she could write it herself. Besides, I said that I was a communicator and not a writer. That was why I only wrote those letters that I had to write myself. After all, I could dictate quickly. That was the way things were done in my day; I never started to type things myself. Of course some things are different today.

Malik: Yes, they often are. And what did you expect of your secretary? How long did you work with one and the same secretary? Was this working relationship of long standing?

Maucher: Very long-standing.

Maucher: Well, I never had a lot of change. I had the same secretary the whole time I was in Vevey, right up to the time when she had to retire, whereupon they sent me a new one from Germany. I told her to become familiar with Switzerland, learn a little of the language and then she would be useful if she had an office in Germany. Otherwise I had no one else.

Malik: Would you say that your secretary found you to be an agreeable boss?

Maucher: Yes, I really am.

Malik: Without moods and quirks? Is that something that never happened?

Maucher: No, a secretary had an easy time of it with me. I really am not a moody person, I'm not violent or anything. Secretaries enjoyed working for me and it wasn't difficult for them. I could explain what I wanted. They knew that jeans were not permitted in my office. If they couldn't accept that, they couldn't become my secretary. And that was the end of it.

Malik: But your secretary arranged all your travel itineraries, didn't she?

Maucher: Everything.

Malik: And your appointments.

Maucher: Everything.

Malik: You had a person who knew everything there was to know?

Maucher: She did everything.

Malik: A person entrusted with confidential information; a person in whom you had every confidence; a classical case?

Maucher: She did everything; all the correspondence; there was nothing she didn't do. She was the traditional executive secretary: discrete, educated and intelligent – and she had good relations to the establishment. She was very popular with everyone without fraternizing with them. I always had secretaries like that. In Germany I had one who had similar attributes. Admittedly, no two people are exactly the same. I still write to her on her birthday and she writes on mine.

Malik: Was your secretary available round the clock? Was that something that was required? After all, you worked in all the time zones.

Maucher: Actually, it wasn't necessary. And that was down to me. I said: »I don't want that; that can be arranged differently«. That's why I did not phone my secretary at four o'clock in the morning – and if I did, then it was because the establishment was virtually on fire. But as far as possible, I respected her leisure time. If I did need a secretary until ten o'clock in the evening, she stayed without any further ado because she knew that I wouldn't ask if it weren't absolutely necessary.

Malik: In the CEO's office there are many, dozens or even more on-going tasks that have to be scheduled etc. Did she do all that, too?

Maucher: My secretary had all the on-going tasks and was responsible for the appointments book.

Malik: Of course. And I assume you could place absolute reliance on your employees or the other line managers; I mean that they could be relied on to keep their appointments and that everything ran smoothly?

Maucher: Yes, I've got to admit that I really had no problems in that respect.

Malik: And what about your meetings? How often did these take place?

Maucher: Well, the first thing was that there should be as few as possible. I held meetings with the Management Board and the General Directors every other Monday as from 10 o'clock. And I was in favor of establishing a ruling that we generally – and that applied to other meetings, too – didn't meet before ten o'clock in the morning so that everyone had time to attPartend to personal reading matter between eight and ten o'clock; had time for interviews or individual talks or time to deal with other matters. Thus a certain discipline developed that wasn't perfect but functioned on the whole. That way we knew that we had certain times when there were no meetings.

Malik: And you chaired the meetings?

Maucher: Yes, I chaired the Board meetings.

Malik: And who prepared them? Did you prepare the minutes?

Maucher: We had a general secretary's office. Although the general secretary was not my assistant, he dealt with all the matters pertaining to the Board of Directors and all the matters that are done in the general secretary's office. He also prepared the Board meetings.

Malik: And took the minutes?

Maucher: And took the minutes.

Malik: And a rhetorical question about virtues such as punctuality: Did your meetings start punctually?

Maucher: Absolutely.

Malik: And finished punctually, too?

Maucher: Yes, of course. I think that in that respect I had learned considerable discipline, so it all worked relatively well.

Malik: And what about abroad where things are perhaps taken a little more easily than in Switzerland, which is only natural? But with you as Chairman of the Board of Directors and CEO, the people were there anyway, I assume.

Maucher: They were there. Besides, I always said I didn't want to spend hours reading charts. I read all the charts and documents on the plane so that my employees could expect me to be familiar with these when I arrived. I was interested in the following: Firstly, I wanted to have a personal report from the boss, describing the present situation as he saw it. Secondly, I wanted to see the management as well as one or two major customers. I also wanted to see the shops where our goods were being sold. I wanted to see the products, we were selling there, on the shelves; I wanted to see the advertising we had for the products and if possible I wanted to spend an evening or have a meal with people from society – for example with competitors or the Prime Minister or the like. When I had done that, I knew all I needed to know; I really knew everything.

Malik: You once told me on another occasion that Nestlé didn't have a company plane.

Maucher: No, we didn't.

Malik: Did you always take scheduled flights if possible?

Maucher: I held the view that we were modest, but we had style. That was an important principle. And I said that if I was flying to America, I would fly first-class with a normal airline. If I had to combine visits to three different places in Germany or visit Paris, Copenhagen and Vienna in the space of two days, I leased a plane. But that was mainly in Europe because if I had to visit three different places in two days then it was worth taking a private plane. But never once did I take a private plane to Tokyo or America.

Malik: Who accompanied you on such trips? Did your secretary go with you?

Maucher: No, never.

Malik: And who organized everything for you or dealt with writing documents on the spot when necessary?

Maucher: Well, when I flew to the markets, I always went with the relevant General Director, a member of the Board, because I didn't wish to take any

decisions without consulting him. And besides he provided me with all the relevant information during the trip and he got all the information he needed on the spot. That meant that I never flew to a country without having the relevant regional manager with me.

Malik: And then of course you could also make use of the infrastructure of the company on the spot, and had the necessary support and all that.

Maucher: Yes, immediately. Everything was in place. The degree of bribery in the respective country could be measured by whether it was possible to put me into a car and drive past all the checkpoints or whether you had to go through the system.

Malik: This quality, perhaps I could call it this down-to-earth approach, this pragmatism, this directness and lack of guile – there's no pomp or anything like that to it. Perhaps that's due to your education and growing up in a village. Learning working methods at university is pretty much non-existent nowadays.

Maucher: I didn't have any money. After graduating from high school I served an apprenticeship at the Nestlé factory. I stuck on stamps and repaired the authorized signatory's bike. After that I worked in Frankfurt; I studied for six years and worked full-time. You learn to rationalize, don't you?

Malik: Yes, indeed.

Maucher: To be able to survive you have to be in a position to do things effectively. That's the way you learn it.

Malik: And now to some things that are quite banal but which I have ascertained are by no means simply to be found in young people; which even tend to be a rarity: tidy e. g. perfect orthography, perfect punctuation, good German. You don't exactly have to be a writer. But you write your essays yourself, don't you?

Maucher: I learnt all those things at school.

The importance of PR and media activities

Farschtschian: With this in mind, did you have an active influence on PR activities at Nestlé?

Maucher: Nothing else is possible; so, yes I did. I gave a lot of interviews, held press conferences and worked closely with our chief PR and press officer. He was in my office frequently because he needed to know what was going on. He needed to be told where we were heading. That is even more important as far as my successor is concerned because it has become even more extreme. But I can tell you one thing: when I held my last press conference in Vevey at the end of my active service, the whole caboodle knew that this was indeed my last press conference. On the whole I got along well these people; the only one to almost have a heart attack nearly every time was my press officer; he always wanted to write elaborate statements for me and I told him that I didn't need all that. I only needed a small piece of paper with the major points on it; I didn't need anything else. He was always in a cold sweat, because I did that at eight o'clock in the morning and went into the press conference at nine. In the course of time he realized that everything would go off brilliantly. As a result, my press conferences were much more spontaneous than others' were. At my last press conference there was a man who ran the trade magazine ›Cash‹ for a while. He could be a bit aggressive at times, but I got along well with the press. At the end he stood up and said: »Colleagues, today we have experienced the last press conference by Mr. Maucher in Switzerland. Take careful note that we will never have any more press conferences in Switzerland like the ones we have had with him.« This man was in no way connected to the company but he felt that no one else would ever do it like Maucher. But I think that my way of spontaneously treating the press properly was appreciated by them in turn, because everywhere else they were treated to elaborate lectures.

Malik: What would still interest me is: in principle all the major departments naturally reported to you because you were the most senior boss. But you told me once – and I was most impressed – how you personally took care of the brand issue of Nestlé.

Maucher: Those are the major issues.

Malik: If I understood properly, it concerned the branding policy – i. e. it concerned which brands would remain autonomous.

Maucher: That is something you can't delegate. Those are major issues. Naturally in the course of time I initiated Mr. Brabeck, as head of Branding and Products, into such matters and we dealt with them together. If you operate in a brand name company, and you are concerned with how to treat brands, how to manage brands, which qualities to put into the brand, and which messages you need for the customers, then you cannot in principle delegate. When the fundamentals are in place, you can delegate tasks but not beforehand. That is one of the major assets we have.

Malik: Perhaps this does not have anything directly to do with working methods, but I have another question: How did things work with the retail trade, Mr. Maucher? The fact that Nestlé is so immensely strong in the brand sector has led me to ask this question – your strengths that are necessary with respect to the retail trade, the tremendously fierce price wars, and private labels and all the …

Maucher: Well, that is of course a topic that I only addressed from a policy point of view at Vevey. But when I was in charge in Germany, the power of the retail trade, the purchasing power of the retail trade, and how we dealt with it were of course extremely important. The same applied to how far we needed to allow ourselves to be blackmailed and how far we didn't need to do so. In principle two things are important: firstly, from a policy point of view, you need to have a cost structure so that you don't need to start with excessively high prices, because if the gap between you and the other cheap products becomes too large, you lose part of the market share. Cost competition is therefore an important aspect in this battle. Moreover, you need to strengthen the brands to such an extent that the trader cannot do without you; that if he doesn't stock your brands, he will lose sales. Those are two very important fundamentals. In addition, you should not harm the brand by manipulating the quality or adjusting the expenditure on advertising.

Secondly, building up relationships with customers is also important – both by your sales staff and you yourself. In Germany I knew personally the ten major retailers who generated 80 percent of turnover. I knew the families; I knew them all. I knew that if there was anything wrong with one of our firms, I could rely on them to phone me first before they made any disastrous decisions. »Maucher, there is something wrong; have a look and see«. And I expanded something that my predecessor in Germany had started: we organized a seminar for couples from Germany. We invited the eight or ten major retailers and their wives to spend eight days with us, and somewhere in Africa or elsewhere we discussed interesting topics with which they would never have been faced otherwise and which also interested their wives. I always participated and made it a rule that there should be no shop talk. I wanted to cultivate an occasion where we could develop our contacts to the people and where they would say how terrific it was that Nestlé did something like that. They really appreciated it; firstly, because their wives also got something out of it; and at the same time, they met their competitors completely informally. Besides, it was – excuse me for saying it – an honor for the people that I was present.

Malik: Very wise ...

Maucher: Apart from that, you need a sense of humor as a salesperson; you need to retain your dignity and be friendly. I have occasionally quoted the famous Chinese proverb: »If you cannot smile, you should not open a shop«.

Management style, motivation and applied leadership

Farschtschian: Perhaps I might take up this argument. You have said, and I quote, that the sales department does not constitute the whole firm but the whole firm should be a sales department. How can this be achieved?

Maucher: Well, I have to motivate and mobilize the whole place so that the employees say: »We want to be a good company. We want to make good products. We want to see to it that things go well in the company«. To achieve that, everyone – no matter what job he does – has to have some sort of interest in how things are going in the firm, and not just with regard to his specific job. That can only be obtained if you take part in management conference and work with the departments. Then the people say: »Yes, sir! Let's give it a go«. This kind of enthusiasm is crucial to the success of a firm.

Malik: I think that today it might be termed applied leadership. Would you also ...

Maucher: Yes, I would agree with that.

Malik: In this practical way.

Farschtschian: It also means a management style with which you can exert influence on the corporate culture.

Maucher: Yes, it does.

Farschtschian: Now we really have a topic that should certainly lead to an interesting discussion between the two of you: Mr. Maucher, you say that to be able to lead you need charisma, but Mr. Malik has criticized the word itself with regard to managers.

Maucher: Well, that is, of course, a wide topic. I think the reason for Mr. Malik tending to oppose charisma is the fact that, to start with, he thinks automatically of people like Hitler and other leaders with charisma, who in the course of history were responsible for the most terrible crimes. But charisma is a must for a good man of character and personality. If he has certain charismatic attributes, he is noticed as soon as he enters a room for example, or when he speaks to people they agree with him. Perhaps charisma isn't the right word; perhaps it might be better to say »strength of personality« or »the gift of persuasion«; »the warmth that you exude and that engenders liking«; »the confidence that you impart«. If it is that, you will achieve more than someone who comes in and says: »Firstly, secondly, thirdly«. There have been studies by psychologists where two people were asked to speak before students – you know the examples. The one held a brilliant, rational and first-class speech and the other talked a lot of nonsense, but he was charismatic. They all said that the second one was marvelous but not the first one. Those are quite simply things that happen in life. However that presents women with a certain problem because evolutionary-wise women have an entirely different task; they are of equal value but they are not equal. Frequently, a woman attracts particular attention when she enters a room and looks good; but it is not because of her charismatic personality. Compared with me she will always find it more difficult, because I, in the same way, can convince people spontaneously. She has an entirely different quality, which it might be better to call harmony. She has a feeling for things that is often missing in men. I don't mean that to be negative but this charisma and showing off that men have is important in leadership, whether we like it or not. As a rule, women do not have it to the same extent and are often put in the wrong pigeonholes even though they don't deserve it.

Farschtschian: Is that your opinion, too, Professor Malik even though you apply the definition somewhat more specifically.

Malik: It occurred to me that the term »charisma«, which used to be used in management studies, had ceased to exist for some time. Suddenly it has turned up again. Naturally I found that interesting in relation to my work. I realized that the concept had come over from America in a rather surprising and disturbingly naïve way, veiled in all the things that have ultimately happened in totalitarian systems, and I didn't and certainly don't want to aid and abet that sort of thing ...

Maucher: Precisely.

Malik: And then we are told we have to be able to mobilize people and fill them with enthusiasm and so on. So I asked the following question: »Where is the difference between the tempters and the genuine, true leaders who are needed so urgently today? « However, I do agree that if someone has charisma, it can help him enormously and that is naturally a tremendous advantage in some situations.

Maucher: ... That's the way of it. We need to distinguish between the good leaders and the pied pipers.

Malik: Correct. But how do I distinguish today between the leader and the tempter on the basis of the current kind of naïve, but no less dangerous leadership theories?

Maucher: True. That ought to be the issue.

Malik: Although you hardly dare to say it even now, it cannot be denied that Hitler knew how to mobilize the masses and create enthusiasm. You only need to look at those party congresses in the 1930s; in most cases, they still send a shiver up your spine. You see that perfect organization and tremendous discipline and so on. After all, it led to untold deaths ultimately.

Maucher: And that is exactly why we need to be able to tell the difference.

Malik: And it is this distinction which I find is missing in almost all leadership theories of today. I mean, what I wished for was to have a theory of personality and a leadership theory which enables me to distinguish clearly between all the Hitlers, Stalins and Maos on the one hand and a Churchill for example or – if you take business– you yourself on the other hand.

Maucher: Churchill is a good example.

Malik: This distinction simply has to be possible.

Maucher: And without the dangers.

Malik: You have charm that is apparently inherent; you speak simply, but you can speak vividly; those are all enormous advantages.

Maucher: Those are all features of good leadership.

Malik: Naturally! But they are huge advantages. On the other hand, there are excellent executives who do not have your stature for example and possibly don't have your charm either. Nevertheless, they have gained respect in their company. If you dig deeper, you arrive at attributes that you have already mentioned frequently: frankness, trust, reliability and integrity of character.

Maucher: Yes, absolutely ...

Malik: You write in one of your principles: »Walk your talk«, as the Americans say. Those are the things that have always interested me – what is it that, in this sense, has an engaging, striking, and charismatic impact on other people? Those are the things that you have described in a most impressive way.

Maucher: Well, I would say that if it goes in the direction of show business, it won't last in the long term.

Malik: That's the way I see it, too.

Maucher: You can't convince others if you aren't convinced yourself because then you aren't credible. I think, that's where it all begins.

Malik: There is another question I would like to ask at this point: Was there a policy at Nestlé, such as existed in other companies that if two employees – a man and a woman – were in a relationship that was also obvious in the company– both of them had to leave?

Maucher: No, we didn't. You have to understand human reactions and find a satisfactory solution if you are the boss. It's as simple as that.

Malik: That brings me to a management situation that can occur in various forms. Let's take a hierarchical, albeit flat hierarchical structure: You have a boss under you and this boss has employees under him. Things aren't working properly, but it doesn't get to your ears. Then someone seeks you out and says: »Mr. Maucher, I need to tell you something about our boss: things just aren't working out. How should we handle it? « How do you handle such a situation yourself?

Maucher: Well, I think I did hold such an important position in the company; but I sensed so many things that any employee would have come and told me such a thing because he would have told himself: »Maucher must know that«.

I think that there was little that I wasn't aware of and I could sympathize with many things.

Malik: That means that a subordinate had the opportunity to come directly to you?

Maucher: Yes. I had a principle, and incidentally, that applied on the market, too. I said: »Every Nestlé employee, and that included senior staff, too, has to be loyal to his boss. And that applied from Brazil to the farthest corner of the world: no one should be disloyal. There was only one thing that had to be reported and that was obligatory: if a boss did things that could cause considerable harm to the company. In that case a conscientious, leading employee at Nestlé had a duty to bypass his boss and inform us«. That was what I said.

Malik: And how did you deal with the situation? If it did occur, what did you do?

Maucher: Well, if it did occur, I had a word with this boss and I transferred either the boss or the employee. In any case, I acted in such a way that the problem was solved. However, I did say that loyalty stopped there; that loyalty to the company had priority over loyalty to the immediate superior.

Malik: And because of this higher loyalty you had to accept the possible danger– that it could result in intrigues?

Maucher: Well, you know when someone is merely gossiping; that's quick and easy to figure out; it's easy to find out when someone just wants to give himself airs and tell some tale or other.

Malik: And then you acted very consistently?

Maucher: Absolutely.

Malik: That means that the people were transferred or dismissed or ...

Maucher: Immediately. I've always said that anyone can make a mistake but I am absolutely against cardinal sins. You know, in that respect I am much more brutal than the others but when it comes to mistakes, I am maybe a bit more human, for anyone can make a mistake.

Malik: These stories get around and then everyone knows that Mr. Maucher acts that way. That goes far beyond the usual way corporate culture is tackled in the textbooks. And that brings me to another topic: From what you have said I conclude that you were seldom on such close terms with people to address them by their first names.

Maucher: Very rarely. We lived in different cultures. I have only a few older friends at Nestlé, some of whom were at the head office and with whom I was on close terms, but right to the end many of them addressed me as Monsieur Maucher. And of course it depends on the culture, In France I was Monsieur Maucher, in America I was Helmut and I called my opposite number Joe.

Measures to promote innovation

Farschtschian: With regard to corporate culture in the wider sense you say – and that is evident in the sources mentioned in this book – that the capacity for innovation and creativity can be promoted to a certain extent by methods, systems and measures. It would be interesting if you could explain how you achieved that. How were you able to promote innovation with the measures you took and with the methods you used?

Maucher: Well, the general attitude in the company was that we only made use of measures and methods to a limited extent. That was the climate. You created innovation not by methods, but by an innovative climate; and you created this climate by encouraging the people to think about life: »What do we make exactly? What is missing? « Then of course you can utilize certain methods; certain groups can get together and say: »Dash it all, let's consider how business is to proceed«. Once a year– I introduced that during my term of office – I went with all of the Board of Executives to Caux above Montreux. A friend of mine owned a hotel and restaurant there and for two days I discussed the following with them: »Quo vadis, Nestlé? « But this was done in a way that was almost entirely lacking any structure but had a very positive impact on the climate. The people grew closer together, talked informally and only had to be encouraged to say: »Well, now I have to put my foot down and say on this subject that we'll do nothing«. I only said: »What's the matter? « We arrived at a lot of innovative ideas in these discussions; we considered: »Where are we falling down at the moment? Where have we fallen behind? Where do we have nothing at present? « In the end we reached decisions such as: »We want to put more money into nutrition research«, or »We need to tackle the relatively weak market position in Africa, for instance; yes we need to tackle that«. It was there that we did a lot of things that were innovative; that we arrived at new ideas; new points of view.

Farschtschian: Actually, that goes in the direction of Professor Malik's syntegrations; are these similar approaches?

Maucher: If you define these as methods, then I would say that they are. Methods do help.

Malik: Yes, it goes in that direction. Today, where it can be seen that very many people – or at least more and more people – are needed if a consensus is to be reached and a sound basis is to be formed, so that everyone can and wants to do his or her bit!

Maucher: Certainly.

Malik: If everything works in your example so that you arrive at good results in an informal situation with a minimum of guidance, that's marvelous. In our case there is a little more guidance, so that the self-organization of information flow can be achieved.

Maucher: Okay but the organization, restructuring is a different matter. You have to adapt the company time and again because people change, the structure changes, dimensions change – you always have to carry out organizational adjustments. It isn't something you do today and then leave for ten years; adjustment is a steady process – according to the people, according to the problems and according to the dimensions. There are continual demands made on a boss. He needs to discuss that with his people; it is essential that he does so. Anyone who waits for ten years until a catastrophe hits and then needs to make a huge fuss to change everything causes a lot of trouble as a rule. Things become very difficult then, don't they?

Malik: Considered still from the point of view of methods: if you now had to put Nestlé on an entirely different track and said: »We are now going to increase our business in China significantly and that means having to withdraw resources here and reallocate them there; that entails many and profound changes«. That would be a challenge to making changes. Or if you had to say: »We need to think about how business would look if due to the crisis we had to manage on 30 percent less... We don't know and we hope it won't be necessary but we need to think about it«. After all, as leaders, we want to be prepared.

Maucher: Well, such things would have to be discussed openly and at length with the entire management. They would all have to be behind any decisions. Everything would have to be taken into consideration (who was against it etc.) until we are unanimous. And then they would have to do exactly the same in their field of responsibility – communication, persuasion, discussion – and say: »If, in your area, things come out of your discussions where you think, let's say, we are on the wrong track or that it won't work that way, then get back to us for it will have to be corrected. After all, we may have decided something which we believe will work«. And then the head of Asian business comes and says: »One thing's certain: that won't work in Japan. Their culture is completely different so we will need to tackle it completely differently or do something else«. All these things have to be addressed and that requires considerable discussion, talks, solidarity, reaching a consensus and frankness because otherwise a mistake will be made or one of these people will not actually be behind it and will boycott it.

Malik: Precisely.

Maucher: In such a case, you have to get the team behind you and make corrections if you notice that there are things that come up which you hadn't thought of.

Farschtschian: Mr. Malik, if I understand correctly, these are precisely the kinds of challenges for which you developed your innovative syntegration methods, aren't they? They were developed for integrating the largest possible number of persons needed for a consensus and making use of the knowledge of all the participants to reach overall solutions and to speed up such a process so that implementation can be carried out more effectively and faster.

Malik: That's correct. These are the really huge and complex over-lapping challenges for which we developed these methods and tools. They provide the top management with 80 times its power and effectiveness and it becomes 100 times faster; for example in the case of huge restructuring measures, post-merger integration, strategic positioning, entering new countries and markets, integrating corporate cultures, improving results considerably, strengthening innovation and so on.

Regarded closely, these methods are revolutionary in their innovativeness and have already been applied successfully around 600 times and there hasn't been a single flop. The reasons for these enormous accomplishments are to be found in the natural laws of communication and cybernetics.

To clarify this somewhat from a historical point of view:

We developed them for the really complex challenges which can only be mastered holistically because they affect most of the company or the company as a whole; because they are all linked to one another and develop a high degree of complexity. Consequently, because they change of their own accord and in a particularly dynamic way, they can derail easily and usually even faster than it is possible to develop solutions to them.

Moreover, in absolute terms, a large number of executives at upper and lower levels are needed – in large scale enterprises several hundred of them – who have the necessary expertise and the necessary socio-cultural powers of persuasion in the organization. Knowledge, speed and social energy are crucial to responding to such challenges successfully. After that, power has to be brought as quickly and effectively as possible to all levels, from the bottom to every management capillary in the organization. With traditional procedures you reach the merciless boundaries of what was customary very quickly, brutally and in a way that destroys values.

Our syntegration processes, however – the name is a combination of synergy and integration – open up entirely new opportunities for action at top management level. They even enable the largest organizations to move and change light-footedly and quickly. In DAX-listed companies they are frequently applied over a wide area. Thus, one of the major carmakers has linked its top global 450 managers multiculturally and horizontally in order to provide new answers to questions on strategic positioning.

It used to be, as you, Mr. Maucher, described so aptly that this would have taken ages and needed lots of discussion forums. We accomplished it in six weeks and the results were excellent; not only at a factual level but also at a cultural level, which is often more important in such issues. There was solidarity, a should-to-shoulder stance, a community spirit, frankness, a common consensus at the level of the greatest common factor and the setting free of an almost unimaginable social energy, a combative spirit as it were for implementing the processes.

Maucher: I would like to underline that. Your so-called »Malik Solutions« with your syntegration methods to the fore are of the utmost importance as they combine in an ingenious way three crucial elements: dialogue, cybernetics and organization know-how.

Farschtschian: Mr. Maucher, you built up a company that had a quarter of a million employees when you retired; today there are more than 330,000. How many people do you need to really stir such a group in such situations? How many did you need?

Maucher: At headquarters?

Farschtschian: Well, I mean, you worked in 80 countries or more, didn't you?

Maucher: First of all, we had certain rules regarding how many we needed in the other countries. While in office, I once carried out an operation with McKinsey and had the feeling that with our current methods we had a few too many employees in headquarters. There were about 1,700 of us. I said: »We'll have to be rational and check what we need. What can we delegate to the markets? What can we do more simply? Where do we not need anything at all?« And I carried out this exercise myself – with McKinsey and their best people. And I said: »Just check!« Then we reached the consensus that we needed 200 people fewer in headquarters.

Then I said: »But it isn't going to be done by getting up in front of the workforce and saying: ›Just so that you all know: from tomorrow on we will need 200 people fewer.‹« I held a management conference and said: »We are probably going to need fewer people. That's the way it looks at the moment. But one thing I can tell you: we are talking about a figure where we won't be creating a catastrophe. We have fluctuation, we have retraining, we have all kinds of possibilities and we don't need to do it all in one year, if it works in three years, too. The main thing is that it is done. But I would like to keep the feeling of security in the company and that is why I say that no one will lose his job for, in view of the number of jobs concerned, we can solve it within three years. I'd rather pay a few cents more for the next two years«. That's the best investment in human resources policy.

Farschtschian: There are very few companies that do that.

Maucher: It's hardly ever done and yet it's so simple. I once said: »Where it does get difficult is when you have to close a factory because you can't transfer all these people somewhere else«. In England, where relatively early on I had to rationalize quite a lot, I had to close a factory. That was in Grimsby.

Farschtschian: But I think you gave it away, didn't you?

Maucher: Well I said: »I'd like to find a satisfactory solution. I'd like someone to take over who can continue to employ most of the people«. That means that I said I would give the factory to anyone who came and guaranteed that he would continue to employ the people – he would get it for a pound. That way we found a buyer and that brought me more image and confidence than many other sayings. Unfortunately it isn't done nearly often enough.

Malik: That would probably take us straight to the works council. You wrote that you yourself had a personnel commission in Switzerland.

Maucher: Yes, I had.

Malik: But you had a works council in Germany, in the major organization here.

Maucher: Of course.

Malik: And presumably they were very much on your side when it came to such measures.

Maucher: I never had problems with them. However, I did tell them: »Listen to me. There are many things that you will tell me, where I will say that you are right because we didn't know about them. But if you try to take me to the cleaners, you'll have a problem with me. So please don't try to get one over on me«. And I worked splendidly with them. We had sensible people, ones who really represented the interests of the people; who also, let's say, elected the labor party and the like. Most people are approachable.

Malik: Yes, if it's done properly, and that seems to be one of your great skills.

Maucher: If you treat people properly, they'll treat you properly, too. I've never really had problems with works councils anywhere. And I've always said that if they didn't exist, they would have to be invented. People need an opportunity to communicate with us generally because not all bosses are able to communicate with their employees in such a way that a works council isn't needed. Of course I had meetings with them regularly and told their Chairman: »Come on and tell me what the matter is! What's going on in the joint? « (laughing). »Where does the shoe pinch? « and so on or »Come on, what shall we do?« You need to know that we often make mistakes and that basically the people are right. I must tell you a ridiculous story in this context – I mean, I could tell you a lot: In Germany a general works council was set up according to the laws etc. at that time and the members from every factory in the whole of Germany met twice a year and held their council meeting etc. The problem was that they said: »Gosh, we'd damn well love to travel first class, wouldn't we? We are somebody now, so why shouldn't we be able to travel first class? « »Human resources department, regulation XY ... no, first class is only intended for so and so, okay? « And then they said: »Why isn't it possible? « »They can do with us ...« To cut a long story short: One day I heard all about it and told the human resources

department: »You really are idiots ...« Being allowed to travel first class is much more important to them than getting a 2 percent or 0.5 percent pay rise. The most important thing in their whole life is being allowed to travel first class from the Allgäu to Frankfurt. So then I said: »That doesn't cost much! You're such idiots...« So then I changed everything and that got me much more consent than I got with many other things. It's true that such an incident is ridiculous but if you have such bureaucrats in the administration, anything like that can happen.

Malik: It frequently happens that matters of principle are made out of such things for the wrong reasons ...

Maucher: Ridiculous things are often more important than you think. And apart from that, when I walk through the factory with the plant manager, then I know exactly how he runs the business. I know by the way the people look and the way he looks at them and I know what kind of contact there is between them. Then I know exactly that he isn't very able; that he is a good technocrat, and that we can forget him. After I've trudged through the factory with him, I know how he leads.

Farschtschian: Just by the reaction of the employees, or ...?

Maucher: Yes; by the way he behaves, by the way the employees behave and by the way they look at him. It's easy to see.

Human resources policy

Farschtschian: That's interesting. Your human resources policy entailed more than just a check list and the HR department. After all you say: »Look more in the eyes than in the files«. How do you recognize really good applicants if you look in their eyes?

Maucher: Well, these are vivid sayings, aren't they? But it really does apply. However, a check list is a good thing, too. I need to know if someone spent three years in prison, for example. But after that, when I have someone like that in front of me and I look at him ... with most people I can see from the way they look at me whether they are to be trusted or not. You can see from their eyes whether they want to make something of their lives or not ... Everyone reveals what he is like, and you need to develop a feeling for that. But you do need to ensure that you are not the only one to look at the applicant. There are subjective aspects which can affect your assessment because either you and the candidate gel or you don't. For that reason I always wanted – in addition to »screening« by means of the staff check list – one or two other experienced people to have a look, to verify whether my judgment was correct or to say: »No Mr. Maucher, you're on the wrong track; I think you saw things wrongly; we need to talk about it again ...«. If you have two or three experienced people who come to the same conclusions, then you have a more certain assessment of the person than you could have obtained from all your check lists and HR departments. That's a fact. But as I said: You need to avoid subjective assessments.

Malik: But that isn't something you learnt at university, is it?

Maucher: Of course not. You don't learn everything there but you do get the requisite know-how. However, to return to leadership skills: You can write as often as you like that people are the focus of attention but if you yourself go through the joint and aren't aware of anyone, you might as well give up.

Malik: How did employees get into the inner circle of future executives to whom you personally devoted yourself? You couldn't possibly supervise hundreds of people with the intensive care that would be necessary for the top positions.

Maucher: Well, I must have known about 300 people, so to speak. But that was naturally in the course of time. I took part in meetings of the marketing department where I saw quite a number of people. I went to Brazil and talked with the management where I spent some time with ten people and perhaps I saw 25 people in a larger meeting or conference. Through time I gathered a lot of information about the people we had. If someone was chosen, it wasn't my decision alone for there was my colleague who was in charge of Latin America and who knew even more people. I talked with him, and he told me: »Yes, so and so would be suitable«. Then I was able to say: »Yes, I noticed him, too. I think he would be the right one«. What is crucial is that you are interested. If you are interested, then you see to it that things happen there. If you aren't interested, nothing happens.

Politics, business and society

Farschtschian: As far as this topic is concerned, there would generally be a lot of positive and negative things to report. However, we don't want to go into that in detail but merely want to leave it at a few remarks. Mr. Maucher, what do you think about our current political leaders?

Maucher: What we need again are more statesmen and stateswomen and fewer prime ministers. Only at Nestlé we say: »We'll adapt«. People always have to be fed.

Malik: That's true, no matter what government we have.

Maucher: There are two things that are naturally discussed by us, too: firstly, if food prices continue to rise worldwide (and that's what'll happen because the supply is lower than future demand), this will lead to less growth in our developments in the Third World. People there already spend 40 to 50 percent of their money on food and if prices rise by another 10 percent, they'll be able to buy even less. That's the first thing; it's a simple fact that needs to be taken into account.

The second is the fact that in the developed world there are certain trends towards nutrition and in addition people want more precise information about where a product comes from. That means that creating an image, the Nestlé brand, our behavior in the world is increasingly important to well-informed consumers. Moreover, quality and convenience are also crucial.

Malik: But you are relying on Nestlé being adaptive, being flexible ...

Maucher: Certainly. I mean, we have 500 factories all over the world and adapt to each country by looking at how things work there. Basically Nestlé doesn't need to worry: we have the position, the markets, and the experience. However, one thing is clear: growth in the Third World will be restricted by the imbalance in supply and demand and the attendant price rises.

Farschtschian: I would like to thank you both for the stimulating debate. We have discussed very important topics in considerable detail with the result that many of our readers will be able to benefit from what has been said,

Part 4

Helmut Maucher's Thoughts on the Future and Proposals for Improving our Democratic Constitutions

Some remarks on future developments

I don't wish to add any forecasts of my own to the many that have been made about the future. However, I would like to say the following: It looks as if we will have no wars between the Great Powers in future but there will still be local wars and terror.

The world population will continue to grow although I believe that it will not grow as much as has been predicted in many different forecasts. The reasons for this are increasing urbanization and the further increase in social security (and an ensuing lower dependence on families); in the enlightened attitude to and the decrease in religious ties (a trend which can be observed worldwide); the influence exerted by the media; the demographic development towards an increase in the older population and the regional shift towards non-European areas with focus on Asia.

Globalization will continue to increase. This means that there will be temporary protectionist trends in individual areas of the world.

There will be an increase in democratization worldwide and in the reduction – i. e. the change – in authoritarian systems; see the developments in the Mediterranean area.

Apart from that, humanity should finally have learnt that those huge socio-political designs like communism and other utopias never contribute to solving our problems but on the contrary end in disasters. In this context philosopher Karl R. Popper said once: »The attempt to make heaven on earth invariably produces hell«.

As already mentioned, resources like water, energy and food will become exceedingly scarce in future. Consequently, it is about time that the nations and regional amalgamations like the EU, the major international economies of the G20, and the UN addressed these issues in addition to the obviously important economic and political questions, and that they adopted suitable measures. Appropriate priorities need to be set; and at some stage, it has to be realized that these problems are more important than deciding whether some monument or a part of a town will be declared a World Heritage Site by UNESCO or not.

Despite all their advantages, Western democracies appear to have difficulty tackling certain necessary problems because they fear they will lose votes and might not be re-elected.

Therefore, we can observe a dramatic rise in public debt, which cannot be allowed to continue.

Consequently, I would like to conclude my remarks with some thoughts on democratic constitutions and make some suggestions as to how these could produce greater efficiency and contribute to politics and society functioning better.

Proposals for democratic constitutions

General thoughts and remarks to start with

Community is more than perceiving common interests.
Helmut Maucher

If common sense were more common, the world would be a wonderful place.
Helmut Maucher

Every social system comes to grief on its own excesses.
Wilhelm Röpke

Bureaucracy hinders; system liberates.
Helmut Maucher

Liberalization over-extends; paternalism incapacitates.
Source unknown

You have to accept people for who they are; there aren't any others.
Konrad Adenauer

Force without justice is tyrannical; justice without force is powerless.
Blaise Pascal

Creating and increasing the efficiency of democratic societies

Despite all the difficulties, I am still convinced that a democratic constitution is the most suitable for states and societies to regulate the co-existence of human beings. We also know, however, that democracies would function better if human beings generally showed understanding and intelligence; were equipped with a basic grasp of all important fields of knowledge and were more community-orientated; and if the political class included people outstanding in their profession and in their character. Since, as we are well aware, this is not always the case, we are faced with a dilemma. Politicians and human beings generally think and act too short-sightedly, are too easily subject to moods and fashions and tend to act emotionally rather than rationally. As a form of government, democracy has also become more difficult in general, because problems have become more complex and are less readily comprehensible and straightforward. Moreover, the media has a greater influence due to modern means of communication and the high level of technology. The power of the media with all its attendant side effects (for example, dramatizing events and fuelling fears and going as far as to generate a sense of doom, frequently distorted information, and so-called committed or investigative journalism etc.) has never been so great. Many people are no longer able to process the overwhelming volume of information in order to form a balanced opinion. Besides, it can be observed that there is a tendency for the left of the political spectrum to be more strongly represented in the media world.

Yielding to citizens' demands and a desire to win the next election tend to also produce an irresponsible level of public debt and a high ratio of government expenditure to gross national product in most democracies.

What could be done at least to partly compensate for these weaknesses in democratic constitutions and to achieve better results? Here is a brief outline of some proposals:

- A presidential democracy should have longer legislative periods to lend it greater authority and achieve more stability and longer-term action. What is also needed is a general strengthening of the highest levels of government (no matter how it is organized) and also an emotional strengthening of the »symbolic power« of the head of state. The method of the constructive vote of no confidence (such as we have for the chancellorship in Germany) should be used more frequently.
- A multiple-party state should be prevented: by introducing (as was introduced here a long time ago) the 5 percent hurdle or going even more in the direction of the British system.
- All in all, more care should be taken in the selection of the political class which, from my point of view, should be paid better. The attendant emphasis on more leadership and authority should be complemented by an

extensive application of the principle of subsidiarity, decentralization and the promotion of federalism. The central political power should concentrate on essential tasks and be more capable of acting in such matters. Therefore, we need a strong but nevertheless streamlined state.

- Furthermore, parliamentary democracy should not be softened by more direct democracy and referendums; there should not be more opportunities to object to things which were already decided in the preliminary stages (see »Stuttgart 21«) or to form civil rights movements about such things. This requirement is also necessary because more direct democracy means more superficial populism; in addition, the influence of the media is strengthened. Here we need a better and more sensible balance between the interests of the community and the interests of the individual. In this context I am, of course, in favor of the classical protection of minorities but I strictly oppose »terror by minorities«.

- We urgently need to introduce a *Schuldenbremse* (a debt brake) to get the steady rise in the level of public debt, which I have mentioned already, under control.

- Furthermore, we need to look for opportunities – particularly in legislation and in some watchdog committees – to point the media more strictly towards their actual tasks or towards pursuing a responsible information and publishing policy; towards perceiving their function as a corrective to criticize and control the state and society in order to prevent negative spin-off and abuse of power.

- I am rather worried about some negative changes in mentality in our society; changes resulting from affluence, freedom and social security. These include an increase in egoism and inconsideration, a lack of respect for authorities and of stamina to cope with the hardships of life. All in all, there is less focus on performance and an increase in a mentality that focuses on one's own wishes and demands. And in general, a decrease in the ability to form attachments or commitments and in loyalty can be observed, too.

- Therefore greater efforts are required in education, in the parental home and in schools and also greater endeavors are needed in all social institutions including the churches.

More proposals for improving democratic constitutions

- In view of the danger from terrorism, I am also in favor of more civil protection and data retention and less general data privacy protection.
- The social market economy should be restored to its original purpose in terms of ordoliberalism as developed by the Freiburg School. The social network should not degenerate into a social hammock. In this context the right to co-determination, the Industrial Constitution Act and the like should be organized so that the employees can look after their interests fairly. However, some of the power political components of these laws should be retracted.
- In general terms, the balance between freedom and equality and between the economy and ecology in terms of the social market economy should be organized optimally and as objectively as possible. (The new energy law with the ensuing premature shutdown of nuclear power stations means that this balance has not been maintained; moreover, the objectives of expanding alternative energy forms are unrealistic and are causing extremely high costs that are impairing our competitiveness).
- With regard to fiscal policy, I would advise reducing the rate of government expenditures to gross national product and simplifying the tax system. Despite the necessity of a moderate redistribution in a social market economy, there should be more tax on consumption rather than performance.
- Investments in education are needed and these are more crucial than ever. Better information and training strengthen democracy. The better people are informed, the more sensitive, discerning and rational they are and the better democracy functions! However, some of the objectives and contents of democracy ought to be reconsidered. For example, people should be better informed about how a market economy functions and what advantages it has. More attempts should be made to reduce hostility towards technology and there should be greater insistence on the rules of conduct that are indispensible in a community. People who are unaware of and do not understand how the community and the world function and who remain uninterested in this are unable to become mature, responsible citizens. In this respect, it is also important to educate teachers appropriately.
- In jurisprudence, particularly in criminal law, greater emphasis should be placed on the protection of the victims and not on the protection of the culprits. The police should have more opportunities to intervene if

there are riots etc.; the protection of rioters and hooligans should be reduced.

- In general, the following question should again be discussed more objectively in public and in science: »How much leadership, authority and how many rules are needed in a community and at which point do we begin to restrict the individual too much in his freedom and rights?« The discussion is very difficult because society as a whole and the individual communities adopt very different positions in this respect.

- So far I have restricted my remarks mainly to the Federal Republic of Germany and now I would like to mention some things which need to be changed fundamentally worldwide. Modern means of communication, the financial world, increasing globalization and the networking of the entire world require us to rethink the question as to which tasks and competences we should hand over to worldwide institutions, regional amalgamations like the EU, individual nation states and the federal states within large nation states. For example, we cannot give free reign to increasing globalization, the free movement of goods and the global financial world without introducing corresponding regulations worldwide in terms of the ordoliberalism that was developed earlier in nation states. For example, we can only tackle issues like the shortage of energy, water and agricultural products or many ecological issues etc. optimally if we discuss and regulate these worldwide. In this respect the UN and the G20 acquire increasing significance. On the other hand, there are many questions and problems that in terms of subsidiarity can be delegated without any difficulty to individual countries, regions or even communities. Such regulations mean that there is greater closeness to the citizens and less bureaucracy. The more the world grows together the more we need a readiness to engage in international dialogue and co-operation combined with the will to weigh up the interests of the individual with the common interest.

- With the steady increase in and the activity of NGOs (non-government organizations), civil rights movements and protests, it is even more important that the enforcement of the constitution, the constitutional state and sovereignty by means of laws and corresponding competences by governments is guaranteed.

- Finally I am convinced (although this is contested in many circles but is based on my own experiences) that every community, every institution, whether public or private, functions better if it has a charismatic leader, whose character is at the same time – and that is the important thing –

first class and beyond reproach. I am not advocating charismatic pied pipers or irresponsible populists. Expressed provocatively, it could be said that we need more statesmen and women than prime ministers.

Concluding remarks

In general, politics and society should be geared towards what people are really like and not towards how they should be so that utopian ideas can be avoided. The famous philosopher Popper said: »So far all the social systems and all the prophets who have promised to make heaven on earth have ultimately produced hell«.

Apart from that, the famous Roman politician and philosopher Marcus Tullius Cicero said over 2,000 years ago: »The national budget must be balanced. The public debt must be reduced; the arrogance of the authorities must be moderated and controlled. Payments to foreign governments must be reduced if the nation doesn't want to go bankrupt. People must again learn to work instead of living on public assistance«.

Part 5
Epilogue

Management –
Doing the Right Thing in the Right Way

At the beginning of this book, I wrote that management can be best understood as that social function that enables everything else to function. Not only this encompasses the diverse organizations of the world of business but also all the other sectors of society. Management is the transformation of resources into results, and managers are in this case the people who work in their profession to achieve these results.

Helmut Maucher's unique achievements in management during his term of office at Nestlé are one of the most brilliant examples to date of the impressive entrepreneurial results that can be generated by management as defined above. Maucher's example is thus a guiding principle for mastering the global challenges of the » Great Transformation 21« with its great risks but with its even greater opportunities.

A vast majority of today's top executives grew up and were educated in a time of collective Anglo-Saxon misunderstandings and illusions about management. Consequently many of them have had hardly any opportunity to learn proper management as depicted in such an exemplary and impressive fashion. However, this era of illusion is coming to an end even if the consequences in the form of emerging turbulent crises worldwide will cause us considerable bother for some time to come because the apparently ultimate truths of yesterday are proving to be a false guide to the future. Seen that way crises have their uses if they are understood in essence and result in new action.

Consequently, the challenges for today's generation of executives is all the greater. There is, therefore, a greater and more urgent need of right management than ever before. One of the most reliable aids to navigation is management as practiced by Helmut Maucher for decades and which now needs to be learned from him – in association with the latest methods – as quickly as possible.

Fredmund Malik

Part 6
Appendix

Earlier Key Statements
made by Helmut Maucher

On the occasion of Helmut Maucher's 60th birthday, the Nestlé Group in Germany issued a publication entitled *Weichenstellung; Ein Unternehmer in Deutschland.* (*›Setting the Agenda; an Entrepreneur in Germany‹*). This publication contains statements made by Helmut Maucher when he worked in Germany before taking office as head of Nestlé in Vevey. The attraction of these key statements lies in the fact that they date from a time more than 30 years ago. They illustrate how profound, comprehensive and subtle the young Maucher's thinking was in what was then his first important executive position. Helmut Maucher's key statements published in *Weichenstellungen* are reproduced below:

»In a market economy the world is redistributed daily«.

»The really social deed performed by the entrepreneur and the free economy is to be found in their entrepreneurial performance and their entrepreneurial activity which is aimed at the consumer«.

»If it is not absolutely essential to make a law, then it is essential not to make it«.

»Reform cannot and should not mean a little less capitalism every day and a little more socialism every day«.

»We need more commitment, ›devotion‹ and obsession for the whole matter in terms of focusing on the success of the company«.

»With short-term tactics you can, at best, win a battle but never a war. For my part, I am in favor of winning the war«.

»We do not want to appear ostentatious but want to remain modest in our social and personal behavior and nevertheless have style and standards«.

»Planning means actively shaping the future in good time and taking the necessary decisions in advance«.

»Stipulating sales targets cannot be a high-handed act but must be based on exogenous data and the opportunities within the company«.

»We don't want a team of leaders but a team with a leader«.

»If marketing means the transformation of market requirements and technological innovations into entrepreneurial performance, marketing needs to be linked even more closely to the overall objectives of the company«.

»It is precisely in times of slight growth that we need to take the offensive and develop more genuine and active dynamic«.

»The manufacturer needs to know more about trade. Understanding trade marketing and the way trade thinks is essential«.

»It is clear to me that the importance of sales has increased in the last few years and it will continue to do so«.

»Anyone who skimps on the costs which enhance the value of a brand-name product, in other words on quality and advertising, is committing suicide in installments«.

»In accordance with long-term strategy, advertising needs to be constant in its message and credible in its assertion«.

»I tend to be more in favor of the company being in a better condition than in favor of better conditions«.

»If efforts to increase work performance result in success, a person and his or her welfare need to be moved into focus and become the guiding principle of our action«.

»Capital and work cannot take decisions against the consumer that are independent of or contingent on interests, without sustaining damage in the end«.

»Personal respect and regard for human beings are not only an ethical and social task but are absolutely essential for operations in a company«.

»In the food industry performance, innovation and efficiency in the broadest sense also have opportunities in the future«.

»It is our ambition to contribute to providing the population in developing countries with better supplies of good and economically affordable food«.

Collection of Helmut Maucher's Aphorisms and Thoughts

Collection of aphorisms

Being conservative doesn't mean keeping the ashes but preserving the flame.
Jean Jaures

There are only two things we can give our children that last: the first is roots and the second is wings.
J. W. von Goethe

There is no fortress so strong that money cannot capture it.
Cicero

A little kindness from person to person is better than a vast love of all mankind.
Richard Dehmel

Where vanity begins reason ceases to exist.
Maria Ebillioner-Eschenbach

It is incredible how much intelligence is used in the world to prove nonsense.
Christian Friedrich Hebbel

The attempt to make heaven on earth invariably produces hell.
Karl Popper

Force without justice is tyrannical; justice without force is powerless.
Blaise Pascal

The politician thinks of the next election, the statesman thinks of the next generation.
William Gladstone

Legislators and revolutionaries who promise equality and liberty at the same time are either psychopaths or mountebanks.
J. W. von Goethe

If the devil wants to create confusion among humanity, he makes use of idealists.
Nicolo Macchiavelli

We all live under the same sky but we don't all have the same horizon.
Konrad Adenauer

Whenever a man does a thoroughly stupid thing, it is always from the noblest motives.
Oscar Wilde

Democracy presupposes an attitude of reason on the part of the people which it is supposed to produce first.
Jaspers

Being tender-hearted towards a wolf is but tyranny to a sheep.
Abdu'l-Bahá

Every social system comes to grief on its own excesses.
Wilhelm Röpke

The state exists to prevent poverty but not to prevent wealth.
Johannes Groß

They reminded him of a dove that regards the air as a hindrance to its flight and therefore it believes it could fly better if only there were no air.
Immanuel Kant in opposition to supporters of absolute freedom

The greater the distance from a problem the more idealism grows.
Rosa Luxemburg

The ability that is most appreciated is the ability to pay.
Unknown

Affluence is the transition from poverty to dissatisfaction.
Unknown

Freedom is understanding necessity.
Hobbes

If you know your enemy and know yourself, you need not fear the result of a hundred battles.
Sun Tzu

This company works without making a profit. (That's not the way it was planned but it's the way it has turned out.)
Seen in an artist's studio

Anyone stepping in his predecessor's footsteps leaves no traces of himself.
Unknown

The more human beings act according to plan, the more effectively they can be hit by coincidence.
Friedrich Dürrenmatt

Planning is replacing chance with error.
Unknown

As a rule, man is the sum of his abilities minus the sum of his vanities and as a rule, the balance is negative.
Alfred Mahler

The strong man is strongest when he acts alone.
Friedrich Schiller on the subject of alliances

An entrepreneur or politician sometimes needs »a trained ruthlessness in looking at the realities of life«.
Max Weber

In our shop either the coat goes or the purchaser goes.
Head of a textile shop

Many journalists have the knack of separating the wheat from the chaff and printing the chaff in the end.
Adlai Stevenson

There are more people who trip over their tongues than over their feet.
Tunisian Proverb

Most people find thinking strenuous but gymnastics comes naturally to everyone.
Arthur Schopenhauer

Romanticism is essential. The absence of kitsch makes life unbearable.
Friedensreich Hundertwasser

A compromise is only perfect when everyone is dissatisfied.
Aristide Briande

If there is nothing but praise, then it must be scrutinized carefully: if there is nothing but condemnation, then it must be scrutinized, too.
Confucius

For the time being, until philosophy holds the universe together, the bustling crowd preserves itself with hunger and love.
Friedrich Schiller

The world belongs to the enthusiast who keeps cool.
William McFee

Committee – a group of people who keep minutes and waste hours.
Fred Allen

Instead of loving your enemies, treat your friends better.
Mark Twain

If you want to drain a swamp, don't ask the frogs.
Popular saying

Helmut Maucher's own aphorisms and thoughts

If all human beings were humane, the world would be a wonderful place.

Hopefully we share more values than just the share value.
Lecture before financial analysts

If common sense were more common, we would have considerably fewer problems and conflicts.

Reform cannot and should not mean a little less capitalism every day and a little more socialism every day.

Competition that functions is still the best means of distributing power.

Many animals are cleverer than we think and many people are less clever than we think.

Unconventional thinkers are sometimes useful but unfortunately most of them are only unconventional windbags or oddballs.

Sometimes you have to have the courage to speak the truth even if it isn't always the politically correct thing to do.

Thoughts on Schiller's Don Carlos: It used to be that critics or intellectual rebels were punished or even killed. Today they receive state awards.

The main difference between my generation and those in power today is: we were a generation of commitments and today's generation is a generation of options (but it has to be admitted that every generalization or sweeping statement is debatable).

Success is not due to the fact that we are good but that the competition is even worse.

Increasing sales are the most effective camouflage of management errors.

Canned food and washing machines have contributed more to women's emancipation than all the demonstrations in their support.

Anyone lacking sensitivity cannot lead, nor can anyone who is only sensitive.

All large companies tend to attach too much importance to staff work. In a market-orientated system we have to do everything to get away from staff-orientation and focus on the consumer.

Advertising is like research: half the money is wasted. Unfortunately you don't know which half.

An appeal to executives: »More pepper, less paper! «

Being an opportunist is something different to being opportunistic.

Frequently, dissatisfaction in a company has less to do with a lack of information and more to do with a lack of confidence.

As the head of a company, it sometimes makes sense to act in the same way a raider would act after taking over a company or probably in the same way your own successor will act!

The strategic vision: Many of the things that were done because the opportunity presented itself or as the result of a sudden brainwave were later invented as strategies for the universities or journalists.

An exchange of views with the boss: the employee comes with an opinion to the boss's office and comes back out again with the boss's opinion.

Mistakes cannot always be avoided. A mistake only becomes disastrous if you are not prepared to correct it.

My attitude in dealing with employees and unions: I'm like the leaning tower of Pisa – I might incline to your point of view but I stand firm.

One way to success: Never say ›yes‹ if you actually want to say ›no‹.

I'm in favor of ethical and social responsibility but oppose ethical and social blarney.

Advice for corporate management: »Keep heads up and overheads down«.

Widespread behavior by bosses: they spend 50 percent of the time talking and the other 50 percent not listening.

Bureaucracy hampers; systems free.

The farsightedness that many people have is overlooking the nearest problems.

The average person: It is unfortunate that the average person is usually below average.

Anyone who is young is not yet able to understand the world; anyone who is old is no longer able to understand it.

If you want to motivate people, you need to know what motivates them. Four motivations are: love, power, wealth and vanity. These probably satisfy 90 percent of the basic needs.

Every career and every life ends as an unfinished symphony.

Fundamentals of human resources policy: more attention to people and less bureaucracy with people

One of the problems in business and society: We have too many regulations and not enough principles.

To counteract our short-term thinking and acting it is worth looking at things »sub species eternitatis« (from the point of view of eternity) now and again.

A German proverb says: »Age doesn't prevent stupidity«. I would add: » and intelligence doesn't either«.

People used to seek salvation; today they seek happiness.

There are some things that you can only understand if you are not an expert.

A well-known proverb says: »The way to hell is paved with good intentions«. I would add: »The way to hell is paved with nice temptations«.

Many PR people behave like the cock that crows at 5.00 in the morning and thinks that it is he that causes the sun to rise.

Paradox: Never have managers thought and acted so much in the short term since the word »sustainability« came into vogue.

If expenditure is increased in a company, you need to check thoroughly if it is an investment or a nail in your coffin for the future.

Honoring the dead and the old, and stretching and promoting youth will keep society stable.

A principle for successful corporate management: think in the longer term but act faster (not the other way round!).

A communication rule: it is better to write the way you speak but don't speak the way you write.

Instead of »wishful thinking« it would be better to heed Max Weber's »trained ruthlessness in looking at the realities of life«.

A form of bribery which is permitted and effective is flattery.

We need more of Friedrich Schiller's »Ode to Joy« and less of »Bonjour Tristesse« (Françoise Sagan).

Biographies

Dr. h. c. Helmut Oswald Maucher, born in Eisenharz (Allgäu), Germany on December 9, 1927

After graduating from high school and completing commercial training in the Nestlé dairy in his birth-town of Eisenharz, Helmut Maucher began a career which even judged in the light of the period of the economic miracle at the beginning of the 50s was absolutely breathtaking. It took him to the head of the Nestlé food group as the first non-Swiss CEO and Chairman. Parallel to various positions at Nestlé Maucher studied business administration in Frankfurt. From 1975 on, Maucher was head of Nestlé Germany; he had been a member of the management at Nestlé in Frankfurt since 1964.

In 1980 he was called to Switzerland as General Director of Nestlé AG and a member of the Executive Committee. In 1981 he was appointed CEO of the Board of Directors at Nestlé AG. In the period from 1990 to 1997 Maucher acted as both Chairman and CEO of the Board of Directors. In 1997 he stepped down from his office of CEO but remained Chairman until 2000.

In 2000 he ended his active service as Chairman and was appointed Honorary Chairman of the Nestlé Group. The *Frankfurter Allgemeine Zeitung* described him as one of »the best-known European managers of the older generation«; *Fortune,* the economics magazine elected him one of the best managers in Europe.

Maucher is the author of *Marketing ist Chefsache* (›Leadership in Action: Tough-minded Strategies from the Global Giant‹), and a *Management-Brevier: Ein Leitfaden für unternehmerischen Erfolg* (›Management Breviary: A Guideline to Corporate Success‹). He was also active beyond the company as, for example, President of the International Chamber of Commerce (ICC, Paris) and Chairman of the European Round Table, a committee of some 50 top managers, who bring their expertise from the top echelons of the economy to bear on the integration process of the European Union. In 2004 he was awarded the Social Market Economy Prize by the Konrad-Adenauer-Stiftung (Konrad-Adenauer Foundation) for his entrepreneurial flair and social commitment.

Mandates on Supervisory Boards, offices in watchdog committees and other institutions

- Chairman of the Board of Trustees of the Institute for Public Opinion Research in Allensbach
- Chairman of the Board of Trustees of the Universität Bayern e. V., Munich
- Member of the Foundation Board of the »Frankfurt Institute for Advanced Studies« (FIAS)

Honors

- »Fortune Magazine Gold Medal« – 1984
- Awarded honorary doctorate by the Autonomous University of Guadalajara, Mexico – June 1989
- Awarded the Order of the Aztec Eagle Mexico – April 1993
- Awarded the Großes Goldenes Ehrenzeichen mit dem Stern (the highest possible decoration) for service to the Republic of Austria – August 1993
- «Leadership Award for Corporate Statesmanship«, International Institute for Management Development (IMD) – October 1993
- IMD – Maucher Nestlé Chair – November 1993
- «Appeal of Conscience Foundation Award«, New York – October 1995
- INTERNORGA Award, Hamburg – March 1996
- Awarded honorary doctorate, European Business School Östrich-Winkel – February 1997
- Manager Magazine »Business Hall of Fame« – May 1997
- The Grand Cross with Star for Distinguished Service of the Order of Merit of the Federal Republic of Germany – September 1997
- Awarded honorary doctorate by the Technical University of Munich – March 1998
- »Scopus Award« by the Hebrew University of Jerusalem – May 1999
- The Austrian Cross of Honor for Science and Art, First Class – August 1999

- »Social Market Economy Prize 2004«, Konrad-Adenauer Stiftung e. V. – November 2004
- Appointment to the »Club of Marketing Excellence (CME)« by the German Marketing Association and the German magazine *absatzwirtschaft* (Industrial marketing) – August 2008
- «Bayreuther Vorbild-Preis« (Prize for Setting Exemplary Standards) by the Faculty of Philosophy & Economics at the University of Bayreuth – October 2008
- Hanns Martin Schleyer-Preis for significant contributions in strengthening and promoting the principles of free and democratic policy – April 2013.

Prof. Dr. oec. Fredmund Malik, born in Lustenau (Vorarlberg), Austria on September 1, 1944

Prof. Dr. Fredmund Malik has developed an all new thinking and management system designed to revolutionize the leadership perspectives of top executives and the functioning of large organizations. His tools apply where conventional management stops. They were created to empower the top leaders of large organizations to reliably master growing complexity and the dynamic new challenges of the 21st century.

After several years of practical management experience, Malik studied business economics, social sciences, logic and philosophy of science. He earned both his doctorate and habilitation in corporate management. He was Professor for General Corporate Management, Governance and Leadership at the University of St. Gallen (1974–2004), and a guest professor at the Vienna University of Business and Economics (1992–1998). He is Special Professor at two renowned Chinese universities In 1984, he founded the Malik Institute in St. Gallen which he heads as Chairman and CEO. The Institute has been among the leading knowledge organizations for cybernetic thinking and management solutions ever since.

In 1984 Malik published his first classic on system-cybernetic management, *Strategy of the Management of Complex Systems*. In 1997, he first described and predicted by the name of »The Great Transformation21« what we experience today: a long and protracted phase of mostly unexpected turbulence including financial collapse and debt crises. Contrary to mainstream opinion, early on Malik has localized the roots of these turbulences not in the world of finance only but much more so in the growing complexity of today's global systems and the inadequacy of conventional management methods.

A key element of Malik's approach is his broad understanding of management beyond profit making as the very societal function that enables society and its diverse organizations to function properly especially under conditions of rising complexity.

Therefore, Malik has based his management on cybernetics and the systems sciences. The result is a novel set of solutions and tools for the great challenges of business and society. These tools include the unique Syntegration® procedures, a new kind of social technology for adapting organizations to even fastest-changing environments.

Malik's management systems apply to all types and levels of organizations as well as teams and individuals. They ensure management compatibility throughout an organization and also shared understanding, language and knowledge which are the pre-condition for speed and effective self-regulation and self-organization of complex systems.

Malik is the author of more than 10 award-winning bestsellers and some 300 further publications. His classic Managing Performing Living was selected amongst the best 100 business books of all time. Prof. Peter F. Drucker, doyen of management, said: »Malik has become the leading expert on management in Europe [...]. He is a commanding figure – in theory as well as in the practice of management«. Business Week labels Malik as »one of the most influential business thinkers in Europe ...«.

Awards (Selection)

- 1975: PhD in systems science with the highest distinction. Amititia Prize awarded for the best PhD of the academic year 1975 at the University of St. Gallen
- 2009: Cross of Honor for Science and Art of the Republic of Austria for his Wholistic Management Systems
- 2010: Heinz von Foerster-Prize for Organizational Cybernetics, German Association for Cybernetics
- 2011: Special Professor of system-cybernetic management and governance at two Chinese universities

Dr. oec. Farsam Farschtschian, born in St. Gallen, Switzerland on May 28, 1976

After graduating from high school where he specialized in Mathematics, Farschtschian pursued his studies in political science, international relations and business administration at the Universities of Geneva, Berkeley and St. Gallen (HSG).

Parallel to his doctoral studies at the St. Gallen University, he was a member of a small founding team to establishing and launching of the MBA-HSG program which was later awarded top ranking. He was responsible for business development and marketing the program internationally, significantly contributing to its ongoing success and popularity.

Farschtschian grew up in a multicultural environment and is fluent in many languages. He began his international career by entering politics and working as a Legislative Aide to Texan Senator Rodney G. Ellis. During this time, he witnessed the acute complications of the governance practice at close quarters, when the huge spectacular bankruptcy of Enron Texas hit the headlines worldwide. This event stimulated his interest in sustainable management, effective leadership and in corporate governance; moreover, he became particularly interested in the management theories propounded by Fredmund Malik in St. Gallen.

On the basis of his experiences, he wrote his dissertation, under Prof. Martin Hilb and Prof. Fredmund Malik at the University of St. Gallen, on the role of the Board of Directors in corporate acquisitions. It is with regards to this important strategy that the highest demands are made of the interaction of the top corporate governance bodies – and especially of the role of the Board as the center of power and organization. With his specific mode of practice, Farschtschian was able to make legitimate use for his dissertation of top-class insider information gained from discussions with leading CEOs and Board members of international corporations. The subject, the research methods and the results of the work led him to draw significant conclusions about the functioning of today's corporate governance and delivered numerous proposals for improvements in strategic management, which earned the work particular recognition by high-ranking business leaders.

For many years, Farsam Farschtschian worked for the investment bank Morgan Stanley in London as an Investment Advisor, where he advised some of Europe´s leading entrepreneurial families and CEOs on investment and wealth management related matters. In his last capacity he was in London in charge of the private wealth management business for German-speaking Europe. Since 2012 Farschtschian has been a Director of Deutsche Bank based at its headquarters in Frankfurt where he is responsible for strategic advice to international entrepreneurs and key clients from Europe, the Middle East and Africa.

Farsam Farschtschian has made a significant contribution to this work as co-publisher and co-author. He is furthermore author of the books *The Secret of Successful Acquisitions: Abandoning the Myth of Board Influence* and *The Reality of M&A Governance: Transforming Board Practice for Success.*

Literature

The following sources are available in German. For the purpose of this book these sources were translated into English. The following bibliographical references are in the original.

Interviews with Helmut Maucher

Christoph Berdi, »Mr. Nestlé« in *absatzwirtschaft. Zeitschrift für Marketing*, Nov. 1, 2008.

Dorit Brandwein, »Tue nichts, was nicht morgen in der Zeitung stehen kann« (*Don't do anything that cannot appear in the press tomorrow*) in *Die Welt* on Sept. 23, 1999.

Peter Brors /Olive Stock, »Aus der Provinz in die weite Welt« in *Handelsblatt*, May 16, 2006.

Marc Brost/Arne Storn, »Man braucht Rückgrat« (*Backbone is required*) in *Die Zeit* on Dec. 1, 2005.

Farsam Farschtschian, *Reality of M&A Governance: Transforming Board Practice for Success.* (Berlin/Heidelberg, Springer, 2012).

Farsam Farschtschian, *The Secret of Successful Acquisitions. Abandoning the Myth of Board Influence.* (Frankfurt/New York, Campus, 2011).

Gabriele Fischer, »Ich habe keine Sehnsucht nach einfachen Lösungen. Aber ich sehe viele Dinge einfacher« (*I don't yearn for simple solutions but I do see many things more simply*), in *brand eins*, issue1/2006.

Werner Funk/Armin Mahler, »Nestlé – ein Multi spielt Monopoly« and »Einige Players erobern die Märkte« (*Some players are conquering the market*), in *Der Spiegel*, issue 20/1988.

Rainer Hank/ Winand von Petersdorff, »Unsere Generation ist länger standhaft geblieben« (*Our generation had more staying power*), in *Frankfurter Allgemeine Sonntagszeitung*, on Aug. 6, 2006.

Wolfgang Kaden/ Winfried Wilhelm, »Man braucht Mut« (*Courage is needed*), in *manager magazin*, issue 12/1996.

Max Leutenegger/ Thomas Holec/Andreas Z'Graggen, »Das Gesäusle liebe ich gar nicht!«, in *Bilanz*, issue 12/1981.

Elisabeth Michel-Adler, »Ohne Druck keine Leistung«, in *Tages-Anzeiger Magazin*, issued on Aug. 29,1987.

Christian Ramthun, »Ablass-Kapitalismus«, in *WirtschaftsWoche*, issued on Jun. 2, 2005.

Florian Rittmeyer, »Bleibt euch treu« (*Remain true to yourselves*), in *Schweizer Monat* (Special edition no. 4), in October 2011.

Hagen Seidel, »Der Wind wird eisiger« (*The frosty winds of change*), in *Die Welt*, on Mar. 9, 2007.

Hagen Seidel, »Top-Manager brauchen zwei oder drei Patriotismen«, in *Die Welt*, on Jul. 3, 2006.

»Von der Kunst, ein Unternehmen zu führen« (*The fine art of managing a company*), in *Ernährungswirtschaft*, issue no. 1/1996 on Feb. 5 1996.

»Wer nicht glaubwürdig handelt, wird scheitern«, in *Outlook*, issue 1/2006.

Speeches, publications and essays by Helmut Maucher

»Auf schmalem Grat (*Walking a fine line*) «, in *Bilanz*, no. 20/2010.

»Bedeutung von Forschung und Innovation für die langfristige Wettbewerbsfähigkeit Europas«, (*The importance of research and innovation for Europe's long-term competitiveness*): a lecture given on the occasion of the Doctoral Conferment Ceremony in Februar 1998.

»Chefsache Markenführung« (*Brand management is the boss's business*): a dinner speech given on the occasion of the anniversary conference of »Die Macht der Marke« (*The power of the brands*) in May 2007.

»Das rechte Maß« (*The proper degree of moderation*), a lecture given on the occasion of the Carl Friedrich von Weizsäcker Talks in January 2008

»Die Aufgabe von Eliten in der heutigen Gesellschaft« (*The task of the elite in today's society*): a lecture given before the Lions Club in September 2003.

»Die Bedeutung von Innovationen und Forschung für die zukünftige Entwicklung oder Lebensmittelindustrie« (*The importance of innovations and research for the future development of the food industry*): a lecture on the occasion of the »Forum Life Science 2007« in February 2007

»Die Schweiz von außen betrachtet – Fazit eines Unternehmerlebens«, (*Switzerland seen from the outside – An entrepreneur takes stock*): a lecture given during a series of talks held by the Schaffhauser Gemeinschaft in January 2001.

»Die soziale Verantwortung der Konzerne im Zeitalter der Globalisierung« (*The social responsibility of companies in the age of globalization*), the opening statement to a panel discussion at the Conference held by the BKU (Association of Catholic Entrepreneurs) in October 2001.

»Erziehung für die Zukunft. Gedanken eines Unternehmers« (*Education for the fu-

ture – Thoughts of an entrepreneur): a lecture given at the Commercial High School, Wangen in October 1998.

»*Fast Moving Consumer Goods: Current and Future Aspects of Marketing*«: a lecture given before the Marketing Club, Düsseldorf im November 2006.

»Glaubwürdigkeit und Kommunikation als Elemente moderner Unternehmens- und Markenpolitik» (*Credibility and communication as elements of modern corporate and branding policy*): a keynote speech given at the presentation of the reward for »Best Brands« in February 2006.

»Herausforderungen an die zukünftige Unternehmensführung« (*Demands on future corporate management*): a speech given on the occasion of Professor Dr. Norbert Wieselhuber's 60th birthday in October 2009.

»Herausforderungen an die zukünftige Unternehmensführung« (*Demands on future corporate management*): a speech given at the annual meeting of the Former Pupils' Association of the Bischof-Neumann-Schule in December 2011.

»Ist der Rheinische Kapitalismus zukunftsfähig?« (*Is Rhineland Capitalism Sustainable?*) in *Rheinischer Kapitalismus und seine Quellen in der Katholischen Soziallehre* (Rhineland Capitalism and its Origins in Catholic Social Doctrine), published by Michael Spangenberger, Aschendorff, 2011.

»Langfristig denken – Werte schaffen für Unternehmen und Gesellschaft« (*Thinking long-term – Creating values for enterprises and society*): speech given at a congress on the occasion of the 50th meeting of the »Goldener Zuckerhut« in November 2007.

»Lohnt sich Moral im Geschäft? – Der Stellenwert von Moral für nachhaltigen Erfolg« (*Are morals worthwhile in business? The importance of morals for sustainable success*): a lecture given at the symposium Bayreuther Dialogue on October 24 and 25, 2008 (printed in the brochure of the Bayreuther Dialogue and entitled *Moralisierung der Märkte. Neue ohnMacht des Konsumenten.* (Raising the moral standards of the markets; the new powerlessness of the consumer)

»Marken- und Produktpolitik zwischen Profilierung und Verwässerung« (*Product and branding policy between image and dilution*): a lecture given at the 3rd International Brands-Colloquium in May 2006.

»Marken richtig führen. Grundsätze für den internationalen Erfolg« (*Proper brand management. Principles for international success*): a lecture given at the 3rd Deutschen Marken-Summit (Summit of German Brands) in June 2009.

»Marketing – alte Wahrheiten und neue Aspekte« (*Marketing – old truths and new aspects*): a lecture given at the special event of the ›Wissenschaftlichen Gesellschaft für Marketing und Unternehmensführung e. V.‹ on the occasion of Dr. Guido Sandler's 80th birthday in July 2008.

»Nachhaltigkeit und wertorientiertes Management. Ein wichtiger Faktor für den langfristigen Unternehmenserfolg« (*Sustainable and value-oriented management. An important factor for long-term corporate success*): a lecture given at a special series by the Chamber of Commerce for young businessmen and women in November 2010.

»Pflege der Einfachheit« (*Cultivating simplicity*), in *Bilanz*, issue 13/2010.

»So etwas tut man nicht« (*There are some things that just aren't done*): a lecture given at the Graduate School of Management, Leipzig in November 2010.

Notes for a discussion at the »Hyatt Tischgespräch« of the Konrad Adenauer Foundation in November 2010.

»Unternehmensethik heute – ein Marketing- und PR-Gimmick oder Bestandteil einer sinnvollen Business Strategie? «(*Corporate Ethics – a marketing and PR gimmick or an integral part of sensible business strategy?*): a speech given before the Rotary Club in August 2010.

»Unternehmensführung in einer globalen Wirtschaft – Gedanken über zukünftige Führungsbedingungen und notwendige Führungseigenschaften« (*Corporate management in a global economy – Thoughts on future leadership requirements and requisite leadership attributes*): a lecture given at the Frankfurter Gesellschaft für Handel, Industrie und Wissenschaft (Frankfurt Society for Trade, Industry and Science) in September 2007.

»Vertrauen statt Krise – Wie man auch in schwierigen Zeiten Kunden gewinnen und halten kann!« (*Confidence instead of crisis – How to win and keep customers in difficult times*): a lecture given at the German Supermarket Congress in June 2009.

»Visionen und Innovationen als wichtiger Erfolgsfaktor bei fortschreitender Globalisierung der Lebensmittelwirtschaft« (*Visions and innovations as a vital factor of success in the advancing globalization of the food industry*): a lecture given at the 3rd International Whey Conference (WHEY) in September 2001.

»Wachstum durch Übernahmen, Akquisitionen, Kooperation, Joint Ventures und Fusionen. Praxiserfahrungen prominenter Wirtschaftsführer« (*Growth through takeovers, acquisitions, co-operation, joint ventures and mergers – The practical experience of prominent captains of industry*): a lecture given at the Goldmann Congress »Managing Change«in February 1998.

Weichenstellungen. Ein Unternehmer in Deutschland. (Setting the Agenda – An entrepreneur in Germany), at Nestlé AG, Frankfurt in 1987.

»Wertorientierung als wichtiger Bestandteil moderner Unternehmensführung. Erfahrungen aus der Führung eines internationalen Konzerns« (*Value orientation as an important constituent of modern corporate management – Experiences in the management of an international corporation*): a lecture at the Personnel Symposium »Authentic and integral management« in September 2005.

»Wie kann die Soziale Marktwirtschaft im weltweiten Kapitalismus gerettet werden? « (*How can the social market economy in global capitalism be saved?*), Hyatt Tischgespräch im November 2010.

Speech welcoming those attending the Gala Dinner in the Marmorhalle in Salzburg in August 1999.

»Wirtschaftliche Chancen für Oberschwaben in der heutigen Welt« (*Economic opportunities for Upper Swabia in the world of today*): a speech at »Talks in Upper Swabia« in May 2010.

Literature by Fredmund Malik (Selection)

Managing Performing Living: Effective Management for a New Era. Frankfurt/New York: Campus 2006 and 2012. (Chosen amongst the best 100 business books of all times)

Series: »Management: Mastering Complexity«:

Volume 1: *Management: The Essence of the Craft.* Frankfurt/New York: Campus 2010.

Volume 2: *Corporate Policy and Governance: How Organizations Self-Organize.* Frankfurt/New York: Campus 2011.

Volume 3: *Strategy: Navigating the Complexity of the New World.* Frankfurt/New York: Campus 2013.

The Right Corporate Governance: Effective Top Management for Mastering Complexity. Frankfurt/New York: Campus 2012.

Strategie des Managements komplexer Systeme. 10th edition 2008. (*Strategy for Managing Complex Systems.* Based on the 10th edition of the German Original 1984. (English translation pending).

Uncluttered Management Thinking: 46 Concepts for Masterful Management. Frankfurt/New York: Campus 2011.

Biomimetics – Fascination of Nature, (ed), mcb-Publishing House 2006

Since 1993 he has been the author and publisher of the most read management letter in the German speaking region of Europe: *Malik Letter (malik on management®-Letter (m.o.m.®)).*

Numerous audio and video productions on the subject of managing highly complex sociotech-nical systems, on bionics, cybernetics, governance and on the development of society and the economy.

Literature by Farsam Farschtschian

Reality of M&A Governance: Transforming Board Practice for Success. Berlin/Heidel-
  berg: Springer 2012.
The Secret of Successful Acquisitions: Abandoning the Myth of Board Influence. Frank-
  furt/New York: Campus 2011

Index